D1597272

Awesome book! There is so many great pearls in *Perpetual Wealth*, I can't list them all. But I can tell you that we took notes and with this blueprint for creating multi-generational wealth we are feeling confident in creating our legacy plans! We also loved the examples of family retreats and the ideas for fostering leadership in younger generations. Well done!

— **Jason Bleick**

"Saving saves families!" That's the core message of *Perpetual Wealth* from Kim Butler. This book shows how to grow a "family fund" and make it last for generations.

— **Richard C. Clouse, Sr.**

As someone who has been working in life insurance for years, I loved the step-by-step detail I found in *Perpetual Wealth*. The book will motivate you to save, show you how and where to save, and how to do it as a family.

— **Theresa Sheridan**

Perpetual Wealth is a stellar handbook for the "family banking" concept. The information on how and why to insure children and the diagrams showing ways to structure policies for multi-generational benefit were very helpful.

— **Billy Hall**

Perpetual Wealth is a delightful and insightful read, weaving stories with financial strategies for generational wealth. This book is full of great ideas and examples, and I can't recommend it enough!

— **Juan P. Cardona**

If you are determined to leave a legacy that will last for generations, run to pick up Kim Butler's latest book with Kate Phillips. *Perpetual Wealth* shows you how to get the whole family on board to create, sustain, and steward generational wealth. It can be done and this book shows you how.

— **Lesley Batson**

Perpetual Wealth is full of actionable ideas. Kim Butler and Kate Phillips show exactly how whole life insurance and a shared family vision can help build multi-generational wealth.

— **Dennis McComb**

I am always looking for ways to explain the family banking concept to my clients. I've researched every other vehicle and method I can find, and I am confident this is—by far—the best way to build intergenerational wealth. *Perpetual Wealth* is a vital resource for families and business owners who want to create a lasting legacy. Well done!

— **Jason I. Henderson, Ph.D.**

If you want to help your family truly succeed over multiple successive generations, provide true "generational wealth" that maintains tax advantages, privacy, safety, and control while teaching effective leadership and stewardship, *Perpetual Wealth* provides the roadmap you need to study and follow. The world needs more wise stewards and effective leaders. Set your family on course to *be* one of those families. **— Jim Kindred**

The *Perpetual Wealth* book provides a sound structure for generational family wealth, both the monetary part (to live fully today) and the legacy part (so you can continue to live on for generations into the future through your families' dreams and the financial security you can impart). It shares abundant guiding principles to assist in educating future generations about money, the belief in strong values, and the importance of life-long learning.

— Mark Bertrang
Author of *Investments Don't Hug:
Embracing the Life Insurance Asset*

I've always liked the idea of *Perpetual Wealth* because… It speaks to my sense of legacy. It's empowering for me to think legacy. Human Life Value and Property Value [come from] financial capital perpetuated by mental capital. Yes, you can leave both [HLV and PV], and by doing so, you are empowered and so are those you care the most about.

— Michael G. Isom
Wealth & Protection Strategist, Creator of Vault AIS

Why do families struggle to create and keep wealth—and what can be done about it? In *Perpetual Wealth*, Kim Butler and Kate Phillips give us the facts. They take the banking strategy beyond a product and beautifully lay out a game plan to build and keep wealth in families and, more importantly, how to create a system of family governance to create financially empowered children. I highly recommend this book. **— Curtis May**

To me wealth is experiencing life at the highest levels. Your mindset is paramount to achieving this, and money is a tool to amplify the results. As society continues to associate wealth with the material world, I feel blessed to have books like *Perpetual Wealth* to even the playing field. **— Patrick Donohoe**

The idea of Perpetual Wealth has always fed my Soul Purpose. "Perpetual" meaning long-term legacy, and "Soul Purpose" meaning what I was put on earth to do/give. Those two go together in a way that drives my energies every day. This book gives you some concrete steps to take with your family to work on both legacy and your own sense of your gifts (and your family's gifts) to the world. **— Garrett Gunderson**
New York Times bestselling author and
Chief Wealth Architect of Wealth Factory

PERPETUAL WEALTH

Also by Kim D. H. Butler

Live Your Life Insurance

Busting the Retirement Lies

Busting the Life Insurance Lies

Busting the Interest Rate Lies

Busting the Financial Planning Lies

Busting the Real Estate Investing Lies

With Kate Phillips

Financial Planning has FAILED
(Download for free at Partners4Prosperity.com)

Also by Kate Phillips

Break Through to Abundance

PERPETUAL WEALTH

How to Use "Family Financing" to Build Prosperity and Leave a Legacy for Generations

Kim D. H. Butler
and
Kate Phillips

PROSPERITY ECONOMICS MOVEMENT
Mt. Enterprise, Texas

PERPETUAL WEALTH:

How to Use "Family Financing" to Build Prosperity and Leave a Legacy for Generations

Kim D. H. Butler and Kate Phillips

©2019–2021 Prosperity Economics Movement. All rights reserved.

Published by Prosperity Economics Movement, Mt. Enterprise, Texas

ISBN 978-0-9913054-7-6 (hardcover)
ISBN 978-0-9913054-8-3 (eBook)

Partners4Prosperity.com

Published in association with:

prosperityeconomicsmovement

PARTNERS④
PROSPERITY

Contents

PREFACE:
A Note from the Authors

When we started writing this book (some time ago), we *thought* we were writing a book that answered the question, "How can a family use whole life insurance as a powerful financial strategy for multi-generational wealth?"

It would have been a useful book for our advisor community and our clients who were already open to permanent life insurance. As you will see, there ARE many distinct advantages—such as tax advantages, privacy, safety and control—to using life insurance to practice what we call "Family Financing."

Yet it would have been missed or dismissed by many who could benefit most from it.

And it wouldn't have gotten to the heart of the matter: why generational wealth fails—and what to do about it.

If we had focused only on a financial product or strategy, we would have missed out on sharing the most important information that can help a family succeed over multiple successive generations—regardless of how wealth was acquired.

It became obvious—*Perpetual Wealth* couldn't only be a guide for using life insurance to build and pass down inheritances. It must also show families ways to build trust and support heirs in becoming leaders and wise stewards. It must help families communicate about "the important stuff"—including money and beyond—together.

As the book took shape, we realized that Family Financing was bigger than a strategy for implementing life insurance generationally. We needed to convey a message that, frankly, is often neglected by many agents or advisors who utilize life insurance for "Family Banking" strategies and focus only on a financial strategy or product.

We needed to start with a bigger context, a bigger question:

"What do most parents WANT for their child, grandchild, and other loved ones?"

You likely have no greater wish for your family than for each member to be happy, healthy, and successful. You want them to be free to develop their potential, pursue their dreams, and contribute their gifts to the world. You hope they'll carry on your values and adopt the traditions that define your family. You desire your family to be close and connected, a place of love and support—hopefully, even after you're gone. You'd like to leave a positive legacy, and you hope your heirs will do the same.

You'll find Perpetual Wealth especially valuable if...

You're unsure of what the future may hold and its financial impact. You don't have a crystal ball that tells you how long you will live or if you will face extraordinary health challenges or medical needs. Regardless of your net worth, you're aware that you could be just a few circumstances away from "losing it all." You desire greater certainty, flexibility, and confidence in your financial matters.

You want ideas. Perhaps you've been better at earning, growing, managing the nest egg than discussing it and preparing your heirs. You've heard about pricey private family retreats with family wealth managers, money coaches, and psychologists, but you're not ready to make that leap. You want some options—what can you do that fits your family, your budget, and your situation? You're just not sure where to start.

You need guidance. Perhaps your family has a good head start with the Family Financing method. You have efficient wealth transfer vehicles in place and you have been educating your family to grow and manage their own wealth. But what more could you be doing? How could money actually serve the larger family legacy you hope to pass on—a legacy of shared stories, values, experiences and mission?

You're starting (or starting over) from scratch. Maybe you are a parent who currently only dreams of things like "generational wealth." Perhaps you're just getting started, or re-started after a divorce, failed business venture, or other loss. You've got the capability to save a few hundred, perhaps a few thousand dollars a month, and you want to make the most of what you've got. You understand the importance of long-term wealth and want to give your children or grandchildren the "leg up" you never had.

If any of these scenarios ring true for you, then we wrote this book for you. We hope you'll utilize it for your family's future prosperity!

Kim D. H. Butler and Kate Phillips

To Patrick Donohoe:
Thanks for the title idea!

INTRODUCTION:
Why Family Financing?

> *"The best time to plant a tree was 20 years ago. The second best time is now."*

This Chinese proverb has a lot to say about generational wealth, which is a lot like a forest, an orchard, or an olive grove.

To create a sustainable forest that can be used for generations, you've got to think in terms of 100 years and longer. No matter how big the forest, if you keep harvesting trees and don't plant more, the trees will not last. If you plant, but you fail to teach the next generation to plant, the forest will eventually be depleted.

A Family Fund—the financial asset part of your Family Financing system—is a lot like an orchard. Most fruit trees must be planted 3-5 years before fruit is harvested. Once the harvest begins, a pear tree will bear fruit for 75 years or more. Trees in an orchard need to be pruned, watered and cared for if they are to produce harvests for generations.

The oldest working orchard in the United States, Applecrest Farm Orchards in New Hampshire, was planted in 1914. That's impressive, for an American orchard. But by Old World standards, it's hardly noteworthy.

In Southern Italy, there are olive trees that are *thousands* of years old. An olive tree is at its oil-producing "prime" when it is between 400-800 years old. Trees are revered and legally protected, as damage done to an olive grove takes many generations to restore. Some groves have been tended for hundreds of years by families who pass down time-honored traditions and expertise.

Whether you have been growing assets for decades that you hope will be used by heirs wisely and sustainably, or you're just beginning, the secret is simple:

Start planting.

Today.

And teach the future generations to do the same.

That's what makes wealth *perpetual.*

And *this* is what Family Financing is about.

What exactly do we mean by "Family Financing"?

In a nutshell, Family Financing is a strategy to grow and keep wealth in your family… *from generation to generation.* It has multiple components:

Family Financing is a *financial methodology* that often utilizes a long-term asset as its foundation—dividend-paying whole life insurance from a mutual company—to build long-term wealth, create an inheritance, pass it efficiently to beneficiaries, and show heirs how to use it well and wisely. It includes both financial *assets* and *guidance.*

Family Financing also represents a *product* (something you buy) along with a set of *strategies* (something you do) wrapped in the *context* of long-term thinking and a big idea:

Family Financing helps families invest in the future of the individuals that comprise the family and the values they share. This is the core philosophy of Family Financing.

We named the book *Perpetual Wealth* because Family Financing is a *repeatable process.* Family Financing makes wealth-building a sustainable, renewable practice that can be duplicated by each generation *"so as to seem endless and uninterrupted."*

And what do we mean by "Wealth"? It is commonly defined as:

> *1) an abundance of valuable possessions or money. 2) the state of being rich; material prosperity. 3) plentiful supplies of a particular resource.*

And yes, we mean financial abundance when we say "wealth." But true wealth isn't *only* about affluence or material prosperity.

According to Wisdom Works: "The etymology of the word 'wealth' is instructive here. It comes from the Middle English *wele* or 'well-being.' Before taking on connotations of financial riches, wealth meant the welfare of people; their general happiness and joy."

We like this more inclusive definition of wealth, because it IS about well-being—the well-being of a family and the welfare, happiness and joy of its members.

Family Financing is much more than just a financial strategy. It's also a *philosophy*, a *mindset*, and a set of *traditions* that can pass on a family's generational *wisdom*—not simply dollars.

Family Financing draws families together and helps your children, their children, and the children to follow, thrive and succeed. It teaches families to use money as a tool for growth and freedom, not a weapon for control or a "gift" that promotes dependency. It allows money to inspire teamwork and cooperation, rather than be the topic of conflicts or the "elephant in the room."

Without an intentional method to build and pass long-term wealth effectively, families tend to default to ineffective, even disastrous methods. Whether or not you realize it—if you are following typical financial advice, you're probably *sabotaging* generational wealth and wisdom rather than fostering it, as you'll see in chapter one.

The biggest financial fear is "running out of money," so most people focus on accumulating as much as they can. Some manage to accumulate more than their lifestyle—however luxurious or frugal—requires. Whatever is not spent during their lifetime is taxed heavily, before the remainder is (typically) quickly spent by heirs on new cars and such. And so, each generation scrambles to earn, invest and spend… earn, invest, spend *until there's nothing left.*

Even significant sums of money passed down can fail to disrupt the cycle for long. Substantial inheritances can backfire. Beneficiaries whose lifestyles are subsidized—even to the point of having no need to earn and invest for themselves—often skip straight to the spending stage. Entitled "trust fund babies" are every parent's worst fear and the inspiration for sayings such as, "Wealth rarely survives three generations."

Large or small—family fortunes rarely last. Future generations start again from scratch. Earn, invest and spend. Earn, invest and spend. And so the cycle repeats… unless it is broken.

Family Financing breaks the cycle.

To solve any problem, you must diagnose it properly. And the truth about generational wealth is that regardless of the financial strategies a family uses, the challenges of wealth go far beyond money itself. Just as a pill prescribed from a doctor can't override a lifetime of poor diet, lack of exercise and negative thinking, not even the best financial strategy will prevail in a family that cannot communicate about money and prepare beneficiaries for success.

Perpetual Wealth addresses both the monetary and non-monetary challenges of generational wealth. Both are essential, especially when you consider what multiple studies and a survey of 2,000 affluent families cited in *The Wall Street Journal* reveal:

- 70-90% of family wealth is lost by the third generation, say multiple studies.

- 60% of families who have seen their wealth dissipate point to a breakdown of trust and communication in the family as the biggest reason.
- 25% of families say wealth was lost because beneficiaries were unprepared to manage or preserve the inheritances that came their way.
- Vanishing wealth was rarely attributed to faulty financial or estate planning advice. Only 3% of affluent families surveyed pointed to this as the primary reason for lost fortunes.

The Family Financing model described in this book is based on long-term thinking and financial strategies. Perhaps more importantly, it helps to foster the type of trust, communication and education essential to the success of future generations.

Family Financing with whole life insurance creates an effective financial foundation and the most efficient wealth-transfer method we know of. Combined with the ideas and philosophy in *Perpetual Wealth*, it can change the way you THINK about money and use it in your family.

The Family Financing ideas and practices in *Perpetual Wealth* can help your family's legacy—financial and beyond—*last*.

The 7 Goals of Family Financing

How do you know if your family will benefit from *Perpetual Prosperity* and the strategies and products it advocates? It's a fair question. To answer it, see if these following seven goals align with your values and priorities.

1. **Create long-term "safe and sure" wealth.**
   Family Financing embraces a 150+ year old method that helps you grow wealth, safely and steadily, utilizing a financial product that has already helped generation after generation do just that. It is *not* intended to *replace* other financial and investment strategies; rather, it serves as an important financial *foundation* that can—

   - instill excellent saving habits

- enhance or create investments
- expand assets through the use of collateral
- eliminate unnecessary expenses
- reduce, defer, even eliminate taxes, and
- help you *keep* more of your money in your control while growing it safely and steadily—*guaranteed*.

2. **Protect against loss and provide for your family in ANY circumstance.**
   How many parents have big dreams and good intentions, but then a tragedy occurs—or LIFE happens—and their "plan" is never realized? The Family Financing method is a practically bulletproof financial strategy that can help you weather any economic storm and nearly any circumstance. It increases your financial privacy and can help protect you from opportunists. And it provides protection that ordinary financial vehicles just don't provide.

   Family Financing is more than just a savings plan. It can provide extra assistance to your family in the most challenging situation, including death, disability, even a terminal illness.

3. **Cultivate long-term thinking and an enlightened view of wealth.**
   The Family Financing method fosters an elevated, big-picture view of wealth. It helps family members think generationally rather than short-term. It rewards perseverance and supports the family's values. Family Financing cultivates an appreciation for the wisdom of the family elders and nurtures leadership at all ages.

4. **Implement strategies for generational wealth creation.**
   Perpetual Wealth gives you financial strategies for *sustainable* wealth, both during and beyond your lifetime. Its practices ensure that wealth is grown and replaced each generation, like a well-managed forest designed to last. Family Financing gives your family the mindset, strategies and skills to forever break the too-common cycle of wealth that is hard-earned by industrious founders, and easily spent by heirs.

5. **Raise children (and adults) who are financially responsible, not entitled.**

   Most parents desire to be generous with their children, yet fear that gifts of wealth might not be used wisely—or worse, may even cripple a child's independence. Family Financing *fosters* responsibility. It encourages heirs to become *builders* and *stewards* of wealth, rather than *consumers* of wealth.

6. **Use wealth to support the people and causes you care about.**

   If you follow typical financial strategies, much of the inheritance intended for your loved ones will end up going to Uncle Sam! Family Financing helps you keep more wealth "all in the family," protecting it from creditors, predators and a government eager to redistribute the money you have earned and saved over a lifetime to others.

   Family Financing shows you how to USE assets to develop the most important capital you've ever met: *the human capital within your own family.* It provides a source of capital for younger and future generations. It can also be used to nurture giving.

7. **Create a legacy of more than money.**

   You'll find ideas in *Perpetual Wealth* for "best practices" to transfer a generational legacy that goes far beyond dollars. You'll be encouraged to define what's unique about your family. You'll find structures to help you (and each member of your family) share your stories, dreams, and unique contributions. Family Financing creates opportunities for each family member to follow their own path to success, with support from each other. And it embraces traditions such as Family Retreats, Councils and Mission Statements that can bring your family closer together and create priceless memories.

If these seven goals seem worthwhile to you, you'll find stories, examples, ideas and specific strategies in *Perpetual Wealth* to reach them.

What you'll find in this book...

In addition to the seven goals, you'll discover in the pages of this book:

- How to use Family Financing to pass on wealth while you are still alive to see your heirs use your gifts, often *free of income taxes, gift-taxes and estate taxes.*
- What we can learn from families who have built and sustained great wealth over multiple generations.
- How to communicate with other family members about generational wealth and use Family Financing to teach essential financial skills.
- How to increase the growth of cash in your "Family Fund" using special life insurance riders.
- Ideas for successful Family Retreats.
- How trusts can be integrated with Family Financing strategies.
- Ideas for family giving and philanthropy.
- How to best structure life insurance for Family Financing.
- A sample letter to heirs.
- Ideas for structure, guidelines, and best practices for Family Lending.
- The what, why and how on obtaining life insurance for adult children and/or grandchildren.
- Additional resources for a prosperous life.

The great majority of this content in this book is new. If you read The Prosperity Blog at Partners4Prosperity.com/blog,[1] you might recognize portions of articles that have been adapted for the book. (For notifications of new articles and podcasts, along with a copy of *Financial Planning Has Failed,* the last ebook we authored together, sign up for our Prosperity Accelerator Pack at Partners4Prosperity.com/subscribe.)[2]

Meet Our Family Financing Guides

Soon, you'll meet John and Carol, who will help us make many ideas and strategies more concrete. John and Carol are "composite" characters from our experience and imagination, rather than a real-life couple. (You might have "met" John and Carol in a special report, *Permission to*

Spend: How to Spend Your Principle, Save a Fortune on Taxes, Increase Your Cash Flow… and Never Run Out of Money! You can download the report at ProsperityEconomics.org/permission.)[3]

Confidentiality would prevent us from revealing details about actual clients, so John and Carol allow us to share stories based on real-world examples. They provide examples of what is possible with Family Financing and act as our guides for practical implementation.

Note: while John and Carol are "upper-middle class," don't get distracted by the numbers. Focus on the *concepts*. Whether your family has significantly more or less than "The Johnsons," the principles and mindset are scalable in either direction.

Some ideas may seem quite basic—like the importance of saving money consistently. If you are already implementing, great! Maybe you can do even better. If not, we challenge you to avoid any thoughts of, "But… I know this already!" Rather, consider—how effective are you at implementing the "basic" concepts you already know?

You may already be a "sophisticated investor" by many measures. And yet, you still may not have built a solid financial *foundation* that can "weatherproof" your family's wealth! (This is not uncommon… investing and speculating can be more fun and interesting than saving and protecting.)

Fortunately, it's not too late. You can prepare today for tomorrow's financial storms.

Whether you are just starting to save or you already have a sizeable nest egg, let *Perpetual Wealth* spark your imagination and inspire you to take action. We hope you'll decide to transform *your* family's future and create a legacy with Family Financing!

A Quick Guide to *Perpetual Wealth*

This book is written in a logical, sequential "order." Each chapter builds on ideas previously established, so we recommend reading it in order. However, we provide the following for those who wish to revisit certain topics, or for those who already have certain products and strategies in place and wish to "skip ahead."

Ever wonder why so few families create and keep wealth? The problem is—commonly recommended financial strategies set you up to fail! Learn why so many Americans fail to grow and keep sustainable wealth in chapter one, "How Typical Financial Advice *Sabotages* Family Wealth."

Not saving 20% or more of your income? Do you struggle to save consistently? Read chapter two to understand "The Simple 'Secret' of Family Wealth." You'll be motivated to save!

Are you a whole life insurance skeptic? If you don't have whole life, aren't sure how it works or don't "get" why people use and recommend it, read chapter three, "The Foundation of Family Financing." You'll understand why whole life insurance is the BEST way to start your Family Fund!

Want the basics of Family Financing? You'll find them in chapter four. To understand how multi-generational life-insurance strategies work, why Family Financing is the new family business, and how to find the cash to fund policies, read "A New Paradigm for Generational Wealth."

Why do families rarely STAY wealthy? What causes even affluent families to *lose* their wealth? For the answers, we examine some compelling research and lessons from two of the wealthiest families in history: the Vanderbilts and Rothschilds. Discover the keys to building and *keeping* wealth in chapter five, "Long-Term Thinking, Lasting Wealth."

Understand the "why" and "how" of life insurance for children and grandchildren. Perhaps you're unsure about life insurance for children—or just not sure how to get your family on board. Chapter six, "Family Financing with Your Children" will answer your questions!

Want the nuts and bolts of using life insurance for your Family Fund? Chapter seven explains how whole life policies work. We also give you an overview of other types of life insurance, a Policy Question Checklist and links to other helpful resources. Don't get life insurance without reading "How to Build a Family Fund that Lasts" first!

Should you leave an inheritance? How can you prepare your heirs? In chapter eight, we glean wisdom from families who have succeeded in building wealth—and keeping it. You'll enjoy the stories and the lessons in "Inheritance Wisdom, Wealth and Warnings."

What traditions have made the Rockefellers so successful? You may be familiar with the concept of the Family Office. The Rockefellers also pioneered Family Retreats—a remarkable way to build unity and leverage the human capital within the family. Read chapter nine, "The Rockefellers' Secret Weapon."

Want ideas for Family Retreats and Mission Statements? In chapter ten, the Johnsons take a road trip to Colorado. Come tag along and learn how our family pulls off an inspiring and successful event in "The First Family Retreat."

How can you best utilize Family Lending to benefit your family? In chapter eleven, we contrast *lending* money to family members with *giving* money. We offer guidelines to help you determine when borrowing against a policy makes sense—and when it doesn't. You'll also learn how to compare borrowing from a life insurance company versus other sources to find the best option in "The Beauty of Borrowing."

Who makes decisions about family money—and how? This chapter is full of ideas you can use to define the governance and leadership roles in your family's strategy. We also give you a sample letter to an heir outlining the ins and outs of Family Financing in chapter twelve, "Family Financing Governance and Leadership."

How can your children grow up to be productive rather than entitled? It is never too early to begin a child's wealth education! Everyday situations provide opportunities to convey financial values and instill positive habits. We give you concrete strategies and suggestions in chapter thirteen, "Raising Financially Responsible Children."

Are you "on track" to reach financial independence? In chapter fourteen, we show you how to utilize "Prosperity Economics" at every stage of life. "The 7 Phases of Prosperity" is your lifelong financial checklist!

How do you preserve and protect wealth for a lifetime—and beyond? Learn how wills, trusts and life insurance all work together. We give you the basics on different types of trusts as well as seven rules that will stop you from making critical mistakes in naming beneficiaries. Read chapter fifteen, "Wills, Trusts and Wealth Transfers."

What are you leaving behind and what is your legacy? Explore the full meaning of legacy with practical tips for communicating more effectively and preserving family traditions and treasures. Learn what *not* to leave your children and how to create a multi-generational legacy in chapter sixteen, "Leaving the Legacy You Intend."

What's the most important key to lasting *wealth?* With a little help from Leonardo da Vinci, chapter seventeen emphasizes the importance of long-term thinking. You'll love the book's conclusion, "Winning the Long Game of Wealth."

We sincerely hope you'll seize the opportunity to not only *read* the information in this book, but to *apply* it for the benefit of your family for years—and generations—to come!

CHAPTER 1:

How Typical Financial Advice Sabotages Family Wealth

Now that John and Carol were retired, they usually enjoyed leisurely mornings together. Carol would fix breakfast (unless it was scrambled eggs with salmon, which was John's specialty) and they would enjoy their morning meal and coffee. In between bites and banter, John would read the Wall Street Journal *and check the stock market on his smart phone, while Carol perused the local paper and played crossword puzzles.*

"Wow, just when I think I can predict the market, it makes a fool of me!" exclaimed John this morning.

"Bad news?" inquired Carol, while trying to think of another word for sailboat that also had 8 letters.

"Oh, it dropped 6% last week! We're still up for the year, and it could bounce back, but wow—6% is no small amount! I hope it's not the start of the next bear market."

"I hate to ask… but what's that drop measured in dollars?"

"What? My wife wants details?" joked John. He was the big picture guy, and he knew that Carol liked to get down to the nitty gritty. "Well, our last brokerage statements added up to just over $2 million, I was pleased to see..."

"—So we just lost over $120 thousand last week while we were in Hawaii!?" Carol responded with a bit of shock, demonstrating that even though she no longer taught middle school math, she could still crunch numbers on the fly. "I thought that was an expensive vacation, but you're right—Wow!"

John looked a little nauseous, just like he had after a couple of hours on the famously curvy Road to Hana.

"Ouch, when you put it that way, that's a tremendous amount!" John answered. "Somehow 'six percent' sounded more palatable than 'one hundred and twenty thousand.' I worked years of my life before I earned that much!"

"I know we've been over this before," said Carol, "but I just don't know if it's smart to have that much money in the market."

"Well, we've got other assets and investments, of course, including the two rental homes and bank CDs, which didn't lose a penny last week."

"Yeah—and I don't think those CDs earned a penny, either!" quipped Carol with a grin.

John had been a bank branch manager, and along with Carol's teaching salary and a little real estate investing, they had done well for themselves. They had "followed the rules" of what you're supposed to do with your money: "Max out your 401(k), invest in mutual funds, save in a bank, and buy a house with a 15-year mortgage." But now that they were finally retired—after both deciding to work longer when their 401(k)s became 201(k)s in the last downturn—they were both questioning if they were on the right financial path.

"Maybe we should have taken the advice of that advisor we met with a couple months ago... the guy that Alex and Jordan introduced us to. He gave an interesting talk about sustainable wealth... using life insurance policies to create generational wealth..."

"Oh yeah, he called it 'Perpetual Wealth,'" said Carol. "It was a system for Family Financing. It was definitely interesting. I remember that the life insurance would immediately raise the value of our estate. I mean, if we're eventually

going to transfer wealth, why not transfer more of it to the people we love? I know I still have his card somewhere..."

"That's right. I've always thought of life insurance as the best means to transfer wealth when you die, but he talked about ways to use it to create a source of family lending, also a way to get our kids saving. It definitely got me thinking outside of the box... or should I say, outside of the bank!"

"That's not easy for a banker!" said Carol as she pulled a card out of her purse and held it up. "Here it is. 'Jerry Lee... Prosperity Economics Advisor,' it says."

"That's right. And it sounded like the method could help us save on taxes. It's depressing to see how much of our retirement accounts could go to Uncle Sam if we don't make some changes," mused John. "Not to mention, it would someday save the kids a ton of tax if we left them life insurance rather than our IRAs."

"The kids" were their adult daughters, Cyndi and Julie, and their families. They were both married and had two sons each. John and Carol loved being grandparents to the four grandsons.

"I wouldn't have thought to start new policies, at our age, but those little policies we purchased when the girls were young have done well for us. Jerry said some things that made sense... maybe we should learn more. Plus I know it's time to diversify into different asset classes."

"I'm in," said Carol. "And I know how stressed you get when the stock market is down. I think we'd both sleep better with less of our money riding the stock market roller coaster!"

While she didn't bring up the topic of money often, Carol thought about it more than she let on. John and Carol still had much of their portfolio in retirement accounts where their money seemed under constant threat from market volatility, taxes and fees. It felt like a big chunk of their money was "trapped" in the IRAs, and they both knew it was a poor strategy for transferring wealth when the time came.

As she cleared the breakfast dishes, she found herself thinking that maybe there was something to this Family Financing idea. She went to fetch her notes from Jerry's presentation. A point he made that had really stuck with her was this: "Wealthy people rarely follow typical financial advice; it's more reliable at helping banks and brokerages build long-term wealth than helping families build long-term wealth!"

"Schooner!" John blurted out suddenly.

"What? Oh, the sailboat word! Thank-you, dear."

. . . . .

Common Advice, Disappointing Results

The financial planning industry only arose in the 1970s, with the first class of 42 certified financial planners graduating in 1973. Since then, the financial planning and advice industry has mushroomed into a $57.2 billion dollar industry in the US alone, according to a 2020 IBISWorld report,[4] and that figure *excludes* "mutual fund companies, hedge funds, discount brokers, [and] insurance brokers." An industry website[5] reports 86,910 CFP professionals in the United States—an increase of more than 10% in 47 years!

Are we better off with all this financial advice, along with the explosive growth of the 401(k), target-date mutual funds, and universal life insurance? Hardly! As boomers retire, many millennials struggle. And notably, we've seen both a decline in generational wealth and a decline in generational giving.

According a 2018 report by the Federal Reserve, millennials have less wealth than baby boomers did at their age, due primarily to debt. Other analysis done by the Young Invincibles using Federal Reserve data showed that median household incomes for millennials were actually 20% less than boomers at this young adult stage of life. Fewer millennials owned their own homes, revealed The Young Invincibles 2017 report, and both young adult assets and net wealth had "declined by half in a generation."

A 2015 Census study showed that "millennials are more likely to have a college degree than Gen X-ers did in 1980, yet there are also higher numbers of millennials living in poverty vs. their counterparts in 1980." And the average college debt of over $32k doesn't help matters.

Many boomers are retiring with more wealth than those in previous generations, partially due to a long bull market in stocks, plus their own inheritances. Meanwhile, young people earn less, save less and are more likely to live with their parents than in generations past. And they are less likely to be married (which correlates positively to wealth) or independent. They are also much more likely to be in debt, and more likely to be spending money on smartphones, data packages, streaming entertainment, designer coffees, and other expenses their parents did not have at their age.

Forbes summarized the situation: "Baby Boomers: your millennial children are worse off than you." And while we won't blame the financial planning industry for rising college costs or millennial spending habits, it's fair to ask—Has typical financial advice helped or hurt?

American workers are encouraged and even incentivized to put money in 401(k)s, IRAs and other retirement vehicles. "Max out your 401(k) plan" has become ubiquitous financial advice. Unfortunately, these popular retirement plans make lousy nest eggs and terrible wealth transfer vehicles. And they are just one way that common financial advice can *sabotage* long-term family wealth.

If your goal is generational prosperity, watch out that these 10 problems don't become obstacles to your family legacy:

Problem #1: Invest Now, Save "Someday."

Our process and priorities are backwards. We're taught to invest first, use that as our savings, often incentivized by ever-dwindling 401(k) "matches" (now often only 25 cents to the dollar). It is inefficient and disruptive to use retirement accounts as emergency funds, yet many people start putting money into their 401(k) before they have their first $1,000 in savings. Should they need money, they'll pay onerous penalties and taxes to free it from a retirement account.

Worse, those who "invest first, save later" have no *liquidity* for *opportunities* as well as emergencies. Trained to delegate their spare dollars to mutual funds as soon as they get a job, workers are dis-incentivized from saving towards a home down payment, a chance to open their own business, or investments outside of the typical brokerage environment. And when emergencies strike or markets fail, they lose dollars, lose momentum, and find themselves starting over and over again.

To build your financial foundation, *save first* before investing. By saving first, you prepare for emergencies, then, for opportunities. What do we mean by "saving"? Prioritize putting money where it is SAFE and where you are protected from risk and loss.

Even BANKS must have savings. If they are undercapitalized, they stand to fail. Banks must have adequate "Tier One Capital" to be financially secure and prepare for the future. And guess where banks save many of their dollars? Yup—life insurance! Up to 25% of Tier One Capital held at major banks—hundreds of *billions* of dollars—are in life insurance cash value. This ensures obligations for future employee benefits will be met.

Saving builds your family's financial foundation, and without it, your investments are on shaky ground.

To further understand why saving is so important, let's look at a primary difference between saving and investing...

Problem #2: The Normalizing of Systemic Risk.

How many fortunes have been lost before they could be utilized or passed to future generations? Plenty! With typical financial strategies and vehicles, money is invested in mutual funds subject to systemic market risk. "Systemic risk" is so named because it affects the whole *system*. Investopedia defines systemic risk as "the risk inherent to the entire market or market segment... also known as 'undiversifiable risk,' 'volatility,' or 'market risk,' affects the overall market, not just a particular stock or industry."

It is a deception to think that if your holdings in the stock market are well-diversified—small cap vs. large cap, different industries, different countries, perhaps even mutual funds from different brokerages—then you're protected from downside risk. Yet Americans are repeatedly told, "Max out your 401(k)"—or, to invest mostly or exclusively in stocks and securities vulnerable to systemic risk.

Financial gurus try to guess the "next hot stock" while financial advisors urge us to bet on the market instead of getting back to basics and actually taking Rule #1 seriously: "Never lose money." The stock market can do well in the long run, no doubt—but the dips can be devastating. When the Financial Crisis hit, businesses failed and would-be retirees and college students were forced to defer their plans. While some risk can be acceptable and nearly unavoidable in a portfolio, your focus should be on steady growth, safety and financial fundamentals rather than risk-taking strategies.

Problem #3: Focus on Net Worth, Not Human Capital or Cash Flow.

Typical financial thinking equates a person's value with their net worth, which trains you to focus on your portfolio balance rather than invest in yourself. As authors Michael Ellsberg and Bryan Franklin argue in *The Last Safe Investment*, "Financial Advice Commonly Derived," or FACD, is a plan that is "broken at every step." Designed to maximize net worth (and assets under management), it separates investments from your greatest asset: your human capital—the skills, knowledge and experience you bring to the marketplace.

The focus on net worth can also compromise your ability to build cash flow sooner rather than later. Unfortunately, building the biggest money mountain possible can be counter-productive if at least a portion of it cannot be quickly and easily turned into a healthy and reliable income stream.

There is a saying, "You can't eat equity." Net worth in a 401(k) and real estate equity are good assets to have, but building your human capital will do much more to help you build long-term wealth. And by creating cash flow, you'll be able to *preserve* wealth rather than "eating" your principle. (Cash Flow is not the primary focus of Family Financing, but it is one of the 7 Principles of Prosperity.[6])

Problem #4: Goal Is Retirement, Not Productivity and Contribution.

Retirement (which means "to be taken out of service") can sabotage generational wealth. Besides, automatic retirement at 65 or any other arbitrary age makes no sense! Many people cannot save enough money during their working years to support themselves adequately for another 20, 30, or more years. They stop work, then end up scrimping and saving rather than enjoying themselves. Some become bored without the structure and meaning of work. And those who keep working, realizing they can't afford to retire, feel like they've failed.

We encourage people to find work they love so much that they would never dream of retiring! We are meant to be productive, to contribute, and to receive in return. So instead of retirement, we encourage you to cut back, perhaps freelance, consult, start a business and/or volunteer. Kim has written an entire book with many examples of creative alternatives—as well as a sobering analysis of 401(k)s—called *Busting the Retirement Lies.*

Problem #5: Temporary Protection that May Come Too Late.

Life insurance protects our most important assets—the people we love and care about, including the breadwinners we rely on. But don't we all know someone who died without a policy that would have provided for their family? And as people age, their chances of becoming uninsurable due to a health crisis increase.

When a whole life policy is put in place, a permanent death benefit is guaranteed as long as the policy remains in force. Yet many people don't insure and protect themselves until they are already married and/or have children who rely on their income.

Millennials are the most under-insured group, even though the ideal time to get insurance is when you're young. As Investopedia points out in "What is the Best Age to Get Life Insurance?" the optimal age for purchasing life insurance is "right after birth." That's because the cost of life insurance is age-dependent as well as health dependent and fixed for the life of a policy. Sure, you can wait and pay more later, but there's a risk of an illness or accident that could eliminate the option of obtaining life insurance.

Problem #6: Expiring Death Benefits.

On the other end of the spectrum, typical financial advice tells us to purchase term life insurance, which is almost guaranteed to end before we need it. Many also buy universal life insurance with rising internal costs and no permanent death benefit guarantee.

"Buy term and invest the difference," is parroted by financial gurus and authors. Supposedly, you'll earn 12% in the stock market and be "self-insured" by the time your term insurance expires. But it doesn't work out that way for most people. They put their money into a temporary term life insurance policy that pays only *if* the insured dies, rather than paying into a policy that pays *when* the insured passes away!

Life insurance is the only type of insurance that covers a "when" event— death—not an "if" event, such as a house burning down. If there was a 100% chance your house would eventually catch fire, would you buy the kind of policy that would remain in place, or a cheap temporary policy likely to expire—like a product warranty—*before* you needed it? Both term and whole life are useful, but some of your insurance should be permanent!

Ironically, typical financial advice to "buy term and invest the difference" fails to protect your family from the two certainties of life: *death* and—as we'll examine next—*taxes*.

Problem #7: Government Rules and Taxes.

As I illustrate in depth with Truth Concepts financial software in the book *Busting the Retirement Lies*,[7] you might end up paying *more* in income taxes than your *total contributions* to your 401(k) or other retirement plan!

Want to use your 401(k) or other qualified retirement plan to start a business or invest in yourself before age 59-1/2? You'll pay a penalty *in addition* to the taxes!

Want to borrow against your 401(k)? Mind the rules and timelines—if you can borrow at all. Oh yes—and you'll repay the loan with *after tax* dollars, not the pre-tax dollars that originally funded the account. That will cost you! And if you want to borrow against your IRA… you *can't*. Government rules don't allow it.

Want to pass on your 401(k) or traditional IRA? Unless you're still working, you'll be forced to take minimum required distributions after age 72—whether you want to or not. And leaving your retirement account to a beneficiary just got way more complicated with the new SECURE Act legislation! Adult children or grandchildren who inherit a sizable IRA could now face a BIG tax bill—especially if they are high earners.

The "stretch IRA"—a strategy that used to allow beneficiaries to "stretch" distributions over their life expectancy—is now only available for a spouse or limited exceptions such as minor children. All other beneficiaries must drain their entire accounts—and pay income taxes on the distributions— within 10 years. Stretching out distributions over a long a period as possible used to minimize taxes. Not surprisingly, the government figured out how to get a larger cut—as soon as possible!

This drives home the fact: *whatever the government gives, it can take away.* The government can *change* the rules of retirement plans—what types of assets are allowable in your retirement plan, when and how quickly assets must be removed, or any other rule!

Then there are taxes. If you pass on your 401(k) or traditional IRA to a beneficiary, you'll probably leave them a tax bill along with it. Unless you have Roth accounts and not traditional 401(k)s or IRAs, heirs will pay income taxes on distributions. If they make a healthy income, they could pay more in taxes on the inheritance than the taxes *you* originally deferred!

IRAs, 401(k)s and other qualified retirement accounts are *growth* vehicles, not *asset transfer* vehicles. They're not designed for the purpose of transferring wealth, so it's no surprise they don't do it efficiently. Life insurance transfers wealth with the utmost efficiency because that's what it was *designed* to do.

Problem #8: Never-ending Fees.

Assets are continually subjected to multiple fees—administration fees, fund fees, management fees, broker fees, etc. Some fees are hidden from plain sight, and most are charged on your entire balance, year after year, increasing with the size of your account. A study done by demos.org in 2012, The Retirement Savings Drain,[8] found a median-income couple pays nearly $155k in such fees by the time they retire—nearly *one third* of their investment returns! Households that earn incomes greater than that of three-quarters of Americans paid as much as $277,969 in fees alone. You might pay more.

Those "tiny little fees" add up, and many investors keep paying them, often for years and even decades after retirement. People keep paying fees to keep deferring the mountain of income taxes that will come due if they move their money out of the IRA environment. This is no accident.

The Palm Beach Research Group (an independent group that publishes investment recommendations and financial education, they don't sell investments or life insurance) published a shocking and controversial study a few years ago comparing those "little fees" and commissions on mutual funds to the "big commissions" people think they'll pay with life insurance:

> *The bottom line is that "little" 1.5% mutual fund fee generated eight times as much fees as the life insurance policy over 40 years. More importantly… that 1.5% mutual fund fee caused a difference of $718,433 in final account value… for a loss of 36%.*

> *After 20 years, the fees in the life insurance policy equate to what would be a mutual fund with an annual 0.50% fee.*

> *After 30 years, the fees in the life insurance policy equate to what would be a mutual fund with an annual 0.25% fee.*

> *After 40 years, the fees in the life insurance policy equate to what would be a mutual fund with an annual 0.15% fee!*

While a mutual fund and a whole life insurance policy are "apples and oranges" in many ways (and both can have their place in a portfolio), it's worth understanding how the fees you're paying work. (See more in our "Life Insurance Commission Shock"[9] article.)

Problem #9: Lack of Liquidity and Control.

Typical financial advice keeps you building assets you won't *use* until you retire. Let's face it—the goal of much financial advice is to accumulate money that banks and brokerages can use to *their* advantage—not necessarily yours!

As we detail in *Live Your Life Insurance*, you want to "have a C.L.U.E." with your money:

- **Control**—don't hand over control of your money to a broker, the government, or a volatile market.
- **Liquidity**—keep a portion of your money liquid so that you can act on opportunities and have protection from emergencies.
- **Use**—save money where you can easily access it, leverage it, and put it to work.
- **Equity**—whether in real estate, a whole life policy or elsewhere, acquire assets you can build equity in.

Many popular investments such as mutual funds in 401(k)s, IRAs and brokerage accounts have rules, restrictions and limitations to using your own money as collateral for loans. This is an essential element of Family Financing strategies, so we use a financial product that can be borrowed against easily.

Another way typical financial advice reduces your control and use of your own money is by teaching you to segment your savings into many different small "buckets" that can't be easily combined. College dollars go in the 529, retirement dollars in the 401(k) or IRA, emergency money in the bank account, healthcare dollars somewhere else, etc.

Segmenting your dollars might help you feel more organized, but it can be problematic. You don't really know *how much* money you'll need to be prepared for *which* future challenges. You can end up saving "too much" in the *wrong* places! Maybe you don't need all the money in your Health Savings Account, but you could really use it for college tuition. Or maybe your child won't go to college, but they could use access to capital to help them start a business.

Problem #10: It Doesn't Prepare Heirs for Success.

Typical financial planning focuses on growing assets so that you can someday retire, live on the money you've accumulated, and (perhaps) leave an inheritance to your children.

Typical estate planning focuses on how to reduce taxes when transferring assets.

These are worthy aims, but typical financial planning and estate planning miss critical elements for successful generational wealth building and preservation.

Neither typical financial plans nor estate plans prioritize the *relationship* between the giver and the receiver of an inheritance, or the *readiness* of the beneficiary. Yet both are essential for the success of generational wealth.

"Just let them sort it out after we're dead!" is a common phrase uttered when it comes to deciding on the critical details of a long-term legacy strategy. But generational wealth tends to fail when left to chance.

Heirs must build their own financial, intellectual and emotional foundations. Some expect large windfalls, and are unprepared to support themselves if they inherit less than they expect, or when a trust places limitations that don't allow them to use funds to subsidize their lifestyle. Others inherit large, unencumbered fortunes, but lack the discipline and skills to sustain it or teach future generations to become wise stewards.

No matter the size of the inheritance, many heirs lack the instruction and long-term vision that would enable them to use and preserve wealth beyond their own lifetimes. The family's financial capital is diluted and dissipated, along with the vision and mission that drove its success in the first place.

It's fairly common for families to fracture following the death of family matriarch and/or patriarch. They fail to transfer and nurture the intellectual, social and human capital of the family, and the financial capital suffers as a result. Only a fraction of the descendants—if any—go on to succeed like their parents or grandparents.

The Perpetual Wealth Solution

If we had to boil down these ten problems causing generational wealth to fail and falter in the great majority of American families, it would come to ONE thing:

Short-term thinking.

When you fail to save and build liquidity... when you take a tax break now in exchange for decades of taxation and fees in retirement... when you roll the stock market dice without preparing for the next recession... when you obtain life insurance that will expire too soon... when you fail to prepare heirs for success and decide to let beneficiaries "figure it out when you're dead," *you are sabotaging long-term wealth.*

So if Family Financing breaks the cycle of generational wealth sabotage, how exactly does it do that!? Through four key elements conspicuously *missing* from typical investing advice and practices—all of them, not coincidentally, characterized by *long-term thinking.*

We created this chart as a visual representation of the Family Financing method:

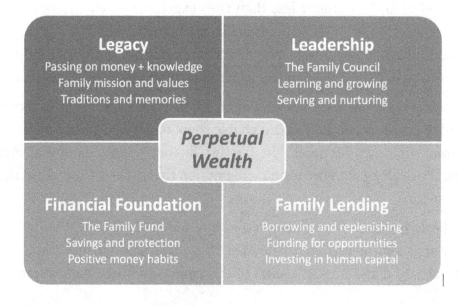

Legacy
Passing on money + knowledge
Family mission and values
Traditions and memories

Leadership
The Family Council
Learning and growing
Serving and nurturing

Perpetual Wealth

Financial Foundation
The Family Fund
Savings and protection
Positive money habits

Family Lending
Borrowing and replenishing
Funding for opportunities
Investing in human capital

Cornerstone #1: Financial Foundation

Let's start in the lower left. We placed the Financial Foundation at the bottom because, after all, it's what all else rests upon.

You've no doubt heard the parable that warns the listener to never build a house upon the sand: "The rain fell, and the floods came, the winds blew and beat against that house, and it fell…" (Matthew 7:27). It's the same with your *financial* house! You must build the proper Financial Foundation for a family—beginning with the simple (yet often overlooked) habit of *saving*.

Your *savings* creates your "Family Fund": the "seed money" for your family's wealth and prosperity. It's the money that's guaranteed to grow—no matter what. This is your fund for emergencies *and* opportunities. It's the money that lets you sleep at night—even when a financial storm is wreaking havoc on most investors.

Because of the unique, centuries-old financial product we use for saving in the Family Financing system, the foundation of your financial house comes with insurance for the storms of life built right in!

Just like saving money, risk management and permanent protection are often not given the full attention they deserve. You probably have car insurance, home insurance, and other types of insurance. But the Family Financing system insures the most valuable treasure possible: the *people* in your family.

Usually, "savings and protection" are NOT the same thing—not at all. But whole life insurance works differently.

Insurance policy premiums for your home, car, and term life insurance policies—except in the rare instance when the insured unfortunately dies before it expires—represent *costs*. You pay the premiums and cross your fingers you won't need the coverage. Either way, the premiums are long-gone. And the more premiums you pay, the less you can save.

Whole life premiums are completely different. Over time, they turn into an *asset*. This makes whole life insurance the ideal foundation for your family's personal economy. The more you save, the more protection you have! And the more protection you purchase—the more liquidity you have available in your Family Fund.

Cornerstone #2: Family Lending

To the right of Financial Foundation you see Family Lending. This is a system for leveraging The Family Fund to invest in the success of the family. This could include investing in your family's human capital through education, training, mentorship, etc. It could include investing in financial assets, such as cash-flowing real estate, or providing a down payment for a first home. It could be used to launch or expand a family business or refinance higher-interest debt so it can be paid off more quickly.

Family Lending serves another, perhaps less-obvious purpose. It gives younger family members an opportunity to learn and practice their money management. Do they want to apply for a family loan? Great, they will need to show they are saving first! Then they will have to apply for the financing they desire using a process that will require them to think through WHY they want that money and how it aligns with the values your family holds dear.

Family Lending provides valuable money management lessons. Young family members will get practice paying back what they borrow! They'll be responsible for determining their repayment schedule and replenishing the Family Fund. They'll also have opportunities to sit on the Family Council and see how and why loans are approved—or not approved.

Cornerstone #3: Leadership

Family Financing leverages more than financial assets—it leverages the experience, skills and wisdom of the founders and other leaders.

Family gatherings, retreats, and governance offer opportunities for younger family members to grow leadership skills and confidence. And while the "financial" part of Family Financing can be done very simply without any of those structures, the chance to nurture family relationships and allow younger members to learn from family elders is priceless.

This cornerstone also reminds us that generational wealth is *not* primarily a process of growing *dollars* that can be passed from parents to younger generations. It's about growing children and grandchildren into *leaders*. Whether they are leading a company, a team at a job, or a household, Family Financing can provide opportunities to:

- work with others towards common goals
- speak and give presentations
- demonstrate discipline and responsibility
- nurture their ability for long-term thinking and consistent action
- evaluate and advocate for non-profits doing good in the world
- contemplate corporate and personal mission and values
- participate in planning events and making decisions
- help guide younger family members.

Cornerstone #4: Legacy

Now we end in the upper left-hand corner, in the place where some people would prefer to begin—with the inheritance! And perhaps this is the point the grid helps to drive home: virtually every parent would love to *give* an inheritance, just as a child hopes to *receive* one. However, very few families have a *system* for creating inheritances with certainty.

If you follow the Family Financing method, it will ensure that each generation saves for the next and one financial legacy leads to another. And true wealth—remember, it means "well being"—extends far beyond a trust fund or inheritance. Your legacy also includes the values and traditions you wish to leave behind, and so much more.

Perpetual Prosperity takes a holistic view of "legacy" and gives you tools and ideas to create a legacy that goes far beyond dollars, far beyond your own capabilities and limitations, and even beyond the confines of your lifetime.

THE BOTTOM LINE

Family Financing practices can help you develop the *financial* capital AND the *human* capital of your family. By understanding how typical financial advice sets you up to fail, you can do better! You can succeed. Your children can succeed, and your children's children can succeed.

Your legacy can succeed.

Typical financial planning—while much better than nothing—leaves much to be desired when it comes to building and maintaining wealth for generations. There is SO much more to prosperity than a balance sheet. That's why the Family Financing method in *Perpetual Wealth* helps you invest in the most important thing you know of... the PEOPLE in your family!

CHAPTER 2:
The Simple "Secret" of Family Wealth

"Should I schedule an appointment for us with Jerry Lee?" asked Carol over breakfast. "We could learn more about Family Financing, and maybe making some other changes with our investments, too."

"Why don't you do that," replied John, peering over his Wall Street Journal. "Our new broker—the guy who replaced Hank—didn't have much useful advice about our financial strategy. He really just offers mutual funds and the types of investments we're trying to diversify away from.

"Hank did his best, but he seemed to have limited tools," commented Carol, recalling their old broker.

"He thought there was a mutual fund for every problem," John affirmed. "They were his 'hammer,' and everything looked like a nail... until the Financial Crisis proved him wrong!"

"He shut down his business, didn't he?"

"Passed it to the new guy and retired. It's tough when your recommendations lose half their value. I hear he's fishing a lot these days, probably still avoiding his old clients! But I can't blame him; almost everyone got caught in that storm."

"Well, even though our investments took a hit, we weathered the storm better than most," said Carol. "I mean, our jobs didn't go away, and we had money in savings."

"I know... I almost just said, 'we were lucky,' but really, we were prepared. It saddens me when I meet customers at the bank and realize they don't even have $200 to their name. I'm not talking about young people just out of high school or college, either—these are middle-aged people and seniors who have probably worked for many years."

Carol thought back to when she taught a personal economics class, hoping it helped spare some students the same fate. "When I taught that economics class at the high school, I always emphasized building an emergency fund that could carry you for at least 3 months. I could tell it was hard for some kids to grasp the concept saving thousands of dollars to keep—not spend. But then, the Great Recession came along and showed me that maybe 3 months of expenses wasn't nearly enough!"

"Yup—I knew a few people who were out of work for a year or more after the big layoffs," recounted John. "I think from the time the girls were small, we always kept $10k in savings—plus the cash value in our life insurance, which is now well into six figures. Of course, that was our life insurance as well as our savings, so that bill got paid every month, right after the mortgage. And anyways, ten thousand dollars would have disappeared awfully fast if either of us had received pink slips."

"No kidding! I'll admit—it wasn't always easy writing that check for premiums. After Julie was born, I recall we had to use policy loans—automatic premium loans, I think they were called—to make the payments for a few months."

"I remember," said John. "Those policies have seen us through good times and bad. I think they taught us how to budget and save in the early days. Then the payments got easier until I would even forget we had the money. I remember *when we had to replace the roof, I thought, 'How are we going to pay for this!?' Then it finally occurred to me… 'Oh yeah, we're covered!'"*

"Haha, literally!" Carol giggled at John's accidental pun. "But I agree about the importance of a safety net. I've watched some colleagues with medical emergencies or unemployed spouses. They inevitably claw money back out of their 401(k)s, in spite of penalties and taxes. It was ugly. I don't think they understood the impact of having to pay back a pre-tax 401(k) with after tax dollars."

"Ouch!" said John, calculating they could be losing 25% or more with that move. "And if the market was down… it would have been double ugly—no chance to recoup losses."

John and Carol hadn't always made winning bets on investments, but they had saved consistently. That was something John had always been adamant about. He'd say, "Your savings is your 'safe money.' It's what you're left with if your investments fail."

The Johnsons understood the difference between "saving" and "investing," and they did both. Their investments in the stock market often grew much faster than their savings, but sometimes the market took big, unexpected steps backwards. Their real estate had done well over time, but without access to substantial savings, they might have been forced to sell one of their rental homes. (They no longer discussed the long eviction or the tenant-who-shall-not-be-named who damaged their property while living there rent-free, but their life insurance cash value saved the day.)

Carol knew the girls and their husbands had 401(k)s, but it didn't seem like they had much in the way of savings that they could easily access. And though they all had life insurance, it wasn't the type with cash value.

More than once, Carol had been approached independently by her daughters with a cash crisis. Cyndi's Camry had suddenly needed a new engine. Then Julie was invited to her best friend's wedding in Bali, but didn't have the cash to book the trip. The girls didn't have their own safety nets—they relied on the Bank of Mom!

Carol didn't really mind, and they always paid the money back. Yet she knew this was not an ideal arrangement. She and John had always been consistent savers. Now they had money to travel and they planned to contribute towards

*college expenses for each of the grandsons: Sheldon, Cameron, James and
Jeffrey. They would likely have money to pass on to the kids, too. But even more
importantly, the girls needed to "inherit" their parents' good savings habits!
Carol realized it was time for their daughters and their husbands to save for
themselves—and stop counting on their parents' cash.*

. . . . .

Saving Saves Families

Saving money—steadily, consistently, and in a safe place—is not the same
as investing. Investments help your money grow for future use, or generate cash flow for income. But good investments are often illiquid. You
might have money trapped in a rental home or a retirement account
which would require cost-prohibitive taxes and fees to access. This is why
families should *save* first—*then* invest.

One of Kim's sayings is, "Saving saves families." Both *saving* (as a verb) and
the resulting *savings* (noun) makes a world of difference. With savings,
people can handle emergencies and build up additional capital to invest
with. With savings, people can get the education, training or mentorship
they need to pursue a fulfilling career. They can purchase a home and not
be at the mercy of a rental market. They can start a business and employ
others. And they can afford the things that are important to them.

Without savings, families struggle and are sometimes even torn apart.
Financial stress and a lack of savings can threaten families and generational wealth in multiple ways:

- Disagreements over finances are cited as the leading cause of stress
  in relationships. According to a Citibank survey, 57% of divorced
  couples named money problems as the primary reason for the
  demise of their marriage.

- Many 2019 college graduates are majoring in debt, with an average
  of $31,172 in student loan debt, says Credit.com. There are more
  than 44 million borrowers with $1.5 trillion in student loan debt in

the U.S. alone. According to Forbes.com, 11.2% of student loans are in default or seriously delinquent.

- Home ownership rates struggle—now 64.6% after a declining trend. Many people live and work in areas in which they can't afford to purchase a home. While renting can be fine for young people and adults in transition, it sabotages personal and generational wealth over a lifetime. Renters can pay hundreds of thousands in rent and have nothing to show for it.

- Bankruptcy still affects many Americans. In 2017, 789,020 bankruptcies were filed, according to UScourts.gov. Less than 3% were business bankruptcies, the rest were personal bankruptcies. In 2020, large company bankruptcies surged.

- 1 in 4 Americans refuse medical care because they can't afford it, according to a 2017 Bankrate.com study. This happens even when people *have* health insurance. Many people just don't have the $5,000–$10,000 saved to cover a deductible. Some have turned to "healthcare sharing plan" alternatives.[10]

- Savings also saves families (and individuals) from the mental and physical stresses caused by financial uncertainty. Besides sleepless nights and ulcers, Princeton.edu studies from New Jersey to India show that when a person is concerned about a lack of money, their cognitive function can suffer—comparable to a 13-point IQ drop or the loss of a full night's sleep.

Life does not *have* to be hard, but if you do not earn and save, it can become difficult indeed. Unfortunately, saving is the thing many people "intend" to do, after they pay their rent, car payment (now averaging $503/month, reports USA Today), phone bill, cable bill, etc. Many families manage to save occasionally, but their savings are spent as soon as an unexpected expense arises.

Families that don't save are constantly at risk. They can end up with multi-layered emergencies, and—in spite of good intentions—no generational wealth.

It's not just that you can't afford to rebuild your transmission or replace your car; now getting to work or picking up your child from daycare is also a major problem.

It's not just that you don't have anything saved towards your kids' tuition; now your children might skip college altogether and choose a lower-paying career, leading to lower earnings and their own savings challenges.

It's not just that Grandma can no longer live independently—she also has no money for assisted living, healthcare expenses, or to hire help. Now adult kids may find themselves traveling for long-distance emergencies, sacrificing their own savings to assist, and/or giving up work to become caretakers to their parents.

Saving money consistently is the first key to personal and generational wealth.

Families that succeed at saving become virtually "storm-proof." They can successfully weather periods of unemployment, a divorce, an economic downturn, stock market crash (the worst time to pull money out of the market) and other disruptions.

Saving sustains families, and savers sustain others as well. Savers are the silent heroes of our society. They're the generous givers who fund hospitals, churches, charities and the arts with their endowments.

Heroes like Robert Morin, the librarian who worked at the University of New Hampshire for 50 years and left the school $4 million when he passed in 2015. A single man who lived simply and drove a '92 Plymouth, few people knew Morin had silently built a small fortune. He put most of his earnings into bank accounts, investments, and life insurance policies which benefited the University, his financial advisor told *The Boston Globe*. Thanks to this humble saver, a new, expanded career center for both students and alumni was created, and the library and football stadium also received upgrades.

Like Morin, savers influence society by funding the causes they care about. They help those in need… *because they can.* Savers invest in the leaders of tomorrow… *because they can.* They fund the projects they are passionate about. During this writing in 2018, an anonymous donor only known as

"Suzanne" left $10 million dollars to KEXP, Seattle's beloved (but never well-funded) independent music radio station... *because she could.*

While we hear "the rich" demonized a lot these days, the truth is that savers enrich our neighborhoods and communities by daring to think, act, save and give with long-term vision.

Savers who leave legacies for future generations provide opportunities for family members to fulfill their potential and change their lives. By providing their children, grandchildren and great-grandchildren with funding for their dreams, savers encourage them to become savers, influencers and change agents as well.

The Great American Savings Crisis

In spite of being a nation of great wealth, the United States is in the midst of a personal and household savings crisis. 57 percent of Americans don't have enough cash to cover a $500 unexpected expense, revealed a 2017 Bankrate survey. In March 2018, 20SomethingFinance.com sounded alarms about the negative savings rate of Millennials—an average savings rate of -1.8 percent. Millennials are spending more than they save.

And the rest of America isn't doing much better. The chart below from the St. Louis Fed and the Bureau of Economic Analysis show that the US savings rate dipped to 2.4% in December 2017—the lowest rate since before the Financial Crisis—bouncing back to a nearly-as-depressing 3.1% in early 2018. (Keep in mind that these savings rates *include* employer-sponsored retirement accounts.)

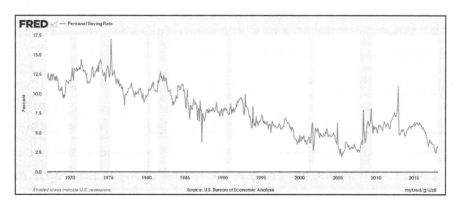

And in spite of what Americans may tell themselves, the problem isn't "not enough income." As recent figures from the OECD[11] (Organization for Economic Co-operation and Development) show, while recent household savings rates for the US have hovered around or below 5%, citizens in other countries put us to shame:

- Germans routinely save between 9 and 10% of their income.
- Luxembourgers save just below 15%.
- Mexicans save just over 15%, in spite of substantially lower incomes.
- Swedes save 16.5% despite much higher taxes.
- Swiss households save nearly 19%.
- And the Chinese, still well behind Americans in income, boast an impressive household savings rate of 37%.

How—and why—do the Chinese manage to save 37% of their income? After all, the average household income in China equates to a mere fraction of the average US income.

One reason for high savings rates is the fact that China has marginally fewer safety nets (social security, unemployment). So there is justified greater fear about the "what if's." Also, there are no credit cards and no ready-made financing for purchases. Homes require a minimum of 30% down payment, which provides strong motivation to save. Saving is also simply part of the culture. It's "what people do."

"I try my best to make life better for my family," says Yuki, a young woman who lives in a tiny studio apartment in Shenzhen, a large city in China. As Yuki explains to an OWN journalist, she earns the Yuen equivalent of $1,000/mo USD and sends half of her earnings to her family. They live on farmland in a poor rural area in China where Yuki says even "a single car would be the envy of all our neighbors."

Simplicity, or what some might call minimalism, is also part of the culture. Kevin Yu, a Chinese-American who worked in China for a few years, noticed how much more simply his Beijing neighbors lived—even though they were a "middle-class couple with great jobs at a major Chinese bank," and Kevin was just out of college. "Compared to my stuffed apartment next door, they lived very simple lives. They barely had any furniture. Their large living room held a television and a dining table. That was it."

When Kevin taught English in Changchun, China he noticed that many people, particularly his students, didn't change their clothes as frequently as Americans do. They would wear only one or two outfits, day after day. One day, a student said something he would never forget: "We think you're rich because you change your clothes every day." Kevin realized how much his life in America has been influenced by advertising and cultural messages around consumption. "It can be hard to see the signal for the noise when we are bombarded constantly with the message that we need to buy."

As Kim presents in the Prosperity Ladder concept in *Busting the Financial Planning Lies*, saving is absolutely critical. It's necessary to take us from subsistence to comfort, and it's a prerequisite to prosperity.

As you can see in the diagram below, *work* is the action that takes you from poverty (or childhood dependency) to subsistence. Subsistence means you're okay as long as everything is "okay"—no emergency car repairs or unexpected vet bills. *Saving* is what takes you to from subsistence to comfort. Being comfortable means you have a cushion. You can afford some wants and not just needs. *Owning* assets will eventually take you to prosperity.

Notice that no matter how much you earn, you cannot get to prosperity without saving:

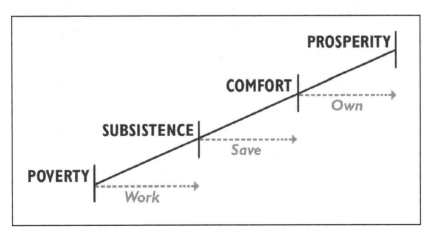

Many millionaires and sophisticated investors have lost it all due to bad bets, fraud, or market swings that wiped out their assets. Kate was invested heavily in real estate (with not enough in savings) and lost her entire net worth in the Financial Crisis. We have an investor friend who has become a millionaire three times—and lost everything three times. This is what can happen when you neglect to *save first*—before investing.

The people of China are climbing the ladder. The Chinese save diligently, realizing all too well that they must make the best of every opportunity. They forego conveniences and wants in order to secure the future of their families.

America used to be a nation of savers. But now it seems our heroes and celebrities are big spenders, high-rollers, and spoiled heiresses. Some Americans are moving the wrong direction, *down* the ladder. Perhaps we could use more self-reflection about wants vs. needs, and greater motivation to save.

The generation that lived through the Great Depression knew true hardship, and became diligent savers. But that generation is dying out. Today, with car loans, mortgage financing and credit cards readily available, many households feel little need to save cash. Many Americans take wealth for granted—or at least, the appearance of wealth.

Incessant advertising urges us to "Buy, buy, buy!" so we can feel more successful, more attractive and, somehow, happier. Cars have to be parked in the driveway because the garage is full of "stuff." Storage units are rented for what won't fit in the overstuffed closets and garage. Americans spend what they make, then spend more on credit. Our government does the same thing. Americans look wealthy—but looks can be deceiving.

You can't leapfrog past saving. It just doesn't work. Your savings creates the *foundation* of your personal economy. Those who build their financial homes on sand often do not survive the next financial storm.

And in 2020, a storm hit. Before we went to press, the personal savings rate spiked along with the shut downs. An average personal savings rate of more than 20% was reached temporarily. However, while some people spent less or were paid more than usual, others fell deeper into debt or were forced to close businesses.

If you wish for your family to do better, realize that the culture around you will not encourage you to save. You *must* create your own culture. To build and keep generational wealth, your family must adopt a *habit* and a *structure* for saving consistently. Without this, even the best of intentions will be short-lived.

(To be clear—you should *invest* as well as save, but it is *saving* that creates the *foundation* of your personal economy... your Family Fund.)

Saving is boring. Fiscal discipline is dull. Nobody watches reality TV shows about savers. It doesn't require great skill, specialized knowledge or a university degree. You don't need special gear, or the latest technological device. You just need to do it!

Your Savings "Cheat Sheet"

Simple steps to get and stay on track:

- Start by saving 15-20% of your income in a bank or credit union savings account until you have a minimum of 3-6 months expenses.

- Use a separate account—not your checking/debit account or a linked account. It's best for your savings to be at "arm's length" from the account you use for regular/everyday expenses.
- Never mind big banks—you'll earn better rates at a credit union or an online bank such as Ally, Synchrony, or Discover.
- After you've built up a modest emergency fund, start saving using a specifically-designed whole life policy. (We'll explain exactly why in the next chapter.)
- Make savings automatic. Set up auto-debit or recurring payments. Our (Kim's) family relies on our bookkeeper to prioritize our whole life policy premiums.
- If you can't find 15-20%, start with whatever amount you can. Some people find budgets, spending plans, or tracking their spending helpful. Others simply "save first"—then spend the rest.

- Start investing *after* you've built up your savings. If you receive a match from your employer, consider investing up to the match level. Additional investments should go elsewhere. (Read "13 Reasons Why Your 401(k) Is Your Riskiest Investment"[12] article by Garrett Gunderson for a summary of reasons why.) Consider a Roth rather than a traditional 401(k).
- Your savings is more than just an "emergency fund." That's how it starts… but it grows into your Family Fund for emergencies *and* opportunities. This all-purpose fund can be used for lucrative investments and it's also your "sleep-at-night money" that gives you the assurance you're "covered"—no matter what.

THE BOTTOM LINE

Your family's long-term prosperity begins with the simple act of saving: *Earn more than you spend and save 15-20 percent of your income.* The habit of saving is the "secret" to family wealth and one of the most important financial lessons you can teach your children.

Of course, it's really no "secret" that earning more than you spend will lead to wealth. The secret comes in actually *doing it.* This is why we love the concept of Family Financing; it provides a *structure* that transforms saving money from a good idea into a priority, a discipline, and an automatic practice.

Saving doesn't require investment savvy or years of mentoring before the next generation can participate. You can help your children and grandchildren adopt good savings habits whether they are in 4th grade or are grown with families of their own. And by choosing the right savings vehicle, you can increase the financial success of your family for generations to come!

CHAPTER 3:
The Foundation of Family Financing

The next morning, John and Carol shook up their pleasantly predictable morning routine and menu with quiche and croissants Carol had picked up from the local bakery.

"This is really good," said John, as he spread some strawberry preserves on the croissant. "I don't miss have to rush off to work in the morning."

"I agree!" said Carol, sipping on a latte from the bakery. They were good at watching their waistlines as well as their money, but it was nice to enjoy a splurge now and then.

"We have an appointment next week with Jerry Lee," said Carol between bites.

"Thanks for setting that up," replied John. "I'm curious what ideas Jerry will have, as he's a registered investment advisor, not just a brokerage rep."

"I know we'll be asking Jerry about Family Financing, and I know he advocates for a type of whole life, maybe similar to what we have. But I did some digging online—"

"Why, that's so unlike you!" said John with a wink. Carol loved to research, and John teased her that if Google were a man, he'd be threatened by how much time she spent with him.

"I know," replied Carol with a bit of a grin. "But I found a lot of contradictory information on life insurance, especially whole life insurance. I absolutely want to do whatever the right thing is for the kids—and of course for us, too—so I really want to have a better understanding of whole life insurance."

"Well, I'm no insurance expert, but I understand the basics of whole life pretty well."

"Great. Now, can you remind me how our life insurance policies did during the Financial Crisis? I don't recall any big changes, I just recall our 401(k)s and IRAs got hit badly."

"Nope, life insurance is steady as a train. I mean, the dividends go up and down a bit. They edged lower after interest rates bottomed out, but in forty-one years, we've never missed out on dividends. And even if we didn't receive dividends, the cash value and the death benefit are both still guaranteed to grow."

"Well, I like guarantees! Speaking of growth… how have the policies done?"

"Well, let's see, it would be helpful to look at a recent statement…"

"Got it," Carol said, as she grabbed a copy from the little desk in the kitchen. "We've had these policies for what, 40 years? I guess 41 years, when Cyndi was born."

"That's right, and they were much smaller policies then. Now let's see… yes, they've done even better than I thought. Would you believe that the face value of mine has tripled in value? And yours… well, yours has increased even more!"

"Face value… is that the same thing as the death benefit?"

"Yup, it's the total value of the policy. You can also see the cash value on the statement, which is like our 'equity' in the policy. That's the portion we can withdraw or borrow against. Of course, the cash value is lower than the face value, as it builds from scratch, unlike the death benefit. But if you lived long enough, the cash value would eventually rise to meet the face value. At that point, the policy would endow, which means you would actually get the whole amount."

"Really! I didn't know that."

"It rarely happens; you'd have to live to be more than 100 years old, I think 121 with the newer policies. But basically, it's a savings plan in which the insurance company takes a big risk in the early years, and a smaller risk as time goes by and your cash value builds."

"Well, I'm actually surprised how much money we've saved in our policies," said Carol, *"and this is in spite of a few big loans we took along the way."*

"They've grown really steadily, which is more than we can say about all of our investments.

"Of course," John continued with a hint of regret, *"the growth has slowed since we stopped funding these at age 65. We're not putting anything into the policies anymore, which is just how we had the policies set up. We thought we wouldn't want premium payments at this age. But I think that was a mistake, because we could really use a good place to store cash right now!"*

"I know—I feel like we could use more in savings and less in the stock market at this stage of life."

"And I don't honestly know about taking new policies at our age," John said. *"I guess that's something we can discuss with Jerry. I'm sure he can get us some illustrations."*

"The illustration... does that show how the policy will perform?"

"Yes—it will show the guarantees and also an estimate of dividends."

"Well, I can see that these policies were a good decision for us. And maybe I shouldn't put too much stock on what self-proclaimed 'financial experts' say on the internet. I know life insurance isn't sexy and it's a definitely not a get-rich-quick scheme."

"You mean, unless someone dies really fast!"

Carol ignored her husband's attempt at humor and took another bite of broccoli quiche. She felt reassured that life insurance had served them well, but she still had unanswered questions. After breakfast, she would research further—this time, seeking out information from whole life experts and advisors in the *field. Carol believed the Family Financing idea could benefit the entire family and she wanted to make sure they built it on the best possible foundation.*

. . . . .

Family Financing—What's in the Family Fund?

Family Financing begins with what we call the "Family Fund." While our focus is on Family Funds comprised of (or at least started) with whole life insurance, Family Funds can use varied and multiple assets. A Family Fund may consist of one or two life insurance policies (generally owned by the fund founder or founders), or many policies insuring many family members. A Family Fund could also conceivably include assets from bank accounts, brokerage accounts, alternative investments, a family home or vacation home, IRAs, etc., though these may vary greatly in liquidity and tax treatment.

Most of these assets can be placed in a trust for the family. A trust has valuable advantages, but is not a requirement. (Policies and other assets can easily be placed into a trust later. See chapter 15 for more on trusts.)

Some advisors or insurance agents may speak of a Family Fund (or "family bank") in terms of *only* life insurance; however, we don't feel that drawing such a rigid line between life insurance and other assets is always practical or helpful. Unless you are starting from scratch with saving, you probably already have assets that must be considered in a will or a wealth transfer. It might—or might not—make sense to treat those assets as part of the Family Fund. (That depends on the asset and your intentions with it.) You could also have policies that remain separate from the Family Fund. No matter what assets end up in your Family Fund, many of the principles in this book will be relevant.

Even if your Family Fund is built entirely with life insurance, money will eventually exit the policy when death benefits are paid. The policies and/ or the benefits can go into a family trust that funds more policies. A portion of the death benefit could be designated for specific purposes within a trust. Alternately, family members can become direct beneficiaries of the death benefit and can use the proceeds as they see fit.

No matter what other assets might eventually be included in a family trust or fund, we highly recommend one type of life insurance as the FOUNDATION of your Family Fund: *high cash value, dividend-paying, mutual whole life insurance.* There are important advantages to using this specific type of life insurance, as you'll see.

Why Save with Life Insurance?

We've made our case for saving money. But why save with life insurance? And why build your Family Fund with "high cash value, dividend-paying whole life"? Why not save with bank CDs, bonds, or in an extra brokerage account?

Building and keeping generational wealth means building a Family Fund that is weatherproof and bulletproof. Your Family Fund should be able to survive stock market crashes and economic downturns. It should offer protection from inflation, money manager mistakes, poor financial habits, your own investing instincts, even premature death. It should be a no-fail strategy for building wealth that you can't lose or outlive.

You want to build a Family Fund that lasts.

There are other secure assets and other types of life insurance, but none work as well for Family Financing. Whole life insurance is poorly understood by most people, and even with whole life, we only recommend certain types of policies. High cash value, dividend-paying whole life insurance is one of the best possible tools when it comes to building generational wealth. Here's why:

Properly-structured whole life is a superior long-term savings vehicle.

Since *saving* is the primary action that builds a Family Fund, you'll want to use the best, most flexible and efficient *savings vehicle*.

There are many benefits to using high cash value whole life insurance as a place to grow and store long-term cash. (By "high cash value" we mean policies with maximized paid-up additions, which help put the most dollars possible into cash value.) We don't know of another savings vehicle that has all of these benefits:

Competitive returns.

It takes some time until your cash value reflects all of the premiums you've paid, so don't begin a policy just to save for a trip to Europe you want to take next year. But we're thinking generationally, right?

When we analyze cash on cash returns beyond the first decade, life insurance typically outperforms bank products and other cash equivalencies—sometimes by a large margin. Over the course of 20 or 30 years, a whole life policy might outperform a savings account, money market fund or bank CDs by as much as 2% annually, or more. And we don't mean just a 2% improvement. If bank rates are at 2% and whole life pays 4%, net, that's a 100% improvement!

Profit-sharing through dividends.

A mutual life insurance company is mutually owned by the policyholders. Why is this important? Legally, *all profits* must be paid to the policyholders, who are the owners. These are paid in the form of dividends. There are no stock shareholders to dilute profits or to force decisions that are only beneficial in the short term. This is why mutual life insurance companies can flourish even in tough times.

While past results are never a guarantee of future results, dividends have been paid by participating (dividend-paying) mutual life insurance companies through *all* market conditions and every type of economy. Whole life insurance dividends have been paid reliably for 150 years *without interruption* throughout the Civil War, both World Wars, the Spanish Flu Pandemic of 1918, the Great Depression, and every stock market crash. *No other financial industry or product can make the same claim.*

Almost zero risk.

There is a guaranteed minimum growth of cash value each year. Once paid, these guaranteed gains as well as gains represented by dividends are locked in forever, raising the "floor" each year. A policy's growth cannot be lost due to a market downturn or changing interest rates.

Even money market funds, which are quite safe, can lose value. Municipal bonds, once a reliable place for "safe money," are now viewed as higher risk after many municipalities have declared bankruptcy.

There is also no risk of rising premiums that would compromise profits or the integrity of the policy. Whole life policies guarantee a level premium payment, and actually, there are ways to reduce premiums if ever necessary. This is one reason we prefer whole life. Other types of cash value life insurance such as universal or variable life can lose cash value or even "implode"—collapsing the policy—when underlying investments underperform, or when costs rise.

Even in the rare case that a life insurance company demutualizes, you won't simply lose the money you've put in. If a mutual company converts to a stock company, it must return its accumulated profits to the policy owners in the form of cash, stocks or policy credits. That's because policyholders are the *owners* of the mutual life insurance company! Their interest must be bought out if the company changes its structure.

Significant Tax Advantages.

Money grows tax-deferred in a whole life insurance policy and in many situations, can help families reduce or avoid income taxes, gift taxes and estate taxes altogether.

If the insurance policy remains in force until a death benefit is paid, the growth of the cash value can become *tax-free*. That's because life insurance death benefits are passed to beneficiaries with no income tax and no capital gains tax! Life insurance policies can also be gifted to children during a policy holder's lifetime without gift taxes (up to lifetime limits.)

Additionally, life insurance as an asset can be passed generationally with no estate tax through a trust, even if your estate exceeds the amount of the estate tax exemption. (For larger estates there are gift and generation-skipping transfer taxes to take into consideration. Please consult with an estate planning attorney.)

Life insurance was designed as a vehicle for passing assets easily and efficiently to future generations. This makes it an ideal vehicle to hold, grow and pass assets to heirs with a minimum of taxes!

Life insurance may be better than "money in the bank."

When we say, "It's like money in the bank!" we mean something is "a sure thing." And if your money is saved in a bank with FDIC insurance, that's rock solid, right? Well, not necessarily.

Privacy.

Bank accounts are anything but safe, secure, and private. Over the years, we have known many clients and friends who have had their bank account garnished for an old debt or affected by a cyber-security problem, credit card fraud or identity theft. Depending on the situation, you might get your money back… or not. In contrast, we've never heard of money going missing from a cash value account.

Saving with whole life insurance gives you additional privacies and protections. Whole life policies and assets aren't reported on your credit report. In many states, a portion of cash value is protected from creditors much like a retirement account—but without the market risk most retirement accounts are subject to.

Saving for college? Cash value is generally not counted as an asset on a FAFSA application, which might help your children or grandchildren qualify for grants or scholarships. In contrast, 529 plans started by parents or grandparents can actually *minimize* a child's chance of qualifying. (We explain further in chapter seven.)

Excellent reserves.

Banks use a fractional reserve system that raises risk and contributes to bank failures, while life insurance companies are required to have solid reserves. After thousands of banks failed during the Great Depression, FDIC insurance was mandated to give depositors some protection. In 2008, Congress passed TARP because there was doubt that the FDIC could provide adequate capital for multiplying bank failures.

Life insurance companies rarely fail, so there has never been a need for an industry equivalent to FDIC insurance needed to restore public faith. In the rare occasions when a life insurance company does go out of business, each state has a Guaranty Association that protects policyholders. If a company is found to be insolvent, they are liquidated, and their policies

transferred to a solvent life insurance company. Due to reserve requirements, a solid business model, long-term planning and actuarial math,
this rarely happens with life insurance companies.

While we are thrilled that FDIC insurance has brought much stability
to banking, don't be fooled into thinking FDIC insurance is infallible.
Having deposit *insurance* is not the same as having *reserves*. If banks had
reserves like mutual life insurance companies, Congress would not have
been held hostage to approve a taxpayer-funded bail-out. In the event of
a large-scale financial meltdown, the FDIC safety net could fail. On the
other hand, well-capitalized life insurance companies would be likely to
survive, just as they did during the Great Depression.

A solid asset.

Today, life insurance is where *banks* keep *their* long-term savings! Banks
must keep a portion of their assets in "tier one capital," which is a core
measure of a bank's financial strength. During the Financial Crisis, banks
of all sizes started drastically increasing their holdings in bank-owned life
insurance, or "BOLI." Now up to 25% of this tier one capital is commonly
held in BOLI life insurance cash value, typically comprised of policies
taken on executives and other key employees. It is held as a long-term
asset to fund future employee benefit programs.

If *banks* save with life insurance, perhaps it's good enough for *your* "family
bank," too.

Whole life insurance is "two accounts in one."

Whole life insurance consists of a savings account plus an additional
death benefit—and possibly terminal illness or long-term care benefit—
that protects us against devastating losses. (The savings portion or cash
value account is actually the available equity inside the larger death benefit, as we explain in *Busting the Life Insurance Lies*.) This is an advantage
that few life insurance critics seem to fully grasp, and it's a BIG reason
why we're fans of it.

Our friend, author and financial educator, John Cummuta, described
Family Funds this way, "A Family Bank (whole life policy) has two accounts:

one for you to use, one to leave a legacy for others." We could also say a whole life policy has an account for "now" and an account for "later." An account to store cash, and another that adds to the value of your estate. An account you grow from scratch, plus a much larger permanent account that is put into place the moment you pay your first premium.

In reality of course, it's ONE policy, and if you lived long enough, the cash value would eventually grow to *equal* the death benefit. The death benefit increases along the way, and the cash value rises at an even faster rate. At a certain age, the policy *endows*. That means you would receive the whole face value—or death benefit—of the policy. Your cash value represents *the equity you can access* in your policy along the way.

There is a common misunderstanding: "The life insurance company keeps your cash value!" No, the face value always represents the TOTAL policy value, which typically increases annually. Meanwhile, the cash value represents your *equity*, which—similar to a home with a mortgage—also *increases* over time. You can't sell your house and collect both the sales price *plus* your equity, right? It is the same with cash value life insurance. The cash value represents the liquid portion of the total asset until it is fully "paid off."

While we're busting myths that stem from a lack understanding... what about those "terrible returns" you've read about on the internet? Surely self-proclaimed financial experts can't be wrong... can they!?

Most analyses you've seen are half-truths. Oftentimes, the comparison is between a *savings* vehicle and an *investment* vehicle. The cash value of life insurance should be compared only to other long-term *savings* vehicles, not to investments with risk.

If you have ever seen the cash value of life insurance compared to stocks, bonds, or some other asset, typically the *entire* (other) asset is being compared to just *part* of the whole life policy (the cash value). Sometimes, the cash value alone (without the additional death benefit) compares favorably to the entire other asset, in terms of growth! Sometimes it doesn't—especially if the time frame is a decade or less.

But that's just *half* of the story. The death benefit and beneficial taxation really change the story, especially in the context of generational wealth.

A comparable taxable account might have to earn 5%, 6%, 7%, perhaps 8% or more—year after year—to produce long-term gains comparable to whole life cash value. (Not easy to do in a safe financial vehicle that won't lose money!)

Then there's the death benefit. (The "second account.")

What happens if you start a college saving fund for your children or grand-children, then pass away a year later? Your saving days would be over. Unless you saved with whole life, your savings plan wouldn't get very far. So life insurance *completes* your savings plan (or college fund) *for you*. In the midst of tremendous loss, life insurance turns a tragically unfinished project into a silver lining miracle.

That's the power of whole life insurance.

With whole life insurance, you start saving *and* guarantee a legacy with your very first premium payment.

Whole life transforms self-sabotage into steady saving!

We've emphasized the importance of having a *structure* that encourages savings. We tend to save what's left over after funding all of our needs and a few of our wants... if we get around to it. The beauty of whole life insurance is that its structure compels policy owners to save *consistently*.

There's a saying in our industry: "Life insurance is like a savings account that shows up like a bill!" Whole life insurance moves "saving money" up in the priority hierarchy so that it's one of the *first* things we pay. We tend to put money in savings after our bills are paid. Life insurance shows up like a bill, and bills get paid. And while there's quite a bit of flexibility for policy owners that need to take a break from (or even halt) premium payments, most of us benefit from a *structure* that motivates consistent saving.

The financial media largely focuses on economic trends, stock picking, and rates of return, yet *investor behaviors*—in this case, savings habits—have a greater impact on results. The fact is, you have more control over your own behavior than economic conditions or markets. And you should always *focus on what you can control.*

There is a good joke we've seen online in various similar forms that reveals the power of saving consistently—by accident:

> "A young man asked a wealthy older gentleman how he made his money. The gentleman fingered his worsted wool vest and said, 'Well, son, it was 1932, the depth of the Great Depression. I was down to my last nickel. I invested that nickel in an apple. I spent the entire day polishing the apple and, at the end of the day, I sold the apple for ten cents. The next morning, I invested those ten cents in two apples. I spent the entire day polishing them, and sold them at the end of the day for 20 cents. I continued this system for a month, by the end of which I'd accumulated a fortune of $1.37. Then my wife's father died and left us two million dollars.'"

It's a funny joke, but the real "truth" of the joke lies in its flawed math! (If you've ever seen the example of the doubling penny, you might notice the flaw, too.)

In his youth, the older gentleman started turning a nickel into a dime, one apple at a time. Then he reinvested what he made, doubling each day, and he did this for a month.

In reality, if someone could double their money every day for a month, starting with one humble nickel, they would have a fortune worth over $26 million dollars on the 30th day! (Sound impossible? See the math for the doubling nickel below.)

.05	1.60	51.20	1,638.40	52,428.80	1,677,721.6
.10	3.20	102.40	3,276.80	104,857.60	3,355,443.2
.20	6.40	204.80	6,553.60	209,715.20	6,710,886.4
.40	12.80	409.60	13,107.20	419,430.40	13,421,772.8
.80	25.60	819.20	26,214.40	838,860.80	26,843,545.6

We laugh at the joke because we think, "How silly to think this wealthy man became rich by doubling his nickels! Of course, the only way to get rich is to inherit a fortune—or maybe win the lottery."

In reality, this is *exactly* how wealth is built. One nickel, one dime, one quarter, one dollar at a time. You start small, you stick with it, and it multiplies with patience. (Perhaps doubling your money every few years or every decade, depending on your savings and earnings rate.)

Meanwhile, if you are saving with whole life, a larger inheritance is put in place instantly—"just in case." The joke inadvertently speaks to the importance of the "two accounts in one" feature of life insurance. The cash value starts you saving, just pennies at a time, it seems. But then it picks up steam! Meanwhile, the death benefit creates a substantial lump sum for beneficiaries.

Of course, the joke is hyperbole. Doubling one's money in a day, week or month should be a warning sign, and nobody can shine a million apples in a day! But don't ever underestimate the power of saving whatever you can—even if it doesn't seem like much—and growing it with patience and the power of compounding interest.

Life insurance can reduce debt and financing charges.

Saving with life insurance gives you the ability to "be your own banker" when needs for financing arise. For some, this is the primary motivation to acquire a whole life policy—it increases your cash and liquidity, creating a safe, dependable, ever-growing pool of money that can be used as collateral when a loan is desired.

Most people "save" in their 401(k)s, then when they need cash for an emergency or financing for a purchase, they use credit cards. If they have business financing needs, they may resort to a high-interest loan or an equipment lease. These types of financing can be extraordinarily expensive! When you save in an asset you can borrow against at a reasonable rate, it can save you thousands, reducing and helping you eliminate debt.

In 1982, many people had whole life policies that allowed them to borrow against their policies at 8%, according to an archived *New York Times* article. That same year, the average mortgage rate was 16.04%! Currently, life insurance fixed loan rates are as low as 6%—that's fixed *for the life of the policy*. Variable rates are lower and of course subject to change. And you don't have to borrow from the life insurance company—you can borrow against your policy at a bank where the WSJ prime rate may be lower.

Another way that life insurance helps reduce debt charges is the fact that cash value *continues to grow even when it is used as collateral*. This doesn't necessarily make your policy the best choice for all loans—you'll still get the growth even if you borrow elsewhere—but it is a feature that helps make whole life an efficient, flexible asset!

We'll explore further the benefits of borrowing, how to determine the best borrowing source, and a big *misunderstanding* about borrowing in a later chapter.

Life insurance helps you control your capital.

Whole life insurance helps policy owners control their own money in many ways.

First, there's no roller coaster ride with whole life insurance. Your money will never be at the mercy of volatile markets. (This is why you *save* before you invest.) There are many uncertainties in life. Your savings shouldn't be one!

Second, there are whole life policy guarantees that keep you in control of your death benefit as well as your cash value. Other types of life insurance may not guarantee:

- level premiums that can never go up
- minimum cash value growth and amounts (net of costs), or
- a permanent death benefit—regardless of how long you live.

Google "universal life lawsuits" and you'll see the problem. People who have paid into policies for years, even decades are in danger of losing their policies because they chose the wrong kind of life insurance!

Third (this one is huge), no more begging to borrow! If your capital is tied up in a 401(k), IRA or home equity, there are often conditions, qualifications, taxes and penalties required for you to gain access your own money. If you don't have money saved, you're at the mercy of finance institutions that can charge what they want or say, "No."

Family Financing with life insurance allows you to lend money for any reason you or the Family Council (your family's board of directors, if relevant) see fit. Since policy loans don't have to fit within narrow bank or mortgage guidelines, constructive uses for policy loans are only limited by one's imagination, the values of the family, and your family's approval process.

A Family Fund built with life insurance increases your control in other ways, too. Your family's legacy won't be at the mercy of the state, the IRS, a probate lawyer or an institution that can invade your family's privacy as banks do.

Family Financing keeps your money—and your decisions about it—in *your* hands, not in the hands of financial institutions.

Whole life insurance is a "smart account" for ultimate financial flexibility.

Do you remember life before smart phones? A dozen years ago, you needed a camera, a pager, a laptop with dictation software, a calculator, a GPS navigation device, an alarm clock and a CD player just to do a FRACTION the things that your smartphone now does. What if your money could be as efficient and flexible as a smartphone?

Typical financial advice positions your dollars to do only ONE job, such as pay tuition OR a medical bill OR accumulate for retirement. Typical financial advice tells you to put money in many different "buckets" that aren't easily co-mingled. But this isn't efficient! You want your dollars to be like a smartphone—a multi-purpose tool that can do multiple jobs.

We call cash value your "emergency/opportunity fund," because we think "emergency fund" is much too narrow. (And besides, opportunities are more fun—and profitable!) Cash value is actually your "emergency-opportunity-education-start-or-expand-a-business-down-payment-dream-vacation-invest-in-yourself-retire-and-leave-a-legacy fund!"

"Financial Flexibility" is a business finance term that Investopedia defines as: "a company's ability to react to unexpected expenses and investment opportunities... Financial flexibility is usually assessed by examining the company's use of leverage as well as cash holdings."

We don't usually refer to financial flexibility in personal finances, yet it's at least as important for families as it is for companies. What will you need money for ten, twenty, or thirty years from now? How much liquidity might be required? Will stocks be up or down when you need the money? You have no idea! That's why you want an *all-purpose fund* that you can use or borrow against at any time for any reason.

Much like a smartphone, whole life insurance is the ultimate multi-purpose "smart account" for your money. Not only can you use your cash value for any purpose, but your policy gives you options to withdraw, borrow against, collateralize, annuitize, gift, sell, and use dividends in multiple ways. A properly-structured policy can fulfill any of the following "jobs":

- A long-term savings vehicle that motivates you to save consistently.
- Your 6 to 12+ months expenses emergency fund.
- A down payment fund for a personal or investment property.
- A college education fund that won't crash with the market.
- Financing for wedding and honeymoon expenses.
- Collateral for a personal or business loan.
- Protection against a personally and financially devastating loss of a loved one. You can cover lost income, final expenses, pay off debt, even take time off work.
- A future income stream for retirement income or funding investments.
- A way to grow assets tax-deferred and gift or transfer them potentially tax-free.
- A place to store and grow cash with greater privacy than in a bank.
- A way to borrow against your assets without impacting your credit.
- A tool to teach younger generations about saving, financing, and using money responsibly.
- A guarantee of future assets or income to a surviving spouse.
- An asset you could potentially sell in your later years.
- Guaranteed insurability you can't outlive.
- A "balancer" in an estate plan for assets such as properties or a business.

- A liquid Family Fund and a legacy for future generations.

Depending on which policy riders you choose—whole life can also provide:

- Financial assistance in the event of a terminal or critical illness.
- A savings completion strategy in the case of disability.
- Long-term care benefits.
- The ability to purchase additional life insurance (and build cash value) without additional underwriting or qualifying,
- Plus other optional benefit riders (consult with Kim at Partners4Prosperity.com[13] or your own advisor for options).

As you can see, whole life insurance is the "smartphone" of financial vehicles and an ideal vehicle to begin building your Family Fund!

Life Insurance allows any family to leave a larger legacy.

Life insurance has several ways of *increasing* an inheritance. As mentioned earlier in this chapter, life insurance turns the first premium payment into a much larger death benefit—instantly.

As the years go by, the death benefit also grows. As you'll see in a whole life illustration, it's not unusual for a policy death benefit to triple, quadruple, or increase many times over through the years. Given how inflation tends to "shrink" money over time, that's an important feature!

Families with substantial assets often appreciate whole life insurance's advantages when it comes to reducing taxes. Life insurance—often combined with trusts—is a common strategy to protect and preserve wealth, helping families transfer assets efficiently. Why not leave more to those you love and less to the government?

If you are middle class (or working your way up to middle class), properly structured whole life insurance can be just as valuable, if not more so. Some family inheritances are possible *only because of life insurance.* You may have good intentions to leave an inheritance, but what if intentions aren't enough? Without life insurance, many intended inheritances are just wishful thinking. Some intended inheritances end up in investments that lose value. Other intended inheritances are saved at first, then later spent when an emergency comes along.

Permanent whole life insurance allows even families of modest means to leave a legacy. Grandparents able to save just $50 or $100 a month can leave an inheritance that can make a difference in the life of an heir. And the simplicity of saving with life insurance also makes Family Financing easy to duplicate, generation to generation.

Building Wealth to Last

Life insurance should *not* be your entire financial strategy (beware of those who say it should). It provides an ideal financial FOUNDATION by providing for emergencies, opportunities, and legacies. Whole life is the "rock" beneath your investments, businesses, or real estate holdings. It ensures your financial house will not be swept away due to a market storm or personal tragedy. Family Financing utilizes the firmest of foundations: companies that have weathered every financial storm for more than a century—including the Great Depression.

Whole life insurance is an ideal foundation because it is a non-correlated asset not tied to the stock market. It does not lose money due to market whims, politics, the value of commodities or housing, or fluctuating interest rates. You have probably never seen a news report about fraud and crime committed by a whole life insurance company, nor are mutual insurance companies under constant attack from cyber-criminals trying to pierce digital banking platforms to steal your money—and your privacy.

If you want a Family Fund that will last for generations, start building it with a proven asset designed to last for generations: whole life insurance.

Skeptical? So were we!

About now, you might be excited—or feeling some skepticism. Perhaps you're rolling your eyes and thinking, "Aha! I KNEW this was a pitch for life insurance!" You feel resistance rising as you imagine we wrote this book as nothing more than a big brochure that we hope will lead to life insurance commissions.

If this thought has crossed your mind, consider that we—Kim and Kate—are OWNERS of whole life and convertible term (convertible to whole life) insurance policies. We are *purchasers* and *users* of the products and strategies recommended in this book.

We were also both once *very* skeptical of the value of whole life! Neither of us purchased or recommended whole life when we started out as a registered investment advisor (Kim) or wealth coach (Kate). We both bought *other* kinds of life insurance and have slowly discovered the value of high cash value whole life insurance.

Kim: I acquired my first policy age 24—a tiny policy for $50 a month. I purchased it primarily because I'd just left the bank and started in the "life insurance" business, and felt I should be walking the talk. (Admittedly, I didn't know what I was doing and it wasn't the type of insurance I would recommend now.)

Now my family and I have over 20 policies! Every family member is insured with one or more whole life policies... along with key employees and parents. I still own two policies each on my kids that I continue to fund (and borrow against if a sizeable need or opportunity arises). Our children in their twenties now have their own policies that *they* own and fund. The last policy we purchased was just a few years ago. After the long-term care riders became available, we purchased a whole life policy with the rider for my husband at age 53.

Kate: My family owned whole life in generations past, but I decided to "buy term and invest the difference" when I was younger. Now I realize the value of using whole life to build liquidity and create a *permanent* death benefit. I purchased a policy for myself a couple of years ago and started the process of insuring my (young adult) daughter while writing this book. It feels really good knowing that I am leaving a legacy—even a multi-generational one! Plus the process has opened up important conversations about the future and about personal finances.

We are writing *Perpetual Wealth* not just to inform you (yes, that, too), but also as part of our learning about creating and keeping multi-generational wealth. (Writing, speaking and teaching about a topic is a great way to *learn* about it!) We also love how a book can take learning that could happen "one on one" and make it "one to many"! We share what we've learned in the hopes that you'll also benefit and apply this information to YOUR family's personal economy.

THE BOTTOM LINE

We recommend saving with life insurance because it *works*. Saving saves families, and death benefits guarantee a legacy. Success is virtually assured when you build the foundation of your Family Fund using a product specifically designed for generational wealth.

Now, if you need an advisor who understands Family Financing—wonderful! Please reach out to us at Partners4Prosperity.com.[14] If you already have a Prosperity Economics Advisor, that's wonderful, too. We hope you'll *both* benefit from this book. We wrote it to help as many families as possible succeed in building and sustaining generational wealth. And if you are an advisor who appreciates the value and proper use of a well-designed whole life insurance policy, make sure you are connected with our advisor community at ProsperityEconomicsAdvisors.com.[15]

For more on the big-picture Family Financing strategies, *who* to insure and how to set up policies… read on!

> *Want to know more about whole life insurance? We have two other books (authored or co-authored by Kim and edited by Kate) that you may find valuable: Live Your Life Insurance[16] and Busting the Life Insurance Lies. You can find them in paperback, Kindle and audiobook formats on Amazon.com.*
>
> *Live Your Life Insurance is a short "handbook" on how to make the most of a whole life policy, with many examples of how a policy can be used to save and build wealth you can use while you are still alive.*
>
> *Busting the Life Insurance Lies covers 38 myths and half-truths about life insurance, especially whole life. The focus of each book is different, although there is some overlap of topics. Both are written to be useful to the general public, life insurance professionals, and our clients.*

CHAPTER 4:
A New Paradigm for Generational Wealth

"It's good to see you in person again," said Jerry Lee, as he welcomed John and Carol into his office. They had only met face-to-face once—introduced by mutual friends at a seminar—although they had connected by phone in recent weeks.

"As you know," started John, settling into a comfortable blue chair in Jerry's office, "we're looking at making some changes in our financial strategy."

"Somehow, we've gotten to our 70s without really having a good strategy for preserving and transferring our wealth," confessed Carol, looking a bit sheepish.

"Don't be embarrassed," said Jerry. "Look at it this way: first, you've got wealth to transfer—that's a good thing! And secondly, you're here now. I'd say you're right on time."

Carol relaxed a bit as she settled into the matching blue chair next to John's.

John and Carol hadn't made any major changes to their finances, although they had recently retired from work to focus on travel, volunteer work, and being grandparents. Currently, as they shared with Jerry, a majority of their financial assets resided in various mutual funds, including managed funds, index funds and ETFs. Those had done well in recent years, but now they desired less down-side risk. They also had a couple of rental homes.

"You mentioned potential strategies to insulate us from stock market volatility," said John. "I delayed retirement when the Financial Crisis hit, but I don't know what we'd do if the market crashed again…

"—Aside from eating a lot of Top Ramen, of course," chimed in Carol.

"We also want to explore the Family Financing idea you presented further," she continued. "We want to do the right thing for the kids, as long as we don't leave ourselves vulnerable. Speaking of which, we've been debating about long-term care insurance, would love your opinion."

"Ideally," added John, "We could maximize the value of our estate and be able to help family members reach important goals—but without giving up control of assets. We want to be able to handle any unexpected financial challenges that come our way.

"Hopefully that's not asking for too much!"

"Not at all," said Jerry, summing up what he had heard. "So you want more balance and stability in your portfolio, and less risk. You'd like to someday transfer assets efficiently—preferably more money rather than less—to heirs, while maintaining financial flexibility in the meantime. You want to support your family's success without compromising your own needs or relinquishing control prematurely. Do I have that right?"

John and Carol both nodded affirmatively.

"Great. Let's take a longer and wider view of family wealth—beyond your own household. We'll pay attention to asset allocation, too. IRAs can be great for retirement income, but they aren't good wealth transfer vehicles.

"It might be a good time to shift some investment dollars into high cash value life insurance for Family Financing as well as your own safety net. We use whole life insurance as a foundation for Family Financing. The policy cash value provides the liquid part of the Family Fund. And the death benefits actu-ally raise the value of your estate, providing a greater legacy and/or additional protection for whichever one of you outlives the other. The policies would also add balance and stability to your portfolio. We'll look at some illustrations."

"Now, where do you store your cash now—your long-term savings?" Jerry inquired.

John explained, "We each have a modest whole life policy now. And much of our cash is in laddered CDs—certificates of deposit with various maturity dates. The best are earning about two percent, and sadly, we won't even get that at renewal time."

"We also have a savings account at the local bank where John worked for years," added Carol. "But it's only paying a fraction of one percent!"

"Taxable, I'm sure," added Jerry, as he fired up some financial calculators on his laptop.

"Now, I see some ways you could reposition assets that might make sense for you. First, you could move money over time from savings and CDs into life insurance. The benefit is that you'll likely end up with more cash in the long run—plus additional death benefit.

"Or you could pay life insurance premiums with IRA withdrawals—after you paid the tax, of course. That would draw down your tax-deferred accounts and shift money from markets with risk into a cash alternative—plus a death benefit.

"Many retirees rely on bonds as the "safe and steady" part of their portfolio, but if you read the article about bonds I sent you, you know I'm not recommending bonds. And because of tax treatment, you'll likely have more income later in retirement by replacing bonds with life insurance. There's a case study video that details the math on this that I'll send you."

"Well, I'm all for more income in retirement!" said John.

"I thought you might be," grinned Jerry. "Now, there would be some trade-offs. There's income tax to pay on the withdrawals in the short term. Then it would take time for the cash to build back up due to initial policy costs. But with the death benefit in place, the value of your estate would increase, plus you'd be moving the money into a more stable environment. The growth inside the policy won't be taxed, and your kids won't owe income tax on an inheritance."

Carol made a note of the pros and cons as Jerry proceeded to outline another option for funding policies and repositioning assets.

"A third option is to use a self-directed IRA to purchase a cash-flowing asset. I like alternative investments such as real estate bridge loan financing or mineral rights leases. Then we'd use cash flow from the investment to fund the premiums."

"I like that idea," said John, "It's the old 'buy a house to get a boat' concept!"

"I don't think I know that one," Jerry said, his curiosity piqued.

"It's the concept that if you want a boat and you have cash to buy it, you're better off using the cash to buy a rental house instead, then using the cash flow from the house to make payments on the boat. You eventually end up with a paid-off boat AND a rental home—plus an ongoing income stream!"

"I love it!" said Jerry. "That's classic Prosperity Economics thinking, right there—putting dollars to work, and moving money 'through' assets, not just 'to' assets."

"That's right!" said Carol. "Your card says 'Prosperity Economics Advisor,' doesn't it?"

"Yes it does! Prosperity Economics represents a movement of agents, advisors and clients who use some traditional financial products—whole life, obviously, also real estate investments and bridge loans, and life settlements—which are the secondary market for life insurance. I thought Prosperity Economics was so 'newfangled' when I first found it, but really, it's a movement away from financial planning towards older, less volatile investments and tried-and-true wealth principles. Financial planning only began in the 1970s as a way to sell more mutual funds."

"Did you say the 70s!?" exclaimed Carol. "That's funny—I've been around longer than the financial planning industry, apparently, but it's so ubiquitous—I've never questioned where it came from."

Jerry smiled. "It surprises a lot of people."

"That's all good to know," said John. "I know one reason we're here is that we'd like to look at how we can start moving some assets out of the stock market."

Jerry made some additional suggestions for re-allocating assets with their goals of reducing risk. Since John and Carol were classified as "accredited investors"— which means having one million dollars in assets, apart from home equity, or

$200k/year income, $300k for couples—they had access to private equity funds and other investments that weren't available to the general public. These were alternative investments that would provide further diversification. Some were growth vehicles, while others could generate steady cash flow to make funding the life insurance policies relatively painless!

"Now about those life insurance policies," Carol ventured, "I know they would assure an inheritance and guard against volatility. But what about the returns? I hear it can take 20 years or more to break even on a whole life policy—that's a long time at our age!"

"First off, I'm going to suggest maximizing paid-up additions riders. That increases your cash value and also death benefit. And it gets you through the funding phase much faster. And let's look at some unconventional options—I think you'll be pleasantly surprised," said Jerry as he reached for the illustrations he had printed off before their arrival.

"Now, we can take new policies on the two of you—and there are some reasons why that might make sense, as it raises the value of your estate. It would also allow you to take advantage of new policy riders. But let's talk about the cash issue first. Whole life insurance can be a very efficient place to store cash. It out-earns bank products, long-term, and gains aren't taxed within the policy. And if we make it generational, that makes it even better! Let me explain...

"With Family Financing, your policies become your own 'Family Fund'—your foundational all-purpose savings for emergencies and opportunities. Of course, there is also a death benefit component, and so your legacy grows along with your cash.

"Now, your policies can also fund opportunities for family members—that's the Family Lending part of Family Financing. Family members could apply to borrow against policies to invest in worthy opportunities such as college tuition, professional development, seed money for a business, or a down payment on a home or investment property."

"That's exactly the type of thing I'd want to use Family Financing for," said John, "—investments that will pay off!"

"And this is critical—Family Financing creates a structure for your kids to build their own Family Funds for emergencies and opportunities. For long-term

success, teach them to practice Family Financing. This is the 'Perpetual Wealth' philosophy you've heard me mention, which just means you're doing Family Financing with multiple generations.

"Oh—and here's the key—make Family Financing something you do 'with' your family, not just 'for' your family."

"I like that idea a lot!" Carol expressed, making a note of it. "I don't think our kids are as disciplined with money as they could be."

"That's a universal problem!" said Jerry. "It's important that saving becomes part of your family's tradition and culture. It's one reason I recommend Family Financing with life insurance. Plus, the policies help people actually DO it. Without a good structure for saving, most people don't follow through. The death benefit and long-term policy benefits motivate people to stick with it. Few people want to save in banks right now because they just aren't paying anything. So people either just spend their cash or risk it in the markets."

"Now, now, those savings accounts are earning plenty, I assure you… for the banks!" said John, drawing nods and chuckles.

"As you know, whole life policies build both cash value and death benefit. For Family Financing, we usually structure the policies for maximum cash value. This helps families save more efficiently than with typical cash equivalencies, over the long haul—while also protecting against devastating losses."

John nodded as Carol took notes. Then Jerry directed their attention to the policy illustrations for a 40-year-old female. (Their daughters were 39 and 41.)

"Now, there are different ways to design and build the policies," Jerry explained. "In your situation, I'm going to suggest that you own and control the policies on your daughters, and they own and control policies on their children. Insuring your kids typically gives you faster cash value growth than with your own policies."

"You had me at faster growth," said John, as Carol nodded.

"Also, Family Financing needs to be multi-generational to be sustainable. This is a good way to do it, though not the only way. I'll give you some information on designing policies that will outline some options." Jerry paused to tuck a handout on "Structuring Life Insurance Policies for Perpetual Wealth" into a folder for John and Carol. (You'll find this information later in this chapter.)

"Perhaps we could make our policies on the girls conditional on them insuring the grandsons," said Carol, "—to make sure the Family Fund doesn't begin and end with us."

"That's an excellent idea," said Jerry, as John nodded. "Now, funding the grandchild's policies temporarily could make sense if there was a period of unemployment or injury. But as a general rule, Family Financing should increase an adult child's independence… not increase their dependence!"

"That makes complete sense…and it's really quite brilliant," observed Carol. "Saving to benefit your kids in a way that motivates them to save, too!"

Jerry then showed them a software analysis of the policy returns. "Now let's look at the nitty gritty. You'll see that that over a period of 30 years, at the current dividend rate, the net returns for cash value are a couple points higher than what most banks are paying."

"And we're looking at only the cash value, not the death benefit, correct?" asked John.

"That's right," continued Jerry as Carol pointed out the different numbers on the policy illustrations and Jerry's screen. "The policy's rate of return is noticeably higher when we consider the policy face value, which is the death benefit. Eventually, whenever an insured passes, the policy pays the higher face value amount—subtract any policy loans.

"And Carol, you had asked about losses in the early years. If you look at what's going into the policy and how the cash value grows, you'll see negative returns at first on the cash value side. Those are the costs I mentioned that allow the life insurance company to operate and take on the risk of a permanent death benefit. After two or three years of premiums and paid-up additions, what I call 'the funding phase' is done. After that, the increase in your cash value each year is always greater than the premiums you pay. Then the growth just picks up steam from there."

"Oh, thanks for pointing that out—I see how the cash builds more quickly with the paid-up additions," said Carol.

"I think it could be worth considering something that can out-earn money market funds or CDs without stock market risk," said John, his body language showing he was interested, but not convinced.

"I realize these are conservative returns, but that's the right comparison," continued Jerry. "We have to understand what kind of asset this is:

- *It's an asset class known for safety and security.*
- *Your gains are locked in and the cash value can never decrease.*
- *It's so reliable that mutual companies have paid dividends every year since before the Great Depression.*
- *Growth is tax-deferred—tax-free in certain situations.*
- *The cash value will be easily accessible through policy loans or withdrawals.*
- *And the death benefit raises the overall value of your estate.*

"I see people compare life insurance to investments, but this is your 'safe money.' Whole life is a vehicle for saving cash, diversifying assets, and protecting against loss. In addition to investments, you always want money that's not tied up in investments or home equity, nor trapped in a retirement account behind a tax and penalty wall. As a banker, I'm sure you understand the importance of liquidity."

"No bank would survive without it, and no household should be without it!" replied John.

"Exactly. Your Family Fund must be accessible when you need it! This is your unshakable financial foundation. It's the money that replaces a roof or sustains a family through unemployment or hardship. It allows you to take advantage of opportunities—such as buying a rental house when you want a boat."

"You're catching on!" smiled John.

"Now, there's one more thing I'd love to show you," said Jerry. It relates to your long-term care insurance question."

"We've been debating about long-term care for several years now," said John. "I've never been able to get excited about it. I've seen companies struggle, premiums increase, and half of the time, people pay into it and don't even use it."

"I guess you'd call us self-insured at this point," said Carol. "But the thought of draining down assets that way would be depressing. I'm not convinced it's worth it, but it's my nature to want to insure against risk."

"Well then I think you might like this," said Jerry. "I'd like to show you how policies with long-term care riders might solve your quandary about long-term care. I've got some illustrations for whole life policies with long-term care riders."

"I didn't even know you could get a long-term care rider on a life insurance policy," John said.

"You couldn't, until recently," Jerry assured him. "Now, what's the biggest down side of long-term care insurance?"

"That we won't use it and it will be money down the drain," Carol answered. "Or if we got long-term care insurance with a 'return of premium rider,' it would just tie up our cash."

"Understood. So what if you could start new whole life policies with guaranteed level premiums for yourselves and—if needed—use much of the death benefit for your own long-term care expenses? In the meantime, the policy is guaranteed to grow. And if you don't need the long-term care rider—or only use a portion of the benefits—you'll just have more to leave to each other… or the Family Fund."

John and Carol were all ears. Jerry showed them how the policy would instantly expand the value of their estate, creating a Long-Term Care asset and death benefit with their first premium payment. The face value or death benefit of the policy would then continue to grow, more or less doubling over the next 20 years at current dividend rates. The death benefit could pass assets to heirs, and with the long-term care rider, up to 90% of the policy's face value could be used for long-term care expenses if needed.

(The specifics vary according to company, current dividend rate and policy size. Contact Partners for Prosperity at Partners4Prosperity.com/contact or the advisor who referred you to ask for your own illustration and details.)

"I like the flexibility of this solution," said Carol after examining the illustrations. "I want to be prepared for anything, without feeling like I'm betting on a worst case scenario."

"I'd definitely rather have life insurance policies that could 'double' as long-term care benefits than throw money into what could be a big black hole," said John.

Jerry let them know that they would have to qualify for the policy and there was a waiting period before benefits kicked in. And he felt hopeful that he had helped some delightful clients tackle a problem with better solutions—a rewarding feeling.

After a few more minutes of discussion, John and Carol felt like they "had a path to run on," as the saying goes. They were interested in funding whole life policies on their daughters and applying for new policies with long-term-care riders for themselves. They would ask their daughters to start policies on the grandsons, which should be affordable for them. Then they would find the best way to make sure their son-in-laws also had permanent coverage. The outlay for six new whole life policies might be a bit of a stretch at the moment, but they knew they could at least purchase new convertible term policies.

"Great. That will get every generation saving, with guaranteed insurability for every family member. Of course, if you do convertible term policies, you still have to convert them within the allowable time frame! But you'll have a few years."

Jerry laid out the big picture of the proposed Family Fund with simple diagrams illustrating who might own and fund the policies. "I know some things could change as you start to have the conversations. You might even find your kids want to own their own policies, if they can afford it. That will put them in the driver's seat."

"Well then... I'd say it's time to have a talk to the kids!" proclaimed Carol.

"I think you're right!" responded John. Then, looking at Jerry, he asked, "Any pointers?"

"The first place to start is a conversation. Let them know of your intentions to start a Family Fund—sort of like your own private family "bank"—for savings, protection and lending. Let them know your reasons why, and be sure to explain how it will help them. Offer to purchase life insurance on the girls and ask them to purchase policies on the kids, if that's what you want. I'd suggest

discussing the big picture first, then specifics. Include the grandkids as much as possible—they don't need the details, but you want to get the whole family on board. And, of course, I'm here to help!"

"We're counting on that!" said Carol.

"Let me send you home with some additional materials that will help you understand the Perpetual Wealth philosophy and Family Financing practices. It's an effective model for generational wealth. I'll send you "7 Ways to Fill your Family Fund" (later in this chapter) and information about different types of life insurance (you'll find in chapter seven). Of course—you can share them with the kids, too.

"And you might share a book or two to acquaint them with whole life… I recommend Live Your Life Insurance, as it's easily readable in a day. It's a great introduction and sort of a whole life policy 'owner's manual.'"

Noting a slight look of overwhelm on their faces, Jerry added, "Don't worry— there's no quiz! Just take it one step at a time. Make a list of questions as they pop up… I'm here to help!"

"You've given us a LOT to think about," said John. "More than I anticipated, and that's a compliment."

"And lots to discuss," said Carol as they rose to leave, "Thanks so much—today was very helpful."

"You're so welcome.

"Oh—one more thing," said Jerry. "Be aware that it takes a few weeks—sometimes longer—from application to approval. During that time, we can tweak many of the policy details… what riders you want, policy size, etc. For instance, we can apply for a large policy, then choose a lesser amount later. We just can't do the opposite! The important thing is to start the ball rolling."

. . . . .

Traditions of Generational Wealth

> *"Give a man a fish and you feed him for a day.*
> *Teach a man to fish and you feed him for a lifetime."*
> —Chinese proverb

Once upon a time, in a not-too-distant past, the family business was used to teach skills, give heirs a "leg up" on a successful life without giving them a handout, and transfer wealth through business equity, assets and know-how.

Before the advent of capital markets, people rarely inherited large sums of money. Wealth wasn't held in a brokerage accounts, it was transferred primarily in the form of an *asset* (property and/or a business) plus *skills* and specialized knowledge.

The *asset* might be a farm, an orchard, a flock of sheep or a fishing vessel. It could be a family business such as a butcher's shop, a blacksmith's business, a doctor's office or a bakery.

The tangible *asset* (property or business) would be passed down along with the *skills*—knowledge, training, ability and confidence—needed to turn it into income. This created a formula for lasting family wealth: **Wealth = Assets + Skills**. Put another way:

> **ASSET** (property, farm or business)
> + **SKILLS** (knowledge & ability to farm or run the business)
> = **WEALTH** (the value exchanged for the goods produced
>   by farm or business)

Much has changed since then. As families become more mobile and as career paths become more fluid, the concept of the family business is, well, going out of business! Children have grown increasingly independent, and family business traditions that have flourished for generations have become increasingly irrelevant.

As family businesses have fallen out of fashion, some families have attempted to simply transfer the *end result* of the family business—the *financial wealth*—to the next generation, *without passing on the critical know-how, mindset and skills needed to create wealth for themselves.*

Unfortunately, this approach has led to many lost fortunes. Without the knowledge, ability and confidence to turn assets into income themselves, heirs become *consumers* of wealth, rather than *creators* of wealth. If you give your children fish but they do not learn to fish, they will become dependent on handouts of fish. Help your children become experts at fishing, and they will never go hungry!

From the Family Business to Family Financing

A November 5, 2013 article in the *New York Times* detailed why "family banks" are becoming the new family business. Like a family business, they provide opportunities to teach financial skills and responsibility while transferring experience, wisdom and know-how. Rather than a focus on a particular business, family money can be used to help family members with education, buying a home, and launching their own career or business. Sometimes they are also used to mentor children in the world of investments and/or philanthropy as well.

Since these Family Funds don't center around one location-dependent business or a particular interest, talent or skill set, they can be implemented with families of diversified interests, geographical locations and career paths. A parent who is a successful farmer, fisherman, or accountant can help a child grow up to become a successful doctor, musician, or engineer. Simply put, Family Funds are an easier fit for most families nowadays than a family business!

There can be many motivations for having a Family Fund to utilize family wealth for the good of its members. Some common reasons are described in the "7 Goals of Family Financing," which are described in more detail in the book's introduction and summarized here:

1. **Create long-term "safe and sure" wealth.** Your Family Fund is the foundation of your family's economy and the stable, steadily-growing part of your portfolio.

2. **Protect against loss and provide for your family in ANY circumstance.** Family Financing is more than just a savings plan or "death insurance;" it is a practically bulletproof financial strategy that can help you weather economic storms.

3. **Cultivate long-term thinking and an enlightened view of wealth.** Family Financing rewards perseverance and helps family members think generationally rather than short-term.

4. **Implement strategies for generational wealth creation**. By teaching the next generation to save, Family Financing helps lay the foundation for wealth. Through Family Lending, legacies and other gifts, families pass on assets along with the skills and knowledge to succeed.

5. **Raise children (and adults) who are financially responsible, not entitled.** Family Financing encourages financial responsibility and empowers each generation to use money wisely. It supports accountability and stewardship.

6. **Use wealth to support the people and causes you care about.** Family Financing helps you keep more wealth in the family through reduced taxes, less consumer debt, greater control of capital, and efficient wealth transfer. Best of all, Family Financing encourages "investments" in the most precious asset you have… your family!

7. **Create a legacy of more than money.** Family Financing and Family Retreats provide structures for sharing stories, dreams, and contributions. They create opportunities for each family member to follow their own success path, supported by the family. They deepen bonds and perpetuate the family's mission, values and traditions.

Life insurance policies for Family Financing can be structured or placed within a trust. They are often administrated by a council or board of directors comprised of family members plus, optionally, advisors or others with particular skills.

High-net-worth families may use a "family office" structure that provides management for the family's affairs: oversight of investments, tax planning, estate planning, and philanthropy, etc. Such structures can work well for families at a certain level of wealth. However, they are not necessary or even practical to begin with.

Family Lending from the policies can be started quite simply, with the founders serving as the sole decision-makers, if desired. However, there are tremendous benefits for integrating other family members.

Family Financing with Whole Life... Step by Step

There are five basic steps to building a Family Fund with life insurance. (This is an overview; we'll go into each of these in more detail.)

Step One: DESIGN the Policies.

This includes your "big picture" strategy and also how the policies will be structured. Your big picture strategy gives an overview of the Family Fund, such as: Will it be comprised of one or several policies? Who will insure whom? How will the policies be funded? Then your agent or advisor will help you structure each policy for your situation. What policy riders do you want? Do you want to maximize cash value, or do you prefer a higher death benefit? How often do you want to pay premiums? And so on.

Step Two: START the Policies.

Once you have your Family Financing strategy, it's essential to move from theoretical to real-world action! This may involve family communication and education, getting permission from the insured (or the parent/custodian of the insured), scheduling physical exams, and applying for the policies by submitting paperwork and the initial payment.

Step Three: FUND the Policies.

Ideally, you'll focus on funding the bank for a few years before you start taking policy loans. Although you could take a loan if needed, it's best to save first. This builds up ample cash value in your policy for emergencies, then opportunities. (See some specific ideas for funding policies for a Family Fund at the end of this chapter.)

Step Four: USE the Family Fund.

This is where the true value of Family Financing comes into play—when you put the dollars to work! The goal is not to simply accumulate money, but to *use* it for the good of the family—*wisely*. By funding education, a business start-up, home down payments and other opportunities, your Family Fund can invest in the future of the family!

Although you don't need to define your lending strategy to start the policy, you should decide on best practices *before* the Family Fund makes any loans to family members (if you intend to leverage your policy). You'll want to lend and borrow selectively. You may also have policies that aren't used for lending, but exist primarily to fund legacies and philanthropy, and/or establish protection and future income for a surviving spouse.

Step Five: DUPLICATE the process.

Ideally, your Family Fund will create sustainable, renewable wealth for generations! We'll delve into this more deeply later in the book with ideas to nurture long-term thinking and create a family *culture* that supports saving and the wise use of wealth.

These are sequential steps, and you don't need to do them all at once. As savings comes first before investing, we recommend completing the first two steps to get the bank off the ground. Then you can focus on the third—funding it—while working towards the fourth and fifth step, perhaps over a period of years. It's good to know where you're heading… and it's a journey that, like many good things, takes time!

In future chapters, you'll learn more about the how's and why's of insuring children, structuring a policy for sustainable wealth, funding the policy, borrowing against life insurance, and nurturing the long-term thinking necessary to build long-term wealth. But first, let's get a "big picture" overview of the Family Financing method.

Structuring Life Insurance Policies Wealth

The biggest key to constructing whole life policie *multi-generational*. Without a multi-generational s eration must start from scratch, scrambling to towards financial independence. Family Financir.o tions to give younger generations a "head start"—sometimes a significant one—not a hand-out.

Family Financing creates sustainable, renewable wealth that *duplicates and grows* with each generation. This is the KEY to creating *Perpetual Wealth*, and there are several ways to accomplish it:

1. **Each generation insures the next generation.**

    In this strategy, parents insure their children, and their children (when adults) will insure their children. The founding generation generally insures themselves, as well.

    This is the model that John and Carol's family are following. The arrows in the diagrams indicate who insures who, or how the premiums are paid:

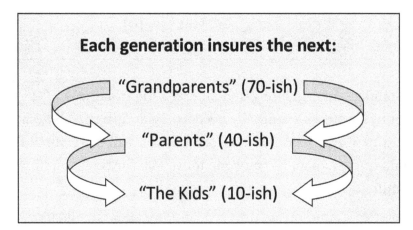

    This is a common model, and it works for a few reasons. Practically speaking, *someone* needs to insure the grandkids, since they're not likely to insure themselves! Plus there are excellent benefits for the policy owner to begin a policy on a child, such as (usually) ease of alification and higher rates of return. At this stage, the focus for the policies is building savings rather than the death benefit, although we have seen instances where families were grateful the guaranteed insurability in place.

And there is more than one way to build a multi-generational Family Fund.

2. **Each generation insures the grandchildren.**

In this strategy, insurance skips a generation, like this:

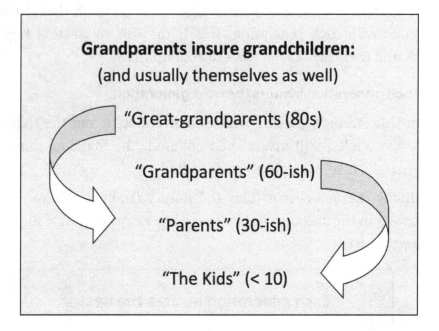

Grandparents insure grandchildren:
(and usually themselves as well)

"Great-grandparents (80s)

"Grandparents" (60-ish)

"Parents" (30-ish)

"The Kids" (< 10)

"Grandparents" insure grandchildren. The in-between generation of younger parents eventually becomes "grandparents" who insure the next new generation of kids. (Permission will be required from parents or custodian, as someone must sign for the insured if they are a minor.)

Note: When minors are insured, another adult should be named as a contingent owner. Should something happen to the policyowner, the child cannot own the policy.

The great-grandparents and/or grandparents would likely insure themselves in this model. If they are not interested or able to do so, consider the next strategy.

3. **Any generation can create a "legacy/safety net" by insuring their parents.**

    Perhaps your parents do not have permanent life insurance and don't desire (or can't afford) to fund a policy. You can insure them yourself, as long as they give your permission to do so. (Permission is always required to insure another adult.) Any generation could do this.

    The example below shows one possible structure for insuring parents:

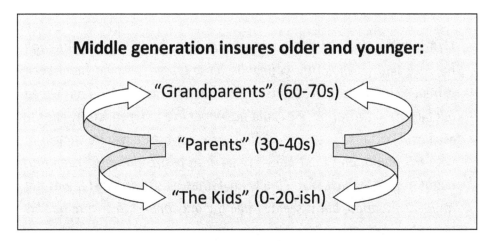

We (Kim and Todd) are like the middle generation in this illustration, with insurance policies on parents (we "split" a policy with Todd's father) and children. And now our children—out of college and working their first jobs—have policies of their own, too.

There are several reasons why an individual or couple might choose to insure their parents. They may anticipate that their parents could need assistance in the future. Perhaps they could become caregivers in the future, which could impact their own ability to earn and save. An eventual insurance windfall will help reimburse adult children caregivers. Policies with terminal/chronic illness rider may also prove valuable, as their parents may need more financial resources should their health deteriorate.

We've described how your own policy functions as an "emergency/opportunity fund." Whether you have an emergency or an opportunity, you're prepared either way. In a similar way, insuring your parents creates a "legacy/safety net."

By owning a policy insuring the "grandparent generation," the adult children originating the policy establish a death benefit that—if needed—can "double" as long-term care insurance. The policy will provide for final expenses and perhaps a legacy as well. So the policy protects both generations from burdensome expenses. At the very least, the policy will provide a legacy that can benefit the entire family.

I (Kate) became my father's caregiver for several years. Although he once had a whole life policy, he let it lapse. It would have been extremely useful to have, as his modest savings had been all but wiped out by a hospitalization. He could no longer live independently, but the Medicaid options for assisted living were not attractive. He moved in with my family and I cut back my work to assist him and "keep him out of trouble," which, if you knew my father, was necessary! It was not an ideal situation, but it seemed like the only option to ensure he was properly cared for.

A few years later, my aunt—my father's sister—passed away. Aunt Carla had kept her whole life policy and included my father in her modest legacy. Now we had new choices! We used some funds to pay for an adult day health program which my father loved. He got out of the house three days a week for Wii bowling and other activities, and I was able to work more. We eventually moved him into a desirable facility where he lived happily for a couple more years. The legacy Carla left made a huge difference in my father's quality of life, as well as mine. I returned to full-time work and started enjoying travel again. I would sometimes say silently, "Thank-you Carla!"

If I had to do it all over again, I would have maintained my father's whole life insurance myself. It would have been VERY helpful to me, especially as a caregiver.

4. **Other multi-generational strategies.**

In the section above, we have neat little diagrams with arrows. John and Carol have two kids, and their two kids have two kids. All of the adults in our story have income. Real families don't always fit into a neat box.

Not every child will have children. Not every adult will have income. Not all partners are married. Not all couples stay married. Not every family is economically "balanced." One adult child may be very successful while their sibling struggles. Therefore, various Family Financing strategies and how your policies are structured may arise from circumstance and necessity more so than tidy diagrams.

Who insures who is ultimately a function of *cash flow*. A parent or grandparent might subsidize a new policy for a time if their adult child is between jobs, pursuing a degree in higher education, or experiencing a temporary cash flow crunch. (When a policy has been established for some time, an automatic premium loan can serve this function.)

In-laws.

Note that the "Parents" in examples #1 and #2 above will likely include an adult child and an in-law (the adult child's spouse or partner). In our example, this would be Sam and Jackson, the husbands of John and Carol's daughters, Cyndi and Julie, who you will meet later in the book.

It is especially important when minors or dependents are involved to have insurance on *both* parents, especially if they provide any financial support to the children.

Depending on the ability of the grandparents ("A") vs. parents ("B"), either generation could fund policies on the in-laws:

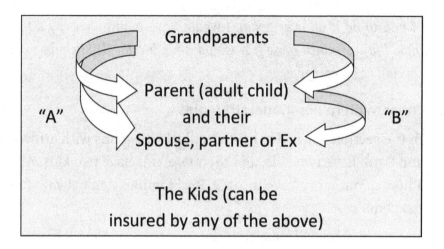

Step-children.

You may be a step-parent or grandparent to a child from a previous marriage. (Be aware that you will need both parents' permission. The same is true if you are divorced and wish to insure your child.)

If you are a grandparent who is insuring grandchildren, you can also insure children of a son-in-law or daughter-in-law from previous marriages. It all depends on your relationship (are you "grandma" or "grandpa" to them?), your ability, and your preferences.

Ex-spouses.

When an ex-husband or ex-wife is still relied on, either financially or for care, it is important to be protected against the possibility of loss. As long as they agree to a policy, exes can be insured. Many exes are eager to ensure that their children will be well-provided for and may even agree to fund their own policies—especially if they understand the benefits.

Gifting strategy.

It is common (but not necessary or required) for parents to gift whole life policies insuring their children to the children. Sometimes this is done when the children are grown and have an established income. Sometimes it is done much later, when the parents are elderly and wish to give an inheritance while living.

In a gifting strategy, it is the policy owner (the parent/grandparent generation) that controls the policy:

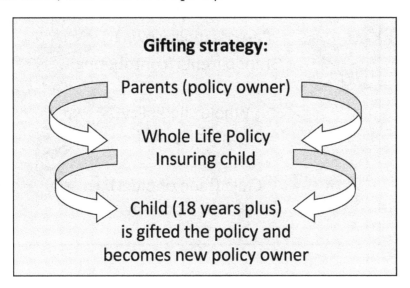

Gifting strategy:

Parents (policy owner)

Whole Life Policy
Insuring child

Child (18 years plus)
is gifted the policy and
becomes new policy owner

"Matching funds."

This concept is similar to how employees can be motivated to save in a 401(k) by an employer that matches a portion of their contributions. (This is not something offered by the insurance company, but a strategy you can create in your family.)

For example: the older generation could fund the base premium and the younger generation can fund the paid-up additions (PUA) riders. Both generations contribute to the policy. This idea can work well with policies the older generation intends to gift to the younger and/or use for college costs or down payment fund for the younger insured.

Another matching funds option: The grandparents could fund a *portion* of a policy, such as the PUAs. If the older (grandparent) generation is someday unable to fund the PUAs, the policies will not be jeopardized.

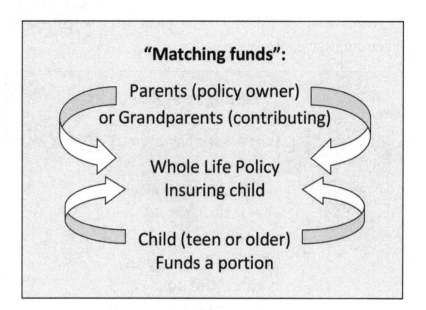

Trusts.

Also note that in order to keep our diagrams simple and useful, we did not try to illustrate the fact that often a *trust* is the owner and/ or beneficiary of a policy. I.e.—a grandparent might have a trust that technically owns one or more policies and also distributes proceeds, for instance, to children and/or grandchildren. (More about this in a later chapter.)

5. **Children (or parents) not required.**

You may not have children (or just not yet). Your parents may no longer be alive, or they may not be insurable. Your family might be you plus a spouse, partner, or sibling. It might be just you at the moment. With any family structure, whole life insurance gives you a powerful way to save and prepare for the future with greater certainty.

In a small family, it is especially important to save and protect each other from potential loss. We have seen people lose a spouse in the prime of their life and have to take on responsibilities they never intended to shoulder alone.

In a couple, each person can insure themselves with the other as their beneficiary. This is what our guides John and Carol have done, also the path my (Kim's) husband Todd and I followed. (You can also own policies on each other, although we don't think there is really added value in this strategy.)

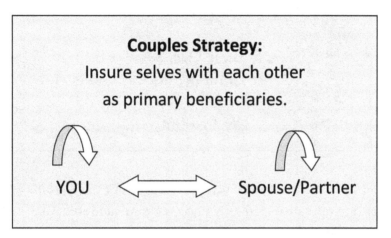

Couples Strategy:
Insure selves with each other
as primary beneficiaries.

YOU   ⟺   Spouse/Partner

Now my husband and I (Kim) have multiple policies on ourselves and each other as well as on our children and key team members. But we each started with just one policy. I bought my first at age 24 with a premium of $50/month. I obtained my first $1,000,000 death benefit policy when we decided to start a family. I always found it curious why "pregnant" parents want to wait until the baby is born before starting life insurance. Once the pregnancy begins, you are technically a parent!

6. Working with lump sums.

Whole life policies are generally funded with monthly or annual payments. But what if you have a sizable windfall, inheritance or lump sum you wish to use to fund a policy? You have a couple of options.

A. Buy an asset or investment, fund the policy with interest/cash flow.

For example, if the grandparents sell a home or a second home, some of the proceeds could be put into in cash-flowing investments such as a bridge loan, rental real estate investment, mineral rights lease, or other income-producing asset. Cash flow from the investment(s) could then fund the policies.

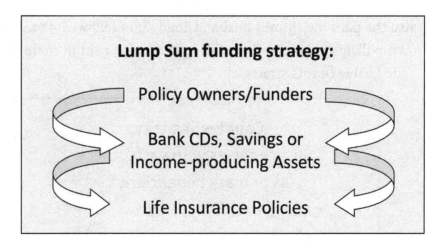

Lump Sum funding strategy:

Policy Owners/Funders

Bank CDs, Savings or
Income-producing Assets

Life Insurance Policies

If you prefer money to stay in conservative or guaranteed environments, you can use savings accounts or laddered CDs rather than a cash-flowing investment with higher risk. Policies can then be funded with withdrawals or by cashing out a CD annually.

B.   Single Premium Whole Life.

It's also possible to use a lump sum to fund a single premium whole life (SPWL) policy directly, as shown here:

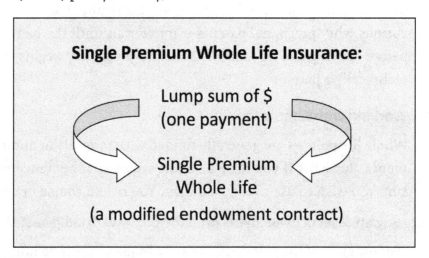

Single Premium Whole Life Insurance:

Lump sum of $
(one payment)

Single Premium
Whole Life
(a modified endowment contract)

However, there are considerations. Such a policy is classified as a Modified Endowment Contract (MEC), which functions differently from a regular life insurance contract.

The upside of a MEC is that it is a wonderful asset transfer vehicle! A single premium policy can multiply a windfall and keep it safely protected and growing until the insured passes away. They are also available with long-term care riders, which allow them to serve functions as both long-term care and life insurance.

The downside of a MEC is that they are not *taxed* as life insurance. Both loans and withdrawals become taxable events, which make them undesirable for Family Lending strategies. (This is important to realize!)

A single premium whole life policy (also a MEC) can still be a powerful part of an overall legacy strategy. A SPWL policy could work well for an older insured who:

- does not wish to borrow against the policy
- has plenty of income and/or assets for their own needs and/or—
- desires additional long-term care protection or other benefit riders
- wants to put a windfall into a safe asset with guarantees, rather than into investments, and
- wishes to maximize legacy gifts to heirs or create funds for family giving.

In a family that already has multiple policies or other assets for emergencies, opportunities and Family Lending, a single premium whole life policy can increase the legacy left behind when the insured passes. The policy could enhance an inheritance for beneficiaries or be used for future family philanthropy. Allowing children/heirs to direct non-profit giving can provide wonderful growth and learning opportunities.

Note: Most whole life insurance companies do not offer true single premium whole life contracts. Some companies have a "two-pay" policy that puts dollars into a non-policy savings accounts or vehicle from which later premium payments are made. This can keep a policy from becoming a MEC, though it can also affect the returns somewhat.

If a traditional policy structure (with smaller premiums over many years) doesn't fit well for you, it can be worth exploring a single premium policy (MEC) or a "two-pay" whole life policy (non-MEC). If you would like an illustration or want to compare various policy options, contact Partners for Prosperity[17] or the person who recommended this book to you for help. Kim and the P4P team can be reached by email: hello@Partners4Prosperity.com[18] or give us a call at (877) 889-3981 ext. 120.

7 Ways to Fill Your Family Fund

At this point, some readers may have a major concern: *"How will I find the MONEY to start a policy for a Family Fund?"*

After all, if you can't find a way to pay for a policy, this will just be a "good idea" that you'll never implement!

There are many ways to fund a policy. The most common way is simply from your regular source of income. If you don't have ample discretionary income, you might need to get a bit more creative. Here are seven ways people have funded policies:

1. **Redirect savings.**

    If you already have an emergency fund in a savings account or money market fund, consider using some of those dollars to fund a life insurance policy. Not only will you likely earn more money with a whole life policy than in a bank, but you will provide your family with the protection of an additional a death benefit.

2. **Money beyond "the match."**

    It can be a good idea to contribute to your 401(k) to take advantage of an employer match. You'll also want to save and invest *beyond* the match, and your 401(k) might not be the best place to do that. Your qualified retirement plan has rules, regulations, hidden fees, plus taxes and penalties should you withdraw money before retirement age. IRAs and 401(k)s are also problematic vehicles for passing assets and can subject heirs to big tax bills, so you don't want all of your money trapped in a 401(k) or IRA.

It is wise to *save* (where money is safe and liquid) before you *invest* (where money is often tied up or not easily accessible, and there may be some risk). So by all means contribute to a 401(k) while you *save* in a policy. As your cash value grows, you'll be able to use it to invest in additional opportunities without retirement plan limitations.

3. Move money from investments to savings.

If your money is tied up where it can't be used for emergencies or opportunities, redirect a portion of it. Perhaps you can use investment dividends or cash flow from an investment. Or utilize the 72(t) federal rule to take early distributions of "substantially equal periodic payments" to take IRA distributions before you reach 59½ without incurring the 10% penalty. (Definitely consult with a qualified advisor and/or a tax specialist before initiating such distributions. Contact Partners for Prosperity at Partners4Prosperity.com/contact[19] or reach out to your Prosperity Economics Advisor.)

4. Reduce debt payments.

There are many ways to reduce the amount of money you pay on debt so that you can free up money to save in a policy:

- Pay off your highest interest/ least efficient debt and redirect money to savings.
- Negotiate lower payments and interest from your creditors.
- Refinance or consolidate debt into a lower payment. (Sometimes you can do this using your policy!)
- Are you pre-paying your mortgage? In most cases, it makes more sense to save and invest that money instead! After all, home equity is not liquid and you can't always access it when you need it.

5. Reduce taxes.

Are you claiming all of your deductions? Do you have the right structure for your business? Can you hire your children or begin a business on the side to lower your taxes? Tom Wheelwright is one of our favorite tax strategists. You can find his advice through his book, *Tax-Free Wealth*,[20] or on his WealthAbility podcast.[21]

Of course, life insurance can be a tax reduction strategy! In chapter 6, you'll learn more about the tax advantages and how to reduce future income taxes using life insurance.

6.   **Redirect other spending.**

As you build your cash value, you can raise your insurance deductibles and lower your premiums. In chapter 6, we cover how your policy might allow you to reduce or even replace a long-term care insurance policy. You can then redirect some of the money that used to go to car, home, or LTC insurance premiums into your whole life policy. This makes your personal economy more efficient!

And sometimes, if you want to save more and build a legacy, it's necessary to change your spending habits. Consider what is truly important to you and prioritize where your money goes. Many people spend more at Starbucks than they put into savings and investments. Yet when they really need cash—they wish they had spent less on coffee!

Go through this checklist of "Twenty Ways to Save $20 (or more!)"[22] to help you shake down your budget. If you don't think you can save, track your spending—every penny—for a month. You'll likely see how you can redirect money from less important things towards your family's financial future. Or you may decide to spend less—even on important things. One of Kim's clients moved out of a big city suburb to a small rural town and slashed her housing costs by over $550 per month!

7.   **Earn extra income.**

Your options to save come down to two simple choices: spend less or earn more. If money is truly just "too tight" to save, it's time to change your financial destiny! Earn more money by:

• negotiating a raise

- working an extra shift
- taking on an extra client or project
- raising your prices
- improving your skills
- changing companies
- earning a degree or designation that opens up new career opportunities, or
- beginning a business on the side. Some of our clients have started "side hustles" that generated thousands of extra income per month!

Where there is a will, there is a way. When you commit to funding multi-generational policies, you're not simply paying a bill. You're committing to something much larger than an insurance policy. You are "investing" in the future of your family!

THE BOTTOM LINE

Family Financing is a Prosperity Economics strategy for building your family's financial foundation. Whole life insurance allows families to pass assets—combined with skills and knowledge—without the traditional structure of a family business. Building a Family Fund with life insurance is a savings and protection strategy that is safe, tax-efficient, and an excellent way to diversify asset classes and reduce stock market risk. Above all, Family Financing is a strategy to build and sustain *generational wealth*. There are many ways to structure policies for Family Financing. The key is to implement a sustainable strategy for *Perpetual Wealth*... generation to generation!

CHAPTER 5:
Long-Term Thinking, Lasting Wealth

John and Carol left Jerry's office with a lot to think about. They were unchar-
acteristically quiet as they walked back to the car. As John put the car in gear
for the drive home, Carol broke the silence. "It really hit me today. I spent a
good chunk of my life teaching school kids math and even personal finance,
but I've spent almost no time helping my own kids and grandkids understand
how money works!

"Money isn't a topic even us bankers address much at home," offered John.

"I think I unconsciously adopted my parents' philosophy about money," replied
Carol. "It was taboo to mention, even with family. You and I have always com-
municated pretty well about our finances. But it hits me that we're talking
about potentially sharing or passing on money... but we haven't been in the
habit of sharing and passing on what we've LEARNED about money... do you
know what I mean?"

"Yes, I think I do. We've learned a lot over the years about money, both from
our successes and our mistakes. We didn't start with much, but we've worked
hard. Fortunately, we've made more good moves than bad. We've gained some

assets over the years—and some wisdom—that are worth passing on. And we probably haven't included the kids in financial discussions like we could have."

"I remember I used say, 'We created our own wealth, the kids can, too.'" said Carol. "But then... the grandsons came along!"

"I know exactly what you mean," said John said with a knowing smile.

Along with the grandchildren had come a growing sense of responsibility towards the family, and a longer view. John and Carol wanted to do all they could to give the boys every chance of success. At this point in life, John and Carol had everything they needed. Now they wanted to steward what they had so they could do more for those they loved the most.

"I'd like to ensure they can have the same advantages we gave the girls," continued John, "such as help with college tuition, or money for a down payment when it comes time to buy a home."

"Obviously, our daughters can help with these things as well, but they also must save for their own futures!"

"Exactly. We're more established and I'm glad that we can help.

"And helping the kids with expenses and leaving a legacy isn't the only reason I'd consider transitioning some of our assets into life insurance."

"Yes?" prodded Carol, curiously.

"I've been thinking, maybe it's time to give up my daily ritual of watching the financial markets. I started that in my early years of working at the bank. I still enjoy following the stock market, but when it comes to our own money, I just want it to grow safely—regardless of the latest headlines!"

Carol nodded. She had noticed this shift in John's priorities: he would rather be volunteering than managing money these days. He often lent a hand with his grandsons' scout troop or their church's Global Group, which helped to construct or rebuild schools abroad. And when they travelled—now several weeks each year—John did his best to "unplug" from the news.

"At this point in my life," continued John, "I want to relax and enjoy the things I love. I have no control over the ups and downs of a market, nor do I want my

own dollars on the roller coaster ride. And could you imagine if we LOST money in a market crash that could have helped the kids out? I'd feel terrible!"

"Or worse," added Carol, "what if we ended up losing money we were really counting on for our own living expenses?"

"Well, I saw that happen to some bank customers in the Great Recession. Those were really lean years for those dependent on their investments. I know a couple of retirees who even moved in with their adult kids to preserve principle when the interest rates fell."

"Let's vow never to have THAT conversation with our daughters!"

"Deal!"

They both laughed... followed by a long silence. After a minute, John spoke in a more serious tone.

"Thankfully, we should have enough cash flow to live comfortably, even to continue saving for future needs and help the kids with a head start. But I'm done with speculation. The longer I live, the more I realize the truth of the old 'Tortoise and the Hare' fable. We need to focus on the long game—for both ourselves and our family."

"Long-term thinking equals long-term wealth..." said Carol, almost under her breath.

"Pardon?"

"Long-term thinking... I'm realizing that's really the KEY to building lasting wealth, isn't it?"

"You know, I think you're on the money! I've always tried to analyze why major banks and companies have failed over the years. It always boils down to the same thing: short-term thinking. Some CEO or key employee thinks they can get away with a short cut. They forget about their long-term goals and loyal customers. They cut a corner, break a rule, or make a risky bet with someone else's money. Inevitably, it backfires. When a bank or a company is in it for the long haul... it matters, and it shows.

"Maybe it's the same when it comes to families!" said Carol. "We've always had financial goals—save for a house, put the kids through college, retire. And

now that we've accomplished those things... the grandkids inspire me to think further into the future.

"When the girls were young, I wasn't thinking long term. We were so busy keeping up with the day-to-day routine. 'Get everyone off to school and work, get home, get dinner on the table, get homework done, and everyone off to bed... then rinse and repeat!' Now it feels like the older we get... the more time we actually have!"

"I understand," said John. "We've got time to be intentional. We've got fewer years ahead of us than we once did, but still plenty of time to build something new."

"Yes—well said!"

"The grandkids also inspire me to make a difference—not just for a day, but for many years to come. The school we helped rebuild in the Philippines last year was an amazing experience. I was so proud of my grandsons... Sheldon and Cameron worked hard. We all worked hard! And it was so worth it. We'll never forget the smiles of the kids, the teamwork, and the satisfaction of helping with a project that will have such a lasting impact. And doing it together... that was priceless!"

"They came back changed kids," recalled Carol. "They had a sense of accomplishment and contribution. It also helped them appreciate their blessings. And if I recall, we used a temporary policy loan for the Global Group trip, didn't we?"

"You're right!" recalled John. "The fundraiser covered a little more than half of the expenses. We kicked in a bit, borrowing against our cash value and repaying it in a few months. Who knew when we started our first life insurance policies that one day we they could help future generations... on two continents!?"

"I remember when we started those policies," mused Carol. I couldn't imagine all the ways we'd use them. I just wanted to solve an immediate problem—to protect each other from the unlikely prospect of being widowed with children. I can't say that I was thinking long-term!"

"Well," said John with a twinkle in his eye, "I was. I wanted to make sure you were always taken care of, whether the kids were grown or not."

"Well, you've done a good job of that!"

"We both have."

"Now here we are—in our seventies—contemplating a new long-term commitment. It struck me today talking with Jerry how this Family Fund is a long-term project. I mean, there's no sense in paying into a whole life policy for a year or two—it's a long-term commitment," Carol noted.

"I guess we've been building a family legacy for decades, so why would we stop now?" John replied with a grin. "But if we are serious about starting this Family Financing project, we've got to get the kids on board."

"Right!" said Carol. Remember what Jerry said… we should do it 'with' them, not 'for' them. I think it's time for a family dinner."

"If you make that sweet potato dish with the brown sugar and pecans, I guarantee you the girls will come and bring the whole crew!"

"Good suggestion… and if saving money is a bit like medicine, a little brown sugar may help it go down easier!"

"I think what will really get them on board is the big picture of the Family Financing," replied John. "I mean, we're asking them to save, but we're also offering them the chance to use the larger Family Fund that we've begun. That's a better deal than a 401(k) match!"

"It sure is."

"Watching a new generation grow is rewarding, isn't it?"

Carol's eyes started to well up a bit as she grasped the impact of their new family wealth project. "This feels like the start of something truly big. I mean, do you understand the significance? We've encouraged the girls and their husbands to save and prepare for the future, but we can only do so much. Family Financing will provide each family with a structure—and a handy premium bill—to actually make it happen. And it will give them the motivation to participate!"

"Yup," added John, "The price of admission for participation in the Family Fund is your own account! Except the grandkids, we can personally 'Grandfather' them in until they are old enough to take over their own policies."

"Haha! Cute, yes, we can 'Grandfather' them in alright."

"They don't call me Grandpa John for nothing—it's what I do best!"

. . . . .

How to Keep the Wealth that Most Families Lose

> *"Rich people plan for three generations.*
> *Poor people plan for Saturday night."*
> —Gloria Steinem

While we love the sentiment expressed in Gloria's quote, as it turns out, planning for three generations may not be nearly long enough. The fact of generational wealth is this: few legacies—even sizeable inheritances— outlive the grandchildren.

"Shirtsleeves to shirtsleeves in three generations" is a familiar phrase to most affluent families. It is a cultural proverb describing a universal phenomenon found in every written language throughout centuries. In Japan, the saying is, "Rice paddies to rice paddies in three generations." In England, "Clogs to clogs in three generations." In China, "Wealth never survives three generations." The Scottish say, "The father buys, the son bigs (builds), the grandchild sells, and his son begs." John Maynard Keynes, the British economist, wrote, "A man of energy and imagination creates the business, the son coasts along, and grandson goes bankrupt."

The sayings reflect a common observation. The first generation (in humble shirtsleeves) earns the wealth with hard work. The second generation goes to work in suits and ties and attempts to maintain it. (That's the best-case scenario.) The third generation blows whatever is left. And so, regardless of the prior generation's fortune, the descendants will find themselves working humble jobs in the clothing of commoners.

Statistically, these traditional sayings have been proven true in multiple ways. Studies quoted by the *Wall Street Journal* confirm that as much as 70 percent of family wealth is lost by the second generation, and 90 percent by the third. CNBC.com quotes an illuminating (if unscientific) analysis combining the Forbes richest family list and the Forbes billionaire lists to figure out what percentage of today's billionaires are first generation, second, third, and so on. Out of 483 billionaires, two-thirds (66%) were first generation. About 20 percent were second generation, and less than 10 percent were third generation. The fourth generation comprised less than 3%. (Robert Frank, "How to Stay Rich for Three Generations," CNBC.com.)

Surely, this dramatic loss of wealth must be the result of faulty financial management, bad investment advice and poor tax planning, right!? Well, not necessarily. Faulty advice from financial professionals was blamed in only about 3% of the cases of vanishing generational wealth, according to research conducted with over 2,000 affluent families over 20 years by the Williams Group (a family-wealth consultancy) and cited in the *Wall Street Journal*. What factors, then, cause so much wealth to vanish by the third generation?

According to the 2,000 families surveyed, 60% of the time, *a breakdown of trust and communication in the family plays the biggest role in lost wealth.* Sibling rivalries and resentments, the inability to communicate on matters of substance, and the failure of heirs to be able to agree on anything from the schedule for the family beach house to which charities should benefit from family philanthropy have caused the demise of many fortunes.

The same study reports that in 25% of the cases, wealth was lost because heirs were not prepared for the inheritances that came their way. Beneficiary education was lacking or missing altogether. In 13% of cases, according to a 2012 by U.S. Trust, parents kept the pending inheritance a secret from beneficiaries. Unfortunately, the element of surprise does not prepare heirs for wealth any more than scratching lottery tickets prepares jackpot winners to become instant multi-millionaires.

The authors of *The Cycle of the Gift* have another explanation for the loss of family wealth reported by the affluent families. Family wealth may indeed live on in trusts and foundations managed by trustees, lawyers and advisors. However, the descendants may no longer see it as "their" wealth. They are disconnected from the money's potential value, have little say in its use and receive little benefit. It may be an advantage that large sums of money cannot jeopardize the independence of heirs. However, it is a tremendous loss that the money cannot be used to nurture their unique talents and ambitions! Perhaps the money goes to worthy causes, but isn't developing the potential of future generations also a worthy cause?

In contrast, the *Perpetual Wealth* philosophy excels when it comes to preserving wealth and putting it to good use. Family Financing encourages families to invest their *financial* capital in their *human* capital. Descendants are supported in finding, following, and succeeding on their own path. However, they are not coddled, spoiled, or subsidized. Adult children who are constantly bailed out don't tend to manage inheritances well.

There is also the issue of dilution. If every family has two or three children (the US average is 2.4, according to Pew Research), and one or more of them marry, each generation is larger than the previous. An individual or couple who begins a Family Fund could have a dozen children and grandchildren, plus spouses and great-grandchildren! This tendency for family trees to expand make it all the more important that descendants learn to do their own saving.

More modest inheritances disappear even more quickly. According to MarketWatch.com, economist and researcher Jay Zagorski, half of those who receive an inheritance tend to spend half of it right away. One-third of recipients will have a negative savings rate within two years of receiving an inheritance, meaning, it's all been spent or lost on bad investments.

The lesson of the shirtsleeves parable is clear: Money given to unprepared heirs tends to be easily spent rather than preserved, managed and grown. Even fortunes can become divided and diluted. When substantial monetary gifts are given to those who no longer have to earn, save and invest, the results are often catastrophic.

Fortunately, it doesn't have to be this way! The philosophy in *Perpetual Wealth* actually addresses every parent's fear: children who spend their inheritances unwisely and fail to be productive themselves.

A Tale of Two Fortunes:
The Vanderbilts and Rothschilds

Railroad and shipping magnate Cornelius Vanderbilt was born to a humble New York family in 1794. Cornelius left schooling at age 11 to work on his father's ferry. He started his own ferry service at age 16 with money borrowed from his parents and went on to dominate the steamboat ferry industry. In the mid-1800s, he went on to multiply his fortune and transform the country by acquiring and expanding railroads.

When Vanderbilt died in 1877, he was the richest man in the United States by a good margin. Upon his death, his heirs inherited the largest fortune ever accumulated—reportedly greater than the sum of money held in the U.S. Treasury at the time. However, his children and his grandchildren lived lavishly, building huge, extravagant mansions on New York City's Fifth Avenue and elsewhere. Some consumed their fortunes completely.

In 1972, the 120 Vanderbilts gathered for a reunion at Vanderbilt University, named for their patriarch who had provided the school its initial $1 million endowment. According to Klepper and Gunther's book, *The Wealthy 100*, there wasn't a millionaire among them. The greatest fortune in American history had all but vanished in 95 years.

Contrast the Vanderbilt story with that of the Rothschild family. Perhaps no other family has been surrounded by so many conspiracies and controversies. Many are quite inaccurate, many are impossible to prove. Regardless, there are still facts to be found and much to be learned about generational wealth from the Rothschild legacy.

Mayer Amschel Rothschild was born in a Frankfurt Jewish ghetto in 1744, one of eight children. Mayer's father was a money changer and silk trader, but a smallpox epidemic left the eight children orphaned when Mayer was 12, according to Investopedia.com. As a teenager, Mayer took an apprenticeship with Simon Wolf Oppenhiemer, a banking firm in Hanover, Germany. Rothschild learned the ins and outs of banking, foreign trade and currency exchange from bankers who served and advised the reigning nobility. After returning to Frankfurt in 1763, Rothschild became a dealer in rare coins and earned the patronage[23] of Crown Prince Wilhelm of Hesse (who had earlier patronized his father).

Mayer married and had ten children; five sons and five daughters. In the late-18th and early 19th centuries, Rothschild established five family banks in key European cities. In Frankfurt, London, Paris, Vienna, and Naples, a bank was assigned one to each of his sons. The family became exceedingly wealthy by providing loans to aristocrats and local governments. This strategy put his family in the position of great wealth and influence and preserved his descendants' power over their assets and affairs for generations. Although Mayer Amschel Rothschild passed away more than 200 years ago—even before all five bank branches had been established throughout Europe—the Rothschild dynasty remains of the wealthiest families in the world. Today, descendents of Mayer Amschel Rothschild are involved in winemaking, the diamond business, farming, hotels, real estate, oil and energy-related investments, asset management, and much more. Nobody knows exactly how much wealth the family still has, although many estimate Rothschild family wealth in the multiple billions.

A Philosophy of Generational Prosperity

Instead of *giving* money to children and grandchildren, the wise use their wealth to increase the success and *independence* of offspring and heirs. Adult children take on the role of *stewards* and *producers* of family wealth, rather than *consumers* of it. This distinction is critical. Instead of passing lump sum inheritances that may not be well-cared for, younger generations are taught to save and manage money. Money can be borrowed and replenished in order to produce more wealth.

When heirs stop producing and contributing, family wealth is at risk. The heir who is no longer productive can also be impacted in devastating ways. When people stop earning money for any length of time, confidence falters. Discipline is undermined. An under-earner from a wealthy family may struggle to fully discover their unique interests and gifts. The challenges of individuation and maturity are magnified. This is why family money must be utilized to help family members succeed and mature—not to subsidize a lifestyle that would otherwise be unsustainable.

As the diagrams in the previous chapter illustrate, Family Financing takes a multi-generational view of wealth. It is this kind of long-term thinking that is essential to the success of future generations. Families who build wealth for generations do not give an inheritance and "hope for the best." They teach and nurture their children and grandchildren to succeed.

The Secrets of Lasting Wealth

Those who have attained generational wealth have left a path for others to follow. While no two families are alike and each will find their own unique path to prosperity, as Tony Robbins says, "Success leaves clues." The recipe for long-term wealth includes these elements:

- The ability to control wealth and liquidity.
- Family Lending (and replenishing) as a means of providing capital.
- The utilization of a family's human capital.
- Long-term thinking about money (financial maturity).
- The "Family Edge."
- The utilization of long-term financial strategies.
- Long-term strategies and structures for family unity.

Let's look at these individually.

The first key to growing long-term wealth is controlling wealth.

Too many people let banks make money off of them—keeping the *bankers* wealthy. Families that save and store capital and act as their own "bankers" are in a very different position. Family wealth can be utilized for private lending, investing, maintaining properties and other assets, educating and training family members, or starting and maintaining businesses.

The Rothschild family is an excellent example of controlling wealth, although we think the marriages of Rothschild cousins—per an edict from Mayer Amschel—may have gone a step too far! Still, the family is known to manage and control their assets with a long-term view. According to

Wikipedia, Baron Benjamin Rothschild said in late 2010 that the family had been unaffected by the financial crisis of 2007–2010 due to their conservative investment philosophy: "We came through it well, because our investment managers did not want to put money into crazy things."

Throughout the years, the Rothschild family has suffered some enormous losses when they have lost control of a portion of their wealth. Hitler, Goering and other Nazis confiscated palaces, property and thousands of paintings and other valuable artifacts from the Rothschilds during the Second World War. Baron Nathanial de Rothschild was taken into custody by the Nazis and reportedly released after payment of a $21 million dollar ransom—the largest ransom paid in history for any individual. The Rothschild bank branch in Paris was nationalized by French Socialists—a devastating blow. (The Rothschilds have since rebuilt a branch in France.) A revolution in Czarist Russia killed the Rothschilds' best client.

In spite of enormous losses, the Rothschild family has proven itself resilient. Descendents of Mayer Amschel Rothschild have worked together to own and control wealth successfully for eight generations. Now diversified in many industries far beyond banking, the family as a whole may have even greater control over their wealth than in previous generations.

Perhaps you are just starting to save and the idea of having a Family Fund that future generations can benefit from seems a long way off. This is where whole life insurance shines. It creates a structure for saving and a much larger, long-term legacy with the stroke of a pen. It takes time to build up cash value sufficient for borrowing, but in the meantime, life insurance will help you *control* and *protect* your family's money.

However grand or modest your legacy is, whole life insurance can make your family's wealth virtually "bulletproof." Whole life protects a family against volatility, risk, unnecessary taxation and even illness and death. Whole life has survived war, depression and every challenge known to man for over 150 years. It is the best "bunker" available to both the affluent and the common person.

Lending to heirs can be more effective than simply giving money.

Mayer Rothschild did not simply give his sons wealth—he gave them *opportunities*. He taught them to *create* wealth through savvy financing practices—borrowing and lending.

You might choose to give gift money to heirs while living or as legacy gifts. There's nothing wrong with that if the receiver is ready. But consider the benefits of Family Lending as a means of providing capital and incentive. When children are allowed to borrow (and required to repay) family resources for worthwhile projects, it gives them practice in using money wisely.

With Family Financing and Lending, family members may have failures as well as successes. While failed projects can be important learning opportunities, of course you will want to increase the odds for success. This is why every Family Fund must have guidelines and rules, such as qualifying criteria for a loan, how it is to be repaid, and what will happen if it's not. (We'll discuss ideas for family loans and grants in a later chapter.) Fortunately for borrowers, loans come with a dose of family guidance!

Lasting wealth utilizes a family's human capital—not just financial capital.

Remember the Family Wealth Formula from the previous chapter:

> **ASSET** (property, farm or business)
> + **SKILLS** (knowledge & ability to farm or run the business)
> = **WEALTH** (the value exchanged for the goods produced
>   by farm or business)

The *Asset* is likely money that is loaned or inherited, although it could be a family business or rental property. The *Skills* that add to it might be taught by a parent, grandparent, mentor, advisor, trustee or friend of the family. These guides provide the human, intellectual and social capital needed for success, such as:

- A prosperous, successful mindset.
- Specific business knowledge.
- Marketing and sales expertise.

- Problem-solving ingenuity.
- A sounding board for wisdom and advice.
- Introductions to others with influence or expertise.

Family wealth goes far beyond financial assets on a balance sheet. Money can be diluted, spent, or lost on a bad investment. Successful families nurture their members so they can avoid most mistakes and recover as quickly as possible from missteps.

The "family edge"—why family enterprises outperform others.

When families give money to heirs without guidance and mentorship, it can disappear quickly. However, when family members work together, adding human capital to financial capital, they have an advantage. This is true in business, in finance, and in life.

Research by Professor John Davis of Harvard and MIT and others demonstrate that family businesses outperform public companies and government entities. Analysts at UBS confirm that family-controlled mid-and small-cap companies have outperformed their peers significantly in the past decade—345% versus 72% in the past 10 years! Additionally, UBS found that family-owned businesses outperformed similar-sized competitors in every region analyzed, including Asia, Europe, Latin America, and the US.

While you don't need a family business to practice Family Financing, some of the reasons found for this family "edge" translate well to the idea of Family Financing:

Long-Term Orientation. Family business leaders have a sense they are "stewarding" the enterprise for the next generation, perhaps as a previous generation did for them. Justin Craig, professor of Family Enterprise at Northwestern's Kellogg school of management told *The Economist*, "When I ask owners whom do they work for, they answer 'for my kids and their kids.'"

This mindset causes family businesses to manage assets differently than corporate peers who may be chasing quarterly returns. Family businesses are more prudent with debt and more cautious with spending. Long-term thinking makes necessary investments while carefully considering costs. It prepares for the future while managing and protecting present assets.

Values-Based Culture. According to Virgin.com, family businesses are more likely to have a strong values-based culture that leads to more loyalty, greater trust, a stronger culture, better investment in training, a clearer purpose, and closer relationships. Family businesses are also more likely to exhibit a higher degree of transparency, reports *Business Insider*.

Long-term thinking, stewardship, prudent money management, purpose-driven culture, trust, loyalty, closer relationships, an investment in developing the next generation... *these are the same qualities fostered by Family Financing.* Heirs are not given money with a "sink or swim" attitude. Those providing capital are, quite literally, invested in both the personal and financial success of their partners.

Long-term thinking is KEY to financial maturity and long-term wealth.

Long-term thinking helps individuals succeed as well as companies. The more "money maturity" we develop, the longer our view of money becomes, time-wise.

Thinking generationally does not come naturally to a young person. To a young child, an hour is a long wait, and a week can seem like an eternity! Long-term thinking becomes more natural for us as we mature and as our assets build.

At the beginning of our lives, we are completely dependent on our parents or others to support us. As toddlers, we don't earn money, but we're capable of throwing a tantrum if we don't get what we want "right now!" We have little capacity to think beyond the moment or delay gratification.

As we grow, we begin to think beyond our immediate needs to "tomorrow." Our timeline extends beyond the present moment. We start earning, perhaps babysitting, mowing lawns, or earning an allowance. The idea of saving up for a toy or a bike over a period of weeks or months becomes a possibility.

As young adults, we learn to be self-supporting. We have to earn at least as much as we spend. Sometimes we find out the hard way that we have to prioritize where the money goes! Unless we want to get evicted from our apartment or lose our car to the repo man, we have to think ahead. We must learn to anticipate our income and expenses.

As we become established, we start to save, invest, and work towards future goals. We save for a home, vacations, perhaps even for financial independence. We might start giving regularly to causes we support. We also might acquire some little ones of our own along the way who need us to be able to earn, save and spend effectively!

Eventually, if we have earned sufficiently and managed our money well, our own needs are more than met. We might keep working if we enjoy it. We might retire, or as many do, transition into a new phase of life that includes travel, volunteerism, freelancing, consulting, or even a new career or business.

Finally, we become givers. This is often the phase during which we start thinking longer-term—beyond our lifetimes—more earnestly. At this point, we have transitioned from immediate gratification all the way to generational thinking.

Long-term thinking grows fortunes, forests, and legacies that last. Individuals who adopt long-term thinking build financial security. Companies that adopt long-term thinking build lasting success. Families that adopt long-term thinking build wealth for generations.

Lasting wealth utilizes long-term financial strategies.

The *Perpetual Wealth* concept is *built* on long-term thinking. As the policy diagrams in the previous chapter illustrate, the very *structures* of Family Financing with life insurance are multi-generational. When you insure a child, you put a legacy into motion for them—and *their future heirs*. You may be insuring your ten-year old child in the moment, but the ultimate beneficiary of the policy may be a grandchild or great grandchild you haven't met yet!

Short-term thinking is costly. Short-term strategies pursue the wrong goals. The Vanderbilt heirs did not consider the long-term impact of their extravagant spending. Enron's spectacular failure was, at its core, an exercise in chasing short-term gains. And every day, families waste money on things that will end up in a storage unit or garbage dump, even though an opportunity exists to invest in future generations.

In June of 2018, *The Wall Street Journal* published a joint editorial by billionaire investor and philanthropist Warren Buffet and JP Morgan CEO Jamie Dimon, "Short-Termism Is Harming the Economy." In it, Buffet and Dimon make the case for reducing or eliminating the estimation of quarterly earnings—a common practice for public companies: "The nation's greatest achievements have always derived from long-term investments… Quarterly earnings guidance often leads to an unhealthy focus on short-term profits at the expense of long-term strategy, growth, and sustainability."

This is one of the many reasons we recommend whole life insurance: *Life insurance companies invest for the long-term.* They are driven by long-term goals, not short-term profits. They are beholden to policy owners, not stockholders who want to see gains each and every quarter.

"A life insurance company should live forever," said Hugo Wesendonck, founder of Germania Life Insurance, renamed Guardian Life in 1917. "It should have principles as unmovable as a rock… Its standards should be high. It must avoid pitfalls that for a time might promise prosperity. Nothing should be promised that can't be carried out."

Hugo's son, Max Wesendonck said, "My father never made a decision without first asking what effect it would have on the company 100 years from now." This kind of long-term thinking makes whole life insurance an ideal tool for generational wealth.

Life insurance companies MUST manage for lasting wealth. When a policy is purchased for a child, the company commits to paying that policy 80, 90, or 100 years or more down the road. They're not focused on short-term profits—they invest to be around for future generations.

Part of building lasting wealth means choosing long-term products. This is why we use and recommend whole life insurance as the *foundation* of your family's economy. Whole life insurance provides the savings and protection that form the foundation of lasting family wealth.

Investments are wonderful, yet they must be built on a solid foundation. Investments are like the engines that make a ship travel faster. It is wonderful to increase your speed, but first, you must guarantee your family will arrive safely. Whole life insurance provides the sturdy hull, the life boats and life preservers your family needs to weather financial storms. As we have seen, even the fortunes of Rothschilds are not immune from storms.

Lastly, strategies and structures for family unity are crucial to lasting family wealth.

Recall the stunning results of the family wealth survey by the Williams Group cited previously. The two biggest roadblocks to generational wealth according to families who had lost significant amounts of it were first, a breakdown of trust and communication in the family and second, heirs who were unprepared for wealth.

Perhaps no other family in history has trumped the three-generation curse as successfully as the Rothschilds. Why? The Rothschilds have consistently managed these challenges. Even when specific financial enterprises failed or when assets were looted and stolen, the Rothschilds worked *together* to overcome challenges.

"The first important strength of the family is unity," said Sir Evelyn Rothschild in a rare 1996 interview published in the *New York Times*. Sir Evelyn was discussing the reunification of the Rothschild London and Paris bank branches as partners again. London had essential financial expertise, and Paris had important continental contacts.

"The point I am trying to make is that today we're one," continued Sir Evelyn Rothschild, as he sat near Baron David de Rothschild, the French banker and cousin who was invited to attend the interview. "As you sit here and you talk to me, you are talking to David, and if you talk to David, you are talking to me."

More than 200 years after the establishment of the original five banking branches, the Rothschilds are still working together, sharing resources and knowledge for the success of the whole family. Even when separated by generations, country borders and languages, the Rothschild family has exemplified cooperation, collaboration, loyalty and unity.

Whether you look at the Rothschilds, the Rockefellers, or lesser-known families of affluence, the story is the same. *They all have adopted long-term thinking about family wealth.* They all have structures—such as family meetings and retreats—to ensure family unity, communication, partnership and mentorship. These families have all capitalized on "the family edge," utilizing both their financial and human capital.

THE BOTTOM LINE

As the "shirtsleeves to shirtsleeves in three generations" saying suggests, few families are able to build and sustain wealth much beyond the second generation. Short-term thinking and strategies have caused the ruin of many family fortunes. Many inheritances are gone in a few short years, and the size of an inheritance is no guarantee that it will last. Transferring money to heirs devoid of the family wisdom necessary to manage and grow it is often a recipe for disaster.

Long-term thinking creates financial maturity in an individual and lasting wealth in a family. Family Financing practices create *Perpetual Wealth* because they are based on long-term thinking, strategies, structures and financial vehicles. Proven financial strategies are only *one* important factor in building and keeping generational wealth. Families must also embrace effective communication, partnership and mentorship. The most successful families grow wealth *together*.

CHAPTER 6:
Family Financing with Your Children

There had been no small amount of speculation leading up to the dinner. When parents say they need everyone present to discuss "family matters," imaginations tend to run wild! Carol had assured her daughters that there was no need to worry—Carol and John were both 'fit as fiddles.' They only wished to present a concept that would help the whole family financially and potentially help with college costs for the grandsons.

After a couple weeks of schedule juggling, John and Carol were finally hosting the family dinner. First to ring the doorbell was daughter Cyndi and her husband Sam with their sons, Sheldon and Cameron. Soon after, daughter Julie, her husband Jackson and their sons, James and Jeffrey, who was still in his little league uniform.

When everyone was finally settled in at the table, grace was said and the food was passed family-style. As calls to "pass the rice, please" and other small talk started to subside, Carol was the first to speak about the reason for tonight's dinner.

"I know our girls seemed a bit concerned that we were convening a family meeting, and I assure you it is for a positive purpose. We anticipate being around for

MANY long years to come!" Carol saw Cyndi—her eldest and sometimes a bit of a worrier—relax.

Carol continued with a slight smile, "However, rumor has it that we might not live forever. Just in case that's true, we've been giving some thought to the financial transitions that may one day take place. More importantly, we want to make sure we make the most of our future years together. We've been thinking how we can best serve the family, not only with our resources, but with whatever wisdom we may have."

Now John joined in. "Part of our preparing for our future has to do with making sure Carol and I stay on solid financial ground. Regardless of what the financial markets bring or what the future may hold in terms of health challenges, we want to make sure we've got all the bases covered… not just for the two of us, but for ALL of us."

Now Carol and John had the full attention of everyone at the table.

"We have decided to start a Family Fund in our trust… a private family bank, if you will," continued John, as he saw a questioning look on one of his daughter's faces.

"Now, I'm not going back into the banking business, mind you! This will be a private resource just for us. Let's call it the 'Family Financing' project. We will use it to save money for things like college tuition or down payments on homes. It will help us prepare for major emergencies or big opportunities. It will also be the main vehicle for eventually passing a tax-free inheritance when the second of us goes.

"The seed money for the Family Fund will be the whole life insurance policies Carol and I established when we were young. We're also in the process of beginning new policies which could provide additional family money.

"Now, you younger boys probably don't want to know ALL of the details of life insurance, but I'm going to ask you to stick around for the start of our discussion—especially because this Family Financing project will likely assist with your college educations! And it's never too early to gain an understanding of money matters and the importance of good money habits. It's a topic we *perhaps haven't given enough attention in the past. But we want to be more helpful in the future. Discussing money shouldn't be taboo in this family."*

The boys nodded their heads as Cyndi spoke up. "Dad, this sounds like a great idea, and I know you know that we can use some help with saving for college. But I'm curious... don't take this the wrong way... but aren't you and mom a little old to be getting life insurance? I mean, I think our policies expire by the time we're seventy! And I guess I'm not clear how life insurance can function as a 'Family Fund'... are you talking about the death benefit?"

"Great questions, dear," said John. There are different kinds of life insurance for different reasons. You and Sam have term policies, I believe. That's a good type of insurance for young families to acquire affordable coverage—just in case the unthinkable happens. I am talking about permanent life insurance—a special type of whole life, to be specific. Whole life insurance—the kind that pays dividends—has been used by families for many generations to store cash and also to leave inheritances. Even my grandfather had a policy!"

Carol proceeded with an explanation that she thought might be more accessible to the grandchildren. "Life insurance may seem a funny way to save money," said Carol. "But it has been used even by presidents and famous business people like Walt Disney and J.C. Penney. It can help us all save and grow money for years to come."

"We tend to think of life insurance as 'death insurance,'" added John. "But it wasn't always that way. Your mother and I established small whole life policies about the time you were born. We have used the cash value quite a few times. We borrowed against the policies for the down payment on our first home, for some of your college costs, and to help us purchase one of the rental houses. The policies helped with a new car and a new roof, too! The death benefit has multiplied over the years, and the cash value has grown to more than we ever anticipated. We always paid back the loans against it. Now, we want these policies to be the start of a larger 'Family Fund' we will create together."

"Those policies really taught us to save in our younger days," reminisced Carol. "If we could pay the mortgage, the life insurance, and buy some food, we were good! We've built almost all of our wealth in our whole life policies, the equity in our houses, and our retirement accounts through work. That's no accident.

These are the bills that got paid 'no matter what'—and the money that was deducted automatically from our paychecks or accounts before we saw it!"

John added with a smile, "Why do you think the IRS takes taxes out of paychecks before people have a chance to spend it on something else? They're not dumb!"

Jackson, the family CPA, chimed in, "The IRS is always first in line, no doubt!"

"Exactly," said John, "which is actually another big reason for the Family Financing project. We can keep more of our money in the family this way. It's a good strategy for transferring wealth—often without paying a dime of taxes."

Now Jackson looked intrigued. As a tax preparer, he felt like he should know more about this tax-advantaged vehicle. He knew much more about taxable accounts!

"Life insurance provides a sound structure for saving, borrowing when needed, and establishing financial security," continued John. "And unlike a regular bank account, it can protect us from the worst of circumstances. Of course, death is a pretty lousy circumstance! But life insurance can also provide benefits in situations of terminal illness or disability."

"We've used it during good times, too," added Carol. "And now our policies can help us invest in the success of the next generation," said Carol, looking at each of her grandsons. "That's you, dear boys!"

"Now, there are some details to be discussed amongst us adults," said John. "But before we let the boys head off to watch a movie, I want to say just a few more things about Family Financing that perhaps everyone should hear.

"In time, we'll establish borrowing criteria for Family Lending—which will be policy loans in most cases. But the big rule is this: Family Funds are for investing in the success of family members. Now, we can grant any kind of loan we want, but the bottom line is this: Family Lending will not be used to buy a fancy car, make risky investments, rescue someone from poor decisions, or pay for a lifestyle you can't otherwise afford. Understood?"

All present nodded in agreement while Sheldon snuck in a wisecrack. "What, no Ferrari?"

"Sorry, Sheldon!" said John with a smile, then he proceeded to use the joke as an example to demonstrate a point. "Actually, one advantage to a Family Fund is that we can make loans that a traditional bank might not make. I've seen people turned down for good loans that didn't quite fit the bank's criteria. Banks aren't particularly flexible, and they don't loan to 13-year olds—even smart ones. But Sheldon—find me a Ferrari worth twice what the owner is selling it for, and we'll talk. But be warned—don't get used to it—you'll have to turn around and sell it for a profit!"

Carol noticed Sheldon's reaction... he smiled, then lit up at the idea of doing a business deal with Grandpa. Maybe there was some entrepreneurial spirit in her grandson that could be nurtured with the right guidance.

"Now, assuming we agree to do it," said Carol, "Family Financing is something we'll do together. Your father and I are willing to help, but every adult needs to participate. That's your entrance fee to the Family Fund—you need to be saving in a policy, too!

"You boys will learn about Family Financing alongside the rest of us, and even potentially apply for loans IF you have a good proposal AND a way to pay it back! Then when you have your first permanent, full-time jobs, you can either start your own policies or take over ownership of an existing policy. Owning your own policy will help you establish savings habits that will serve you the rest of your life.

"Now, as far as you big kids go," said Carol, addressing her daughters and son-in-laws, "your families may already have savings or emergency funds. But that doesn't mean you stop growing your savings. More savings means more opportunities for you and your family."

John added, "There's a saying, 'Opportunity comes to those with cash.' As a banker, I can tell you that's true!"

"Lastly," said Carol, "this Family Financing project is much more than just a financial framework. It's helping your father and me really think about the legacy we want to leave. And I don't just mean money! We want you to have the best of the family's wisdom, ideas, memories, habits and traditions. Our intention for this project is to help all of us grow, learn and support each other

to be our best. Nothing is more important to us than seeing each of you thrive and succeed!"

"Well," said Julie, as her husband Jackson nodded his head in agreement, "This sounds like an amazing idea so far. I'm in, and I'm excited to learn more!"

"Thank-you, Julie," said John. "Carol and I have done a few things right. If we have any wisdom or advice that can help any of you, we want to pass that along. And I'm sure that we can learn something from you 'younguns,' too."

John paused for a long, thoughtful moment before he continued. "I'm a blessed man. We've been able to raise a wonderful family and put away what we hope is plenty for ourselves for retirement. But having grandkids... well, it has changed us. It's made us consider the future in ways we hadn't before, and start to think long-term—even beyond our lifetimes."

Carol put her hand on John's as he continued his thoughts. "This little family we started... it's no longer just the two of us—or the four of us anymore. There are ten of us at the table tonight. And God willing, it's going to keep growing for generations to come!"

"And do you know why this little family got started? I just wanted a date with a pretty girl!" said John, smiling at Carol. "But the best deal I ever got was a pretty girl plus two daughters, two son-in laws and four grandsons. Like I said—I'm a blessed man."

"We're grateful for this family, too, and for all you and Mom do for us," said Cyndi. She wasn't used to her father being quite so sentimental, but she appreciated it.

"You're welcome, dear," said John, before changing gears. "Now that you boys have an idea of what we're up to, you are free to go find a movie to watch in the family room!"

The boys hustled off after thanking their hosts for dinner. John fetched coffee for all who desired it. Then the crew settled in for the next round of discussion, eager to hear more about this Family Financing idea.

"Now, we didn't want to bring up too many details with the boys present, but let me share more about why Carol and I are getting new policies. I also thought we were probably 'too old for life insurance,' but we were wrong about that! Our advisor Jerry said he has even helped people in their young 80s."

"It was actually the long-term care riders that made it a no-brainer," said Carol. "The new policies we are obtaining will be doing double-duty, providing both life insurance and potential long-term care benefits. Of course, I hope we'll never use the long-term care benefits. But that rider will help protect the rest of our assets from medical costs—without tying up money for long-term care premiums we may never need."

"Hmm," said Jackson, "I can definitely see the advantage in combining the benefits of life insurance and long-term care."

"It definitely solved a financial catch-22 for us!" said Carol. We're healthy and didn't want to bet against our good health… and these policies provide us with a lot of flexibility.

"Now, you may or may not have picked up on it, but we would like the grand-kids to have life insurance, too."

"I was wondering," said Julie. "We've never seriously considered getting them insurance at their age."

"Now, this wouldn't be term life insurance," clarified John. "This would be whole life insurance optimized for cash value. It's also a long-term savings vehicle that can help them through college, or help fund a car, a wedding, or other expenses. And it locks in their insurability for life—regardless of what happens in the future."

Carol explained, "Whole life cash value earns more than a savings account in the long run—sometimes a lot more, over time. And unlike a 529 college savings plan or a 401(k) or IRA, your money isn't at risk in the stock market. And you can withdraw or borrow against a policy for any reason—not just college expenses."

John could see that college expenses were a big concern for both families. "Now, do you know what happens if you save and save in a 529—then one of your boys decides not to go to college?"

"I've seen that happen with clients," said Jackson. "If you still have another child to educate, you can transfer the money. If you don't, you'll end up paying taxes and penalties to free up the money. Plus—I've seen 529s take big hits during bear markets."

"Yup—there's a real value to saving in a safe, all-purpose fund. Plus 529s tend to work against you when it comes to qualifying for financial aid."

"That's important to know!" said Julie, who had considered starting 529 accounts.

"As parents," said John, "we were able to give you girls some marvelous advantages. We were able to pay your college tuition—although your summer jobs did help—and gift you down payments for your first homes."

"Those were truly great advantages," Cyndi interjected with appreciation. "Some friends my age are still paying off their college debt and trying to get into their first home!"

"I think you did a great job with your daughters," piped up Sam, Cyndi's husband. "You've raised two fine women!"

"I second that!" said Jackson.

"I appreciate that," said John. "Now that we've got these beautiful girls launched successfully out into the world, it's time for a structure to ensure that we—our family—can do the same for the boys, and for future generations."

"And we can't do it alone!" said Carol.

"Of course not," said, Julie. "So how can we help?"

"That's where the life insurance policies come in," said John. "While we could easily fund policies for the boys—whole life policies are quite affordable for children—we have a proposal that we think you'll like even better."

The girls and their husbands all looked wide-eyed and curious now.

"Your father and I think it's time to upgrade your policies as well," said Carol. "I believe you all have term life policies?"

"Yes, that's correct," said Cyndi.

"Ours are also term," said Jackson, "but I think they might be convertible."

"Great," continued Carol. "Your father and I would like to help fund new policies for the four of you. We would be the owners of whole life policies on the *girls, and eventually, we'd likely transfer ownership to you as the insured. And we want to make sure you men also have permanent protection, whether that's convertible policies or helping you fund whole life. We'll have to get some quotes to see what's doable, as far as our cash flow, but we don't want to leave insurability to chance."*

They all looked pleased but surprised.

"That's really generous of you," said Julie, the rest nodded in agreement.

"Well, this will be your inheritance," said John. "And some of it can be used to help with college. Right now, we've got big retirement accounts—and we've learned that should anything happen to us, this would be a terrible asset to pass on!"

"Oh? How so?" asked Cyndi.

"Taxes," volunteered Jackson. "Whoever inherits an IRA will pay income taxes on any money withdrawn. So heirs end up splitting their inheritance with the government. It can be a rude surprise. Believe me—I've had to break the bad news to a few people."

"Yup—Uncle Sam has a plan for our money… and I have to be honest, as patriotic as I am… I'd rather keep it in the family!"

"Agreed!" said Julie.

"Thank-you—again, that's very generous," said Cyndi.

"You're welcome," said Carol. "And there's a big bonus for us, too. Family Financing will let us put our money to good use while we're here to see it and enjoy it!

"Now, you've got your part to do as well. Our request is that YOU obtain the policies for the boys. They'll be quite affordable, as the younger you are, the lower the premiums!"

"We can definitely do that," said Jackson, while the rest nodded affirmatively.

"You see," explained Carol, "This is how Family Financing works. Every family member is insured. Often, each generation saves for the next. Even if you are funding your own policy—you're saving an inheritance for the next generation!

Then ownership of the policies can be transferred to adult children when the time is right.

"We have some illustrations we can show you give you a better idea of how the policies work. And our advisor, Jerry Lee—he can answer any questions we can't answer."

"Now, as the owners of the new whole life policies, Carol and I will have access to the cash value if we ever need it. We may decide to use the policies to help fund a Family Retreat or other Family-Banking-related expenses. For the most part, our intention is for the policies to establish flexible, tax-advantaged savings that can be borrowed against if needed. The policies will also create an eventual inheritance—and allow us to pass money without unnecessary taxes."

"The policies you'll start for the boys will be similar—the cash value it grows will be yours to access through loans or withdrawals for college tuition or other major expenses, opportunities or emergencies. It's an excellent savings strategy that provides higher returns and tax advantages you won't get from your bank."

Carol added, "When the boys are old enough, you'll have the option to pass the policies to them. Or you may want to keep them and help the boys start their own policies.

"Questions? Comments? Have we completely overwhelmed you?"

"A little," said Julie, nodding her head while she spoke. "It's a new concept for me—using life insurance to save money for ourselves and our children. But it sounds amazing!"

"Yes, agreed," said Cyndi. "And this will give us incentive to save. I love that we'll be saving as a family. I'm embarrassed to say that saving is not our strong suit—although Sam does have a retirement account. But we used up our emergency fund the year the Camry needed an engine rebuild and we had all the vet bills for Buddy."

Carol nodded with understanding. She had suspected that Julie and Jackson were probably financially ahead of Cyndi and Sam, although their incomes were somewhat similar. Jackson—a CPA—was more of a "detail" guy. He appeared to run a tight budget and was careful with spending. Sam and his son Sheldon were both very active, and Carol suspected that a lot of dollars went into skis and bikes and other sporting equipment. It was a good thing they were starting the policies, because it was time to kick start their savings!

The conversation shifted to the process of obtaining life insurance and the next steps to get the policies started. Carol let them know that they would need written consent from their daughters and their husbands before they could be insured by John and Carol. No such permission would be required from the boys because they were minors and their parents would own the policies. The policy owners would all need to fill out applications, which would include medical questionnaires to be completed by the insured. The parents could complete the questionnaires for the boys.

John and Carol were delighted with the interest and commitment they saw from both their daughters and the son-in-laws—both in regards to the policies and the larger Family Financing idea. They were especially pleased to see the kids readily commit to paying premiums. While John and Carol could have funded the grandsons' policies themselves, they were glad they wouldn't have to shoulder the burden alone. More importantly, the girls and their husbands would have a personal investment in creating this bank. It was critical for them to have "skin in the game" and to be contributors and full participants—not simply receivers—in the Family Financing project.

· · · · ·

Insuring Children and Grandchildren: The Surprising Benefits

> *"The sooner you save,*
> *the faster your money can grow..."*
> *—Forbes.com, "The Five Most Important*
> *Money Lessons to Teach Your Kids"*

An article on Bankrate.com states, "If you want to start an argument, ask a group of financial advisers what they think about buying life insurance for children." Consumers can have strong opinions on the matter, too.

Perhaps the main argument *against* insuring children is: *"People only 'need' life insurance if they have a family to support!"* Yet this looks at life insurance from a needs-based viewpoint, which is limiting and problematic.

You could argue that youngsters don't "need" savings accounts. After all, they are supported by their parents! And savings accounts aren't really a "need" anyway—but they are objectively desirable.

Similarly, you could say that the only automotive insurance you "need" is liability insurance, since it is illegal in most states to drive without it. Yet most people obtain optional comprehensive, collision, and uninsured/underinsured motorist coverage. Why? Because they WANT the coverage!

In the same way, we believe that life insurance is a *want*, not an absolute *need*. Many responsible, savings-minded people *want* whole life insurance for their children or grandchildren.

By the time my (Kim's) kids were born, I understood the value of life insurance for all generations. We purchased policies on my children at ages one and two at the time, and later again at ages six and seven. (My kids are one year apart.) I still own, pay for, and borrow against these policies even though my kids are in their mid-twenties. Whole life policies are where we store our cash/keep our liquidity in our personal economy.

Below are ten reasons we *wanted* (not "needed") life insurance for our children.

1.   **Affordable premiums that will never go up are locked in.**

   Polices for children are typically issued at the lowest rates available, and with limited underwriting. As a general rule, the younger the insured is, the lower the cost of insurance.

   The advantage for the policy owner is extremely affordable premium payments. Putting as little as $100 per month into a policy with paid-up additions for a child can eventually turn into hundreds of thousands of dollars in cash value based on conservative policy guarantees. And at current dividend rates (not guaranteed but historically reliable), even middle class families have a chance to build million dollar policies over time with reasonable premiums.

Many people believe that multi-generational wealth is out of reach for them. In reality, nothing could be further from the truth! It's simply a matter of prioritizing financial security and implementing a proven strategy. Many families spend many hundreds each month on non-essentials such as cable TV, eating out frequently, etc. The average car payment is now over $500/month, and some families have two or three car payments. Many families could build lasting wealth simply by driving vehicles longer, car sharing and/or purchasing less expensive or used models.

2. **Optimized growth of savings (cash value).**

The cost of insurance (the mortality cost) is lower for younger people, so whole life cash value grows more quickly at a slightly higher rate of return. At the time of this writing in 2019, the internal rate of return (IRR) on a whole life policy on a child or young adult engineered for maximum cash value (maximizing paid-up additions) is around 4.5 percent, long term. That's at least twice the best bank CD rates—and ten-fold what the big banks are paying now.

Yes, *investments* typically earn more. But keep in mind this is tax-advantaged *savings*, not an investment with unpredictable returns that might put your principal at risk.

3. **Flexibility and liquidity of savings.**

In a whole life policy, the policy owner retains the ability to withdraw or collateralize the cash value—even when the insured is a child or grandchild. As a policy owner, you can use cash value for yourself or for the child. It can serve as:

- Your fund for emergencies or opportunities.
- Collateral you can leverage for an investment or a major purchase.
- A first-car or college savings fund.
- A wedding, honeymoon, or home down payment fund for your child.
- Money for your medical expenses, home improvement, or a business start-up.

There are no limits to what you can use the money for. And unlike money from an IRA, 401(k), 529 plan or home equity, you don't have to meet qualifying criteria to have access to your cash value.

4.   Multi-generational benefits.

My (Kim's) sister and her husband bought a policy for their son, Seth, when he was a young child. They started it at my suggestion as a way to save for their family and for my nephew's future. They used the cash value themselves when they needed it, taking loans and paying them back.

When Seth was a bit older and was driving, they used the policy to purchase a car for him. He was an unemployed teenager with no credit at the time, so he was not going to qualify for an automobile loan! However, there's no qualification required when you take a policy loan, and you even get to determine your own schedule for repayment.

Now in his young 20s and financially independent, Seth's parents gifted him the policy, which he now maintains. I had a couple of meetings with Seth and also asked him to read my short book, *Live Your Life Insurance*. After that, he understood what he had and was really grateful for it! And because his parents began the policy at a young age, it gave him a head start while also helping his parents when they needed cash.

Ownership of a policy can be transferred to your child after age 18, or at a later point, up to and including your own passing when secondary owner designations are identified. You may wish for your child to take over premium payments as a young adult, or you might keep ownership of the policy well into your senior years. Depending on your total estate value, you may want to be aware of gifting limitations.

When the transfer is made, the policy can then serve as:

• Your *child's* fund for emergencies or opportunities.
• Your child's business start-up fund.

- Your child's first car, college, wedding or down payment fund for *their* children.
- Your child's safety net in the event of a terminal illness or other serious diagnosis, depending on policy riders.
- Your child's future legacy for children, grandchildren, spouse and loved ones.

5. **Virtually unparalleled estate planning benefits.**

If you wish to transfer wealth to heirs, life insurance for grandchildren or children is one of the very best ways to do it. You can pass nearly unlimited amounts of cash to the next generation via a "transfer of the policy to the insured"—*income-and-often-gift-tax free*. (If a family's situation does create a gift tax, they can use their lifetime exemption to offset it.)

There are no income taxes when giving a life insurance policy, no matter how much cash value it holds, back to the insured. And for most families, there is no gift tax. There's no interference from the IRS or the state, no probate, no requirement for a trust or even a will with life insurance. (Although we recommend that everyone has a will, and trusts can be very useful.)

6. **A college savings plan with flexibility!**

Is your intention is to save for future college tuition for the insured child? Parents are typically advised to save money in the ubiquitous 529 savings plan. But there are numerous downsides to 529 plans, such as stock market risk, strict plan rules that must be followed, and a lack of flexibility on what the money can be spent on.

529 plans have attractive tax savings benefits up front. But if the child decides not to attend college, this can backfire. In order to get your money out of a 529 plan, you'll pay penalties and taxes if the money is not withdrawn for qualified education expenses.

When saving in a whole life policy, policy loans or withdrawals can be used for college expenses or for alternative education experiences such as a self-designed internship, volunteer work or travel. Cash value can also be used to help the child purchase a car, a home or start a business. In addition, the policyholder can choose to withdraw or leverage cash value for his/ her own needs or retirement.

If the child goes to college as planned, the money saved in a whole life policy is not typically counted as an asset on the FAFSA if they apply for financial aid. That may increase the financial aid package for qualified students.

Unlike a parent's 529 plan, a grandparent-owned 529 plan is not counted as an asset on a grandchild's FAFSA application. However, any 529 withdrawals ARE counted as income for the student, which then must be reported on the FAFSA. According to a recent *Washington Post* article on grandparent-owned 529 plans, this can create an even larger problem. "Because up to 50 percent of a student's income is considered available to pay for college, money used from a grandparent's 529 can reduce aid by as much as half of the distribution amount."

I (Kim) have used policy loans for tuition. It does increase the cost of the tuition by the amount of interest, yet that is where our liquidity was when we needed it. It worked and we kept it reasonable. And keep in mind, the cash value is always growing. You can even use dividends to help pay off the loans. As policy loans get paid back, your cash value becomes freed up to use again. And all the while, the cash value keeps growing, largely unaffected by the loan.

You can also do a withdrawal if paying back the loans would create a hardship. Just be aware that withdrawals reduce the size of the policy.

7. **Future insurability is guaranteed.**

Insurability is rarely an issue for a minor. But how often do young adults in their 20s and 30s "intend" to get life insurance, then never get around to it? Guaranteed insurability is a life-long benefit for the insured at every age.

Not only does a whole life policy guarantee permanent life insurance coverage (provided that premiums are paid and the policy is kept in force), but many policies offer a guaranteed option to purchase additional insurance in the future.

Your policy is also guaranteed to grow over time, increasing your insurance coverage. The $100k policy you purchase for a child may be worth several times that in future decades. You're not simply "insuring your child"—you are insuring their future ability to build financial security for their own family, no matter what.

We have seen friends and clients become uninsurable—usually after a major medical incident. Sometimes, this happens to even young people. We have a friend who fought two battles with cancer shortly after getting married. The good news: he survived the cancer, and he had some convertible term he was able to convert into whole life insurance. The bad news: much of the policy's convertibility had expired and he can no longer obtain the life insurance he desires to protect his family. As he shared with me, "That cheap term insurance turned out to be not so cheap."

8. **An effective tool for teaching valuable financial skills.**

As a child matures and begins to utilize or manage their policy, they develop consistent savings habits that are critical to financial security and success. Policy loans can provide important experience in money management, budgeting for repayment, etc. Family Financing practices also offer opportunities to learn about money from more experienced family members.

As I mentioned a few pages ago, my nephew Seth has a policy that his parents started for him as a child. Since they gifted him the policy (an option, not a requirement), now he makes the premium payments. He also has the option to make additional PUA (paid-up additions rider) payments to save a little more when he wants, because that is how we set up the policy. And he is completing the policy loan payments for the loan used to purchase his first car.

The policy has made Seth a consistent saver. He knows he is building an asset he can use in the future for emergencies, opportunities and an eventual legacy. It has given him valuable money management experience and a sense of responsibility.

9. **Insurance covers expenses in the rare case of such a devastating loss.**

This is the life insurance benefit that nobody wants to think about. Insurance for children is inexpensive, but funerals, memorial services, and other final expenses are not. Nobody deserves to be burdened with expenses or debt in a time of grief.

I (Kate) lost a young, healthy friend to a sudden accident last summer. His parents and other family lived far away and had to make multiple trips to mourn the loss, claim and transport his remains, sort through and pack his belongings, relocate his dog, etc. Expenses added up, and many days of work were missed. Besides being an extremely difficult personal situation, it was an enormous financial burden—one they were not prepared for. The family had to ask for donations to meet their many expenses.

In recent years, we have noticed this unfortunate trend on crowdfunding sites such as GoFundMe. Increasingly, people who have lost a loved one—a child, parent, or spouse—are *fundraising* in the midst of tragedy to cover final expenses. It is a blessing that such an option exists, however, the trend is both saddening and maddening. Such moments of grief should not be spent worrying about money when the sudden financial burden was *completely preventable*.

In contrast with crowd funding for final expenses, parents who *have* insured their children "just in case" have sometimes used life insurance benefits to fund charitable works or scholarships in honor of their child. They find that the ability to leave such a legacy gives some meaning in the midst of loss. We pray that no one reading this will ever know the loss of a child. But if you do, we hope you won't have to worry about money in such a moment.

Final expenses aren't the only financial concern that motivates some parents to obtain life insurance for their children. The parent or grandparent purchasing the policy is also insuring their *own* income, which they know would be affected in the event of such a loss. As one mother put it when a financial advisor asserted online that you should "never" purchase insurance for children:

"I am a mother of two, and the primary breadwinner for the family. And I can tell you right now, though the chances are slim, if something were to happen to either of my children, I'm not sure when I'd be able to return to work. I can't even make a guess. So for me, having a financial cushion to make it possible for me to grieve without the worry of when and if I can return to work is a priceless safety net."

Why do we buy car insurance, home insurance, and health insurance? We purchase it "just in case" of a car accident, house fire, illness or injury. Just in case of a devastating loss. In the case of life insurance, we know that sooner or later, death *will* occur. And when it does, the personal and emotional aspects of death and loss are worthy of our full attention.

10. Peace of mind.

We can't imagine not having every member of our household insured. We want protection from life's storms and "savings for a rainy day." (We desire savings for sunny days, too!)

Life insurance is often thought of as "death insurance." Yet properly used, whole life insurance provides *lifelong benefits* for the policy-holder. Some of these benefits, like peace of mind, are hard to put a price-tag on.

Jamey and Robyn Koonsman met in college, were married, and obtained insurance in their 20s for themselves and their daughters. As Jamey told LifeHappens.org,[24] they never expected to use it. They planned on gifting the policies to the girls once grown.

The girls were both active and seemingly healthy. But while she was just a teenager, their daughter Hope died suddenly—the result of a birth defect the family thought was long resolved. Adding to the tragedy was Robyn's fight with breast cancer. Less than two years after Jamey's daughter Hope died, he lost his wife, Robyn, too.

In the wake of Hope's death, Jamey and Robyn were able to establish a foundation and scholarship in Hope's name because of the policy. When Robyn passed, her life insurance allowed Jamey to pay their substantial medical bills and final expenses while continuing to live in the home they had shared without financial concerns.

Jamey's message to others is simple: "You're never too young to get life insurance, because you never know what will happen. Make sure you take care of your family, so if something does happen, they won't struggle."

Getting Whole Life Insurance for Children

If you wish to insure adult children or grandchildren, you'll first need to get everyone "in the same boat"—like John and Carol. Your adult children may not understand why their parents are getting life insurance, so it is important to help them understand your reasons and intentions for the policies.

It can be helpful to share the research you have done, even policy illustrations. And of course, share this book! The "Family Financing" concept can be very helpful. (For a shorter, simpler read focused on using whole life insurance—start with *Live Your Life Insurance*. It's available in multiple formats on Amazon.com.)

There are many good reasons to insure a child, but there are also rules, restrictions and procedures for insuring a child. Some important things to know beforehand…

The child's parents will need to be insured first. It doesn't have to be both (sometimes there is an issue with the insurability of one parent). It also doesn't have to be whole life. A combination of whole life and convertible term is often best unless you have adequate cash flow to insure your HLV (human life value) with whole life alone.

You will need permission from the child's parents or guardians. If you wish to insure a grandchild who is a minor, both grandchild's parents must give written permission for the policy. (If divorced, just the custodial parent's permission is needed.) The only person you can purchase insurance for without receiving their expressed written consent is your own minor children.

There must be insurable interest. If you have no children or grandchildren, you cannot insure a nephew or niece. You may, however, insure a business partner or a spouse.

You can't get as much life insurance on a child as on a parent. As children aren't usually income earners, they will qualify for usually half or less the face amount. However, the policy will grow, plus there are opportunities at various ages to purchase more.

Low premiums will limit cash value. Even though the IRR (internal rate of return) is typically higher for children, you won't build cash value as quickly because the premiums are so low. It is hard to accumulate substantial cash on a 10 year old.

Finally, not all insurance is equal. There are well-known companies selling life insurance for children that will NOT achieve the same results as whole life that is properly structured and funded with maximum paid-up additions. Two companies we are aware of have such low limits that their policies are not very useful if you want to save for college, home down payments, and so on. Companies with streamlined applications ("No exam required!") and aggressive advertising campaigns tend to not be as competitive, pricing-wise.

LifeHappens.org puts it this way: "Don't buy the first policy that crosses your mailbox. The same marketing clearinghouses that make sure you get updates on your pregnancy week by week are also making your contact information available to firms that market life insurance. Be sure to compare prices, and… talk to an insurance professional or advisor who can help you navigate through choices before committing to a policy." (Of course, we invite you to contact Partners for Prosperity[25] for assistance!)

In the next chapter you'll find "12 Things to Know about Life Insurance for Family Financing." This is a more comprehensive guide to life insurance for the whole family.

The Process of Obtaining Life Insurance

The process is similar for an adult or child, except a child may not require an exam, and only adults fill out paperwork. (A child cannot own their own policy until they are 18.)

Obtain an illustration.

The first step is to consult with an advisor or agent about a new policy. Especially if you want whole life policies to use for Family Financing, you want properly-structured policies from an appropriate mutual company. Your agent or advisor should be familiar with Prosperity Economics. (If not, you might end up with a policy that doesn't build cash value as quickly, or worse—one that is even dependent on the stock market and capable of losing cash value!) If you do not already have a trusted agent or advisor, we encourage you to contact Partners for Prosperity.[26]

Once you and your advisor know what type (or types) of policies you are interested in, they'll provide a quote in the form of an illustration. An illustration shows you how the policy might perform and estimated cost. The exact cost may fluctuate depending on health or risk factors, but you'll know the exact premium before you authorize the policy.

An illustration will show both the *guaranteed* amount of cash value and a projection based on *current* dividends. Of course, dividends can change and may be less or more in the future. However, it is not accurate to say you can only rely on the guaranteed amount. We have NEVER seen a policy that did not earn dividends (though not guaranteed) and dramatically out-perform guarantees!

If you're not sure exactly how large of a policy you want—or how much you want to pay in premium—you can apply for a larger amount and scale down during the application process. Typically, we do illustrations for either a specific death benefit amount or a specific premium amount (with maximum or minimum PUAs, depending on if you wish to maximize for cash value or for death benefit).

Fill out the application.

After you have consulted with your agent or advisor about the type of policy you want and reviewed an illustration, this is the next step. An application can be mailed or emailed to you to be filled out. Although your agent cannot answer the questions on the application for you (such as questions about your health), they can help explain any questions that might be unclear. Then the exam, if required, will be arranged.

This is also the stage when you'll need to start making decisions. For instance, who will your beneficiaries will be? What riders you want for the policy? Will you pay the premium monthly or annually?

Physical exams and medical history.

Children will not get examined at all (depending on the company, up to age 14 or beyond). Insurability is simply determined through medical records. The child's parents (or the child, if they are over 18) must authorize the insurance company to obtain an "attending physician statement" from their primary doctor.

For some teenagers and all adults, an exam is required. A licensed nurse or paramedical professional will come to your home for your convenience. For younger adults, this will be a very quick and simple exam, involving short paperwork and a blood and urine sample. Older adults (or those with higher death benefits on the application) may have to go through a more thorough exam which can include EKG's and other steps.

This all happens as part of the qualification process, before the policy premium can be finalized and the policy initiated. Agents do provide policy quotes and illustrations at the start of the process based on average policy costs for healthy individuals. They will be able to correct or confirm that pricing when you (or your child) have been qualified.

The insurance company will pay for both the exam and the physician's statement. There is no financial cost, risk or obligation in the process of qualifying for life insurance.

Paying the Premiums.

You will verify who will be making the payments with the insurance agent by phone (or possibly a third party verification service). Payments can be made annually (the best option if that works for you) or monthly. You will also get paperwork in the mail to sign.

Note that the policy begins when the first premium payment is made—not when you apply. Typically the first payment is made by a personal check from the policy owner. After that, the company can set up automatic drafts for subsequent payments, if monthly. You can make annual payments directly on the insurance company's website.

The Family Financing Begins!

On a Saturday morning, several weeks after their initial dinner to discuss Family Financing and life insurance, Carol met with her daughters at their favorite coffee shop to exchange "status updates" on the new policies and discuss the project. Although Carol had communicated every week with the girls to make sure the new policies moved along, it was nice to meet and enjoy a sense of camaraderie in the new family project.

Jackson and Julie had proceeded promptly and their boys' policies would soon be issued. However, before signing the application, Jackson (the CPA of the family) had grilled Jerry Lee with a long list of questions to his satisfaction. Carol smiled... knowing Jackson's passion for details, she was pretty sure that Jerry's Truth Concepts software had gotten a workout!

Julie shared that Jackson had originally had a few reservations about using whole life as the primary Family Financing vehicle. He was familiar with popular advice to "buy term and invest the difference" and had assumed that would be their plan. However, once Jackson got his questions answered, he was fully on board.

As a matter of fact, Julie had surprising news: in addition to the policies that John and Carol were starting for them, Jackson and Julie had decided to convert a portion of their own term insurance to whole life. They were already saving pretty steadily, but their savings account didn't come with all the benefits of life insurance! Plus, Jackson and Julie wished to save more aggressively than the smaller policies on the boys would allow. They were grateful for the policies John and Carol were starting for them, but Jackson saw a benefit to owning and paying for their own policies as well. They would be able to redirect money already going into savings accounts into the policies, where it would eventually outpace their savings account.

Cyndi and Sam were very easygoing about the policies. They didn't ask many questions, trusting the advice from Cyndi's parents and their advisor. However, they required a few reminders—both from Carol and Jerry Lee. Carol realized that just because they agreed to get policies for the grandsons didn't mean the policies would happen automatically! She needed to follow up and make sure they moved through the steps.

Carol let them know that policies for adults might take a bit longer, as they involved detailed medical questionnaires and exams. Both Cyndi and Julie had received calls to arrange for physical exams to be performed at their houses. Julie had already had hers and said it was painless, with only simple paperwork, a little blood drawn and a urine sample required. It was easy to schedule and the nurse taking the test was polite and professional. The boys' information had been obtained through their family physician via an "attending physician statement" that the insurance company paid for.

Carol knew Julie and Jackson's policies must be getting close, as John had received a call from Jerry's assistant about them. Since John and Carol would be the owner of the policies, they had to verify by phone that they would be making the payments. Soon they would receive paperwork in the mail to sign as well. Cyndi and Sam would have their exams in a few days, so their policies would not be far behind.

There were still a few details to iron out, such as whether or not they wished to add some favorite charities as beneficiaries. Jerry had been helpful answering quick questions via email and they were scheduled to talk again soon. Carol now had a list of her own questions for Jerry, along with notes on topics and ideas for coffee dates or future discussions with the husbands or the whole family.

Carol was really enjoying these coffee dates with the girls. It was fun and fulfilling to be able to combine her love for her family with her math skills and knack for educating others! Now that she was taking a proactive role as financial mentor to her daughters, she realized how much there was to know—and share. The girls both discussed money with their husbands regularly, but they also appreciated and respected their mother's wisdom and advice in this area.

Sometimes their discussions ranged far beyond finances, to marriage, parenting and life. Carol came to realize that these discussions were just as much a part of Family Financing as the life insurance. As she learned more about the Perpetual Wealth concept and how successful families helped future generations succeed, one lesson stood out to her: NEVER pass an inheritance of "just" money. Leave a legacy of wealth AND wisdom—along with good dose of love, discipline, and good habits. THAT was the recipe for generational wealth and success!

· · · · ·

THE BOTTOM LINE

Family Financing utilizes whole life insurance to:

- Multiply assets and increase net worth.
- Increase a family's long-term financial certainty.
- Insure and protect every member of the family—for life!
- Create resources that can help both owners and heirs.
- Give families a safe, flexible alternative to 529 plans for college saving.
- Establish healthy savings habits for all generations.
- Allow older generations to put assets to work for the whole family—without losing control of them.

There are many benefits to insuring children, including extremely affordable premiums, a streamlined application process, and guaranteed insurability. However, Family Financing is much more than just a financial strategy. It is also a compelling opportunity to:

- Deepen a family's relationships.
- Strengthen communication.
- Nurture leadership.
- Help future generations succeed and learn about money.
- Share family wisdom, values, priorities, habits, and more.

It is important to get the family on board by sharing the benefits of a Family Fund and the founders' intentions. Involve family members of all ages to an appropriate extent. To last for generations, Family Financing is a project best done together!

Interested in life insurance for a child or grandchild?

As you can see, there are significant benefits to insuring children. We can't imagine not insuring every member of our family! We value peace of mind and having "our ducks are in a row." We want all-purpose, tax-advantaged savings vehicles that benefit policy owners, the insured, and beneficiaries. And we want our children and grandchildren to know how to protect their children and loved ones.

Maybe you would like a quote in the form of an illustration that shows how a policy might grow. We can show you the guaranteed gains, projected dividends and death benefit. Or perhaps you still have questions about the process or how life insurance fits into your larger investment portfolio as your financial foundation and the place you store cash.

Whatever You Do… *Get professional help and advice. Don't be a life insurance "do it yourselfer." We are often contacted by people who wish they had gotten advice before they purchased the policy they have now. Some were given unrealistic expectations; others were guided into a type of policy that they now regret. Some have been given poor advice about how to properly use their policy for long-term financial security.*

Contact your Prosperity Economics Advisor who referred you to this book for assistance. We're happy to help those who don't already have an advisor or agent familiar with Family Financing. Fill out Partners for Prosperity's contact form at Partners4Prosperity.com/contact[27] and we will be in touch.

CHAPTER 7:
How to Build a Family Fund that Lasts

A few weeks after their initial face-to-face meeting with Jerry, John and Carol had more questions than ever! For convenience, they "met" Jerry online on Zoom so they could see each other as well as Jerry's computer screen.

"I hear you've got questions. I'll do my best to answer them!" said Jerry.

"It's kind of a random list," explained Carol. "We've been jotting them down over the last few days over breakfast."

"Fire away—and know that there's no such thing as a dumb question."

"My burning question is this," started John. "I recall looking at the calculators and seeing that at current dividend rates, we could be earning a couple points more than the banks will give us. But bank rates are low now. What happens if the they start paying 5 percent again?"

"Great question. I don't have a crystal ball, but what's happened in the past is this: when the banks were paying 5 percent, we'd perhaps see whole life paying 6 or 7 percent—that's net cash value growth—perhaps even 8 percent on a child. So when banks have paid more, we've seen whole life giving higher

returns. And vice versa—when banks pay less, we see insurance dividends float downward.

"Long-term cash value returns tend to float a couple points above bank rates—and you can add or subtract a bit for age and health. So you'll notice that the rate of growth will typically be best on a child's policy, and better on a younger adult's policy than your personal policies. But grandchildren typically have very small policies, though they grow with time. One upside of insuring adults is that you can obtain much larger policies—and thus save more—on a breadwinner than a child."

"Makes sense; thanks. And when I see whole life dividends announced at 6 or 7 percent or whatever the current rate is, is that the cash value growth?"

"Those are gross dividends," Jerry explained. "The numbers in the policy illustrations are net, which is obviously lower. The Truth Concepts software analyses we've looked at are based on the net gains. That's after the costs of insuring the death benefit, running the company, and our commissions."

"Thanks, I like seeing the bottom line," said John.

"Of course," replied Jerry.

Carol asked the next question. "Now, you mentioned that life insurance could help us have more income to spend later in retirement. But we're not exactly sure why that is or how that works. And maybe it's especially important to understand now that we're committing to fund some new policies!"

"Good question! Let's look at the big picture. When you use a tax-advantaged life insurance policy for your savings, it allows you to spend other assets more efficiently. You might say your policy is a 'permission slip' to spend other assets first."

Jerry could almost hear the wheels turning in John and Carol's heads as they contemplated this concept.

"Most people make the mistake of trying to take a little bit from each of their assets in retirement. A better strategy is to sequence spending down your assets, one after the other, in the most efficient way. Tax-deferred retirement accounts and funds with risk should be drawn down first. Meanwhile, keep growing the more stable and tax-efficient assets—like life insurance—for later use.

"By properly sequencing how you consume assets, you spend down (using interest and principle) your taxable accounts more quickly. This reduces your income taxes, which translates into more spendable income."

"I think I get the concept... can you go further with the example?" asked John.

"Of course. Let's say instead of trying to live on 'interest only' or stretching your retirement account disbursements out over a lifetime, you spend down your retirement accounts first. Start with them because they are taxable and problematic to pass on. You consume them completely over the first 10 to 15 years, using principle and interest. Next, focus on other taxable accounts and spend them completely the next 10 to 15 years.

"Then maybe you still have another 5 or 10 years—or more—to go! That's when you start using your life insurance for income. Depending on your situation, you might choose to withdraw, borrow against, annuitize a policy, even sell a policy. Since life insurance is a stable asset and cash value grows tax-free within the policy, you want to save that for last!

"That makes sense," said John, "and I have to admit, we haven't been very focused on income strategies while we've been earning."

"You're not alone," assured Jerry. "Most people focus on building and climbing the biggest 'mountain' of assets they can. Yet few people have a good strategy for getting down the other side of the mountain safely! I've seen this strategy save people in your situation six figures in taxes during retirement, which gives you a LOT more spendable income."

"That's rather brilliant!" said Carol. "And I'll bet advisors with assets under management either don't know this or won't tell you."

"No doubt. Very few brokers and advisors understand how to use life insurance, and most are happy to let you keep paying fees to keep assets under management."

"Of course!" nodded John.

"And there are other ways life insurance can increase your cash flow in later years," Jerry continued. "Most people balance stocks with bonds, yet life insurance cash value growth can often match or out-perform bonds in the long run.

Then the additional death benefit gives you freedom to spend down other assets and still leave a legacy.

"Some people even use the death benefit as a 'permission slip' to do a reverse mortgage on their home in their later years. This gives them another asset they can use for income, if needed. Then they have the option of giving heirs life insurance dollars instead of a property that might frankly be more of a burden to them.

"That's the 30,000 foot explanation. For a more detailed answer, I've got some resources I can send you—a special report and a video that illustrates the importance of properly diversifying assets and sequencing how you spend them. You can see an example of how the numbers crunch using Truth Concepts financial software." (Truth Concepts is a suite of specialized calculators developed by Todd Langford, Kim's husband.)

Carol tended to worry that they could run out of money someday, so the idea of saving on taxes and stretching their money was appealing.

"Now I recall these policies aren't taxable, correct?" asked John, seeking clarification.

"That's true in many situations," said Jerry. "The gains aren't taxed as long as the policy remains in force. Neither are loans," said Jerry. "And there's no income tax on the death benefit for the beneficiary. There's also no income tax involved if you transfer ownership of the policy to your kids, which parents typically do at some point.

"Now, there are situations where gift taxes or estate taxes could be paid if you exceed the exemption limits, unless the beneficiary is a trust," Jerry added, wanting to set accurate expectations. "You're fine at the current limits; it's just something to watch and make sure your estate planner is aware of the policies.

"Something else to keep in mind—if you change ownership of the policy to your daughters at least three years before you die, you can actually pass unlimited amounts of cash to your kids—without income taxes or even estate taxes."

"Wow—that's a great benefit!" said John, as "Grandma Carol" perked up.

"That's the big picture on taxes. There are details that can matter such as the 3-year transfer rule that I referred to. It can be beneficial to also work with

an estate-planning attorney and possibly a CPA who understands whole life insurance." (If you need a referral, reach out to the Prosperity Economics Movement at Hello@pem.email.[28])

Carol, who had been studying a Truth Concepts analysis Jerry had run on a policy, now spoke up. "If a policy averages say three or four percent over thirty years, then after the early years when costs are much higher, the policy growth has to be even greater than the average to make up for the 'funding phase'—correct?"

"I was going to show you that on my financial calculator, but you beat me to it!" said Jerry, sincerely impressed.

"You can't stump the math teacher!" added John.

"And since cash value can grow tax-free—or at the very least, tax-deferred," continued Carol, "we'd have to earn more in a taxable account—perhaps an extra percentage point—to have the equivalent of what we'd have in the whole life policy, right?"

"Absolutely, that's an astute observation," said Jerry.

On his laptop, Jerry showed them on Truth Concepts calculators what they'd have to earn in an alternate taxable account to match the results of the income-tax-free death benefit of the proposed policy. As he did so, John leaned forward with increased interest.

"That's a respectable return for a stable asset that's guaranteed to be worth more each year than the last," mused John. Nothing I can get from a bank is going to come close.

"Now, as far as WHO should own the policies, should it be Carol and myself, or a family trust?"

"Good question—one that you should discuss with your estate planner. You can certainly own your own policies. There are also advantages to putting policies in a trust, or having a trust own the policies. (There can be disadvantages as well… please seek expert advice.) Setting up a trust is something you can do right off the bat or later, since you have the ability to change ownership as well as beneficiaries.

"*Typically, you'd also be the beneficiaries of your daughters' policies—or a trust could be—in the unlikely scenario that anything should happen to them. Your daughters would likely be the secondary or contingent owners of the policies. That means that if something happens to you, they become the policy owners.*"

"*That's good to know!*" said Carol, pausing to add to her notes.

"*Actually, there's a list of 12 things that you should know about setting up whole life insurance for Family Financing. I'll email you the list so you can have it and also share it with your kids.*"

"*Perfect,*" replied Carol, "*That sounds great.*"

"*Any more questions about the policies on the kids? And did you decide yet if you'd like convertible term or whole life for your son-in-laws?*"

"*Yes, we're going to get whole life policies, and we've decided to maximize for death benefit rather than cash value, with just a minimum amount of PUAs. That keeps our cash outlay for the policies a bit more reasonable, and as we told the kids, they can always maximize the PUAs later. We'll probably give them the policies in another ten years.*"

"*We wanted to do the same for each of them,*" added John. "*But as you know—Julie and Jackson are also starting small policies of their own. They're really ramping up their savings, and you helped them realize whole life insurance had some distinct advantages over a bank savings account.*"

"*Yup,*" said Jerry. "*Last I checked, my savings account didn't come with an additional permanent death benefit!*"

"*Neither does ours!*" said John with a smile.

"*Well, I'm sure you both feel good knowing that in a couple weeks, the kids will all have permanent life insurance in place.*"

Carol didn't share the story at the moment, but a memory flashed through her mind from the birth of Julie's first son. Only a few days after James was born, Julie's husband Jackson was right behind a car that was hit head on by a truck coming the other direction! Jackson swerved to avoid the crash and was the first to call emergency responders, who arrived quickly. He never found out if the drivers survived the ugly accident, but the very next day, Jackson and Julie both applied for their first life insurance policies. But what if it had been too late?

The close call wasn't lost on Julie. "Mom," she had told Carol at the time, "I know the odds of either of us dying anytime soon are incredibly small. But why in the world do we have our cars and our home insured—things we can obviously replace, as inconvenient as it would be—and not each other?"

Carol hadn't even realized that they weren't insured. It made her realize that she should be taking a more proactive role in her daughter's lives. She knew her daughters were smart, but life gets busy, and sometimes even the most important things don't get done.

Carol's attention was pulled back to the conversation as Jerry continued.

"Whole life is a great long-term savings vehicle whether you have kids or not. But when it comes to parents or anyone with dependents—or even a business for that matter—it's so important to put permanent protection in place sooner rather than later. Otherwise, a change in health could stop them from obtaining life insurance later. Convertible term can do the trick for awhile. But you've got to watch your time frames and remember—you don't start saving until you start the whole life policy!"

"I know," said John, "I was telling Carol, I wish we had started policies on the girls decades ago!"

Soon all of the policies would be in place. Carol was grateful, but also eager for this part of the Family Financing project to be done. It was necessary but sometimes tedious, and the real fun was ahead! She and John were already planning the "next step"—a surprise for the whole family. When the policies for each family member were all issued, she and John were planning a dinner to celebrate—with a special announcement!

· · · · ·

12 Things to Know about Life Insurance for Family Financing

Keep in mind the following valuable information—it will help you immensely when setting up life insurance policies for your family's *Perpetual Wealth*!

1. **Life insurance is a powerful wealth transfer or estate planning strategy.**

    You can leave your death benefit to the next generation income tax free and often free of gift and estate taxes. You can also *give* a policy you own (say on an adult child) to that child so it becomes theirs to use via a "transfer of the policy to the insured." These strategies can help you take advantage of a lifetime gift tax exemption. (The lifetime gift and estate tax exemption limits are currently $5.6 million for individuals, $11.2 for couples, though subject to change.)

    Life insurance streamlines the process of wealth transfers. Policies held in trusts can help you transfer unlimited amounts of cash to future generations. Families of wealth will want to seek professional advice. Please contact your estate planning attorney or the National Network of Estate Planning Attorneys.[29]

2. **You can own insurance on someone else—IF there is "insurable interest."**

    There must be an "insurable interest" between the parties for it to work. You can't own insurance on me, but you can own it on your parent, child or grandchild. You can also own it on a spouse or business partner. There are other situations which constitute insurable interest, such as owning property jointly or any situation in which one party depends on another and would suffer a financial or other type of loss if the insured person were to die.

    For example, a grandparent could own and be the beneficiary of a life insurance policy on a grandchild. While the grandparent was living, the use of the cash value is theirs to use as a savings account for emergencies or opportunities. When the grandparent dies, the ownership transfers to the grandchild (or the parents if the child is under age). The policy then becomes *their* policy to use as their Family Fund for vehicle purchases, college tuition, down payments on houses, etc.

Nephews, nieces and friends are not considered to be an "insurable interest," unless there is a direct business or financial relationship.

3. **It is important to remember that there are three parties in a life insurance contract.**

    - The *owner*, who initiates and pays for the policy, is the primary role. The owner controls the cash and everything about the life insurance policy.
    - The *insured*, who the owner selects, is the person who the death benefit is actually placed upon.
    - The *beneficiary* is the person or trust chosen by the owner to receive the death benefit. The beneficiary can be changed at any time.

    Typically you don't want three different people playing these roles, although it is possible. And note that while you can change beneficiaries and even owners of a policy, you can never change the *insured*.

    A common arrangement is to have the owner and the insured be the same with someone else as beneficiary. In our family example, husband (John) would own and be the insured on his own policy, and his wife (Carol) or a trust could be the beneficiary.

    Another typical arrangement is for the owner and the beneficiary to be the same. The owner of a policy on a child or grandchild is likely to be the beneficiary. For instance, John or Carol could own and be the beneficiary of life insurance policies on children or grandchildren. And as mentioned, a trust can own and/or be the beneficiary of a policy.

    Note: Consider naming a "contingent" owner. If the owner of a policy is different from the insured, there should be a *contingent* owner. This way, if the owner of the policy dies, ownership of the policy passes easily to the contingent owner. For instance, a grandparent can own the policy on a grandchild. If the grandparent passes, the insured adult child can become the contingent owner.

This is especially important if the policy insures a minor. A child can be insured, but they cannot *own* a policy. You don't want the courts to decide who owns it. This could happen if a grandparent buys a policy on a grandchild and then dies while the grandchild is still minor. Even if your desire is to ultimately gift the child the policy, you would need a contingent owner until the child was at least 18. (You may want a contingent owner after that as well… that's up to you.)

4.   **You need permission to take out a life insurance policy on someone else.**

This is simply the way that insurance works, for everyone's benefit. Adult children or grandchildren must give their own consent to be insured. A minor's parents must give permission. If a couple is divorced, the custodial parent of a minor can give permission for their child to be insured.

5.   **There is a maximum amount of life Insurance face value or death benefit that can be purchased on any one person.**

This is not the modified endowment contract or MEC limit from the IRS, but a limit from the insurance company of how much insurance someone can qualify for. This is usually referred to as "human life value," or HLV, which is an industry term that indicates how a person's monetary "worth" is measured for the purpose of life insurance and also wrongful death lawsuits.

HLV is typically expressed as 15-25 times income OR—for those more established, perhaps even retired—1 times gross worth. (Gross worth equals assets, not net-worth which is assets minus liabilities.) Therefore, buying a large life insurance policy on a 40-year-old that isn't earning an income can be problematic. It can be done, but the strategy must be clear and the policy must make sense to the insurance company. The same is true with a 10-year old without assets.

Typically, children will be qualified for a smaller face value (perhaps one-quarter to one-half) compared to their parents.

"Needs analysis" is a common way to determine how much life insurance to purchase. Although it can help make sure there is an adequate death benefit to pay off a mortgage or replace a breadwinner's income, it's not a very helpful guideline for the policy that will serve a family best. Needs analysis strives to provide the *minimum* protection necessary, while the purpose of a multi-generational Family Fund is to *optimize* a family's savings and wealth-building potential.

One example that shows why using human life value makes more sense: According to governmental agencies, wrongful death lawsuits can result in claims between $7.9 and $9.1 million, states a Missouri legal blog. Why insure a spouse or loved one for the minimum when, objectively, their human life value is many times higher? Most of us wouldn't even do that with a house or car. We want "full replacement value."

6.   **Purchase life insurance on the oldest generation first.**

We suggest life insurance be purchased oldest generation first, then next, then next, etc. This helps with qualifying, as companies like to see parents properly insured before insuring children. It also ensures you are creating multi-generational wealth!

Policies on children are excellent long-term savings vehicles, while policies on adults allow the policy owner to accumulate more cash in a shorter time period.

For example, a policy with a $100k policy face value and maximum paid-up additions (to build cash value faster) will have a maximum premium and PUAs of about $1568/year for a 10-year old boy. The image below, taken from a policy illustration, shows a projected policy cash value of $37,271 at age 29—the 20th year of the policy—based on the current (2016) dividend scale.

$100k Whole Life Policy for a 10-Year Old Boy:
Dividend Option: Paid Up Additions (D)

			Guaranteed			Non-Guaranteed – Current	
POL YR	AGE AT START OF YEAR	ANNUAL PREMIUM #	CASH VALUE ##	DEATH BENEFIT ##	NET PREMIUM #*	CASH VALUE ##*	DEATH BENEFIT ##*
5	14	1,568	6,179	139,978	1,568	6,678	143,701
10	19	1,568	13,464	173,539	1,568	14,897	183,456
20	29	1,568	31,414	222,984	1,568	37,271	253,539
61	70	753	179,769	290,425	753	336,197	534,959
66	75	753	201,598	290,425	753	409,185	582,278
71	80	753	222,258	290,425	753	492,621	637,569
76	85	753	293,991	290,425	753	585,243	703,167
81	90	753	254,005	290,425	753	682,983	777,258

While the illustration is proportionate (meaning if you double the premium, everything else will double as well) it is still limiting if you want to use whole life policy on a child to store any significant amount of cash.

(It's worth noting that premiums for similar-sized policies for girls/women are generally 10-20% less, due to longevity differences.)

In contrast to a policy for a 10-year old boy, the premium for a $100k policy on a 40-year old man with maximum PUAs would be just over $4,440/year. Projected cash value would be nearly $116k in the policy's 20th year.

$100k Whole Life Policy for a 40-Year Old Man:

Dividend Option: Paid Up Additions (D)

POL YR	AGE AT START OF YEAR	Guaranteed			Non-Guaranteed – Current		
		ANNUAL PREMIUM #	CASH VALUE ##	DEATH BENEFIT ##	NET PREMIUM #*	CASH VALUE ##*	DEATH BENEFIT ##*
5	44	4,432	19,486	145,894	4,432	20,833	149,504
10	49	4,432	43,269	184,723	4,432	48,098	197,109
20	59	2,869	93,402	233,167	2,869	115,935	278,153
31	70	2,689	151,373	259,132	2,689	222,541	369,215
36	75	1,942	180,412	270,139	1,942	287,946	420,304
41	80	1,942	201,950	270,929	1,942	357,161	469,395
46	85	1,842	226,853	279,125	1,842	442,802	536,639
51	90	1,842	241,852	279,125	1,842	528,290	603,750

(These illustrations are from 2019 and may have changed. We can provide you with current quotes.)

Premium for a new $100k policy on 60-year old would approach $8,500/year with maximum PUAs. At age 79, the policy's 20th year, the projected cash value would be nearly $197k.

$100k Whole Life Policy for a 60-Year Old Man:

Dividend Option: Paid Up Additions (D)

POL YR	AGE AT START OF YEAR	Guaranteed			Non-Guaranteed – Current		
		ANNUAL PREMIUM #	CASH VALUE ##	DEATH BENEFIT ##	NET PREMIUM #*	CASH VALUE ##*	DEATH BENEFIT ##*
5	64	8,473	32,183	135,651	8,473	37,947	144,861
10	69	8,473	69,651	166,928	8,473	87,698	194,570
11	70	8,225	76,766	172,357	8,225	98,060	204,434
16	75	5,818	191,037	180,404	5,818	143,166	238,508
20	79	8,473	130,644	200,179	8,473	196,992	285,688
21	80	4,700	134,493	200,179	4,700	208,051	293,570
26	85	4,700	152,072	200,179	4,700	267,695	337,618
31	90	4,700	167,105	200,179	4,700	332,344	387,185

If it is not feasible to insure the oldest generation due to health concerns or other qualification concerns, that individual or couple can still be a policy *owner*, provided that there is someone else in the family that they would have an insurable interest in, such as a child or grandchild.

7.   **Policies can be optimized for cash value or death benefit.**

If you wish to save more rather than less in a policy, you will want to maximize your PUAs (paid-up additions) which allows you to put as much as possible into the policy. If your priority is maximizing death benefit or keeping the premiums low relative to the death benefit, you don't need the PUAs.

We are also asked if there are ways to *reduce* the commissions on a policy. Although agents and advisors don't control commissions (they are set by the insurance companies in compliance with state regulations), a policy owner can direct more of their premium into cash value (and a substantially smaller percentage to commissions) by maximizing paid-up additions. Nearly the entire amount of a PUA goes straight to cash value, which helps your savings build faster. PUAs also increase all future dividend payments, making the policy more efficient and profitable.

Most of our clients want to maximize for cash value, but it really depends on your situation. You can also pay a varying amount of PUAs, starting with a lesser amount, then saving more as you are able.

8.   **Policies grow, premiums don't.**

You may have noticed in the illustrations above that the face value or death benefit of a policy grows over time. This helps policies keep pace with inflation as well as the expanding nature of people's lives. Therefore "small" policies insuring children may have their face value multiply many times during the insured's lifetime. And even policies taken on a 60-year old can triple or quadruple.

However, one reason we love whole life insurance is that your *premiums* are guaranteed to never go up! It's even possible that the limit for paid-up additions—which is a way to "overfund" the policy for maximum cash value—will even *decrease* during certain years in order to keep the policy under the MEC (Modified Endowment Contract) limitations. So your premium (including PUAs) might even decrease over time.

Contrast that to universal life policies, which sometimes experience sharp premium *increases* as the insured ages—one of several reasons we don't recommend UL policies.

If you've heard, "Once you start a whole life policy, you'll lose the policy if you can't make a premium payment," this is not entirely accurate. There are multiple ways to decrease, temporarily suspend, or even halt premiums if necessary, especially after a policy has been funded for a few years. See the article on ProsperityEconomics.org, "Reduce or Stop Premium Payments... and KEEP your Whole Life Policy!"[30] for details.

9.   **You can choose various payment options for each policy.**

Policy owners can select annual or monthly payments, and sometimes quarterly. There are different benefits and considerations for each. Paying annually is more efficient than quarterly or monthly and optimizes the rate of return. However, do what works best for your family and know that payment options can be changed later.

There are also various options for the LENGTH of the policy payment period. Some policies are a "10-pay," meaning that you'll pay premiums for only 10 years. Other policies may be longer, such as 20 years, or they may be payable until a certain age, such as 65 or 90 or 120. Be aware that it is impossible to *extend* a policy payment period, and much easier to *shorten* a policy payment period. (You can reduce or even eliminate premiums after about 10 years, if you have paid the maximum PUAs into the policy). We recommend longer pay options since many people end up earning money longer than they anticipate and find themselves wanting a good place to store and grow cash later in life.

On the other end of the spectrum, as covered in the previous chapter, there is also a Single Premium Whole Life option (SPWL). This can be a good way to use a lump sum to immediately enhance net worth while assuring the safe and steady growth of cash. However, single pay policies are classified as MECs (Modified Endowment Contracts). Loans and withdrawals from MECs are taxed as income and, like an IRA, can trigger penalties if you withdraw before age 59-1/2. Therefore single premium policies aren't useful to borrow against, although they are excellent wealth transfer vehicles.

Note: Pay attention to your paid-up additions! If maximizing the growth of cash value is a goal of the policy owner, it is imperative that the policy be set up with the proper Paid-Up Addition riders (PUAs). Policy owners should understand how their premiums and PUAs are to be paid in order to ensure the optimal rate of return. That said, it's perfectly fine to have a policy without PUAs or to decrease PUAs to accommodate cash flow. Just be aware that the policy will take longer to build cash value.

You'll need to follow the insurance company's instructions to not fund the policy beyond its limits. Overfunding may turn it into a MEC, or modified endowment contract, with less favorable tax law. As the PUA schedule often changes during the course of a policy, sometimes decreasing after the first few years, you'll want to pay attention. Basically, take care to read any correspondence from the insurance company so you don't miss something important!

10. **You're probably not "too old" for life insurance.**

Policies can be purchased on oneself up to age 85 as long as you are reasonably healthy. This is a pleasant surprise for many people! (We have also seen "final expense" policies available beyond age 85.)

Not everyone qualifies—but there is no cost or obligation to apply. And sometimes, people who have had resolved health challenges in the past (such as cancer that has been in remission) are pleasantly surprised.

Post-retirement policies make sense if the owner/insured:

- wishes to maximize the value of their estate, and/or
- wants a safe and flexible savings vehicle with an additional death benefit
- desires to combine life insurance and a long-term care rider into one policy
- and have adequate cash flow to fund a policy.

For more on this topic, see "Why Seniors Are Getting New Life Insurance Policies."[31]

Life insurance in one's later years is *not* for someone who needs immediate extra income to live on or does not have the ability to save. If this is your situation, contact Partners for Prosperity[32] or the advisor who sent you this book for other options. You may have existing assets that could be deployed for greater cash flow.

11. Multiple smaller policies are common and often helpful.

You may not have "one perfect policy." Many people "start small, go slow." They add policies as their financial capability expands, as they have more children, and as they come to trust, appreciate and use their first whole life policies.

Depending on how long you have been using life insurance as a savings vehicle, your family may technically have multiple policies that comprise your Financial Foundation. The multiple policies may operate under a single set of rules or principles, if that's how your family decides to govern the use of the policies. Or you could have policies that are part of the Family Fund (potentially used for Family Lending) and others that are not. And as we will discuss in chapter 15, "Wills, Trusts and Wealth Transfers," some families even utilize multiple (different kinds of) trusts. The trusts could hold different policies.

Since few people can insure their Human Life Value with one or even multiple whole life policies (due to the total amount of premium), many people have both whole life and term insurance (preferably convertible term insurance that can be converted to whole life). Over time, term policies can be converted or replaced by whole life as your financial capability builds.

Different policies may also be started for different purposes. For instance, you might obtain:

- Policies on yourself that you use for long-term family savings and protection.
- Policies on adult children or grandchildren to store and grow multi-generational wealth.
- Policies on a business partner and/or key employees.
- A whole life policy on yourself and your spouse that doubles as long-term care protection.
- A convertible term policy to insure your full HLV affordably.
- And a whole life policy for legacy giving to your favorite charities that maximizes death benefit, not cash value.

I (Kim) also like to have different anniversary dates for different policies, so that I have premium payments in different months and seasons, rather than all at once.

12. Choosing the right TYPE of life insurance (and TYPE of company) is more important than which life insurance COMPANY you insure with.

A common question we hear is, "How do I choose the right life insurance company?"[33] or, "What's the best life insurance company?" In truth, there is no one "right" or "best" company. There are quite a few excellent choices. The right *type* of company will be:

- A mutual company that pays its profits to policy holders in the form of dividends.
- Well-established with a solid track record. Most whole life companies have been in business (and paying dividends) for well over 100 years.
- Highly rated, with ratings of "A" or better (such as AA, A++) by the rating agencies such as Moody's, Fitch, A.M. Best and Standard &

Poor's. (Established mutual life insurance companies tend to have excellent credit ratings.)

A common question is also "which company pays the highest dividends?" The answer to that question is much less important than people imagine because:

- Dividend rates declared by various companies are *gross*, not net.
- Dividends can change every year (and are not guaranteed, though they may be historically reliable).
- Whole life is a long-term product. Whatever company is paying the most right now isn't likely the company paying the most a few years from now.
- Frankly, the net returns from the top whole life insurance companies over time tend not to differ very much.

We work with multiple life insurance companies, and there are times when we recommend one over another because of factors such as:

- Flexibility of paid-up additions.
- A client preference for fixed vs. adjustable rate policy loans or direct-recognition vs. non-direct recognition. (Any of those options can work fine.)
- The type of policy or rider offered. (For instance, one company offers a single premium whole life policy, another offers a two-pay policy.)

There can be wisdom in diversifying your policies amongst a few insurance companies—especially if you have multiple policies and/ or a substantial amount of life insurance. Some people like to have one policy with a fixed loan rate and another with a variable rate loan. People with older existing policies may wish to acquire a policy with a new rider. (We did this when the long-term care benefits rider became available.) Or you may have traditional whole life policies plus a "10-pay" or a single premium policy.

For more details on questions you may have about companies and policies, be sure not to miss the Policy Question Checklist and links to other resources near the end of this chapter. But truly *most* important decision is choosing an advisor or agent you feel comfortable with and buying the right *type* of policy. (Of course, we are happy to help if you do not already have an advisor or agent you know and trust. And we work with several life insurers—all who meet our criteria.)

What about other types of life insurance?

One question that comes up often when discussing life insurance is, "What TYPE of insurance is best?" Here is a brief overview of the main types of life insurance:

Term Insurance.

Term insurance is straight forward and easy to understand. You purchase life insurance for a "term," such as 10, 20, or 30 years. When the term is ends, so does your protection. A term policy can't be used for Family Financing, as there is no cash value or permanent death benefit with term insurance.

However, term insurance can still be useful in many situations. It is an inexpensive way, for instance, for young parents on a budget to protect their family against the possible loss of a breadwinner while their children are dependents and before they have the ability to purchase whole life in desired amounts.

Convertible Term Insurance.

Often people want to start saving with life insurance—or simply purchase permanent life insurance—but they just don't have the cash flow to properly fund whole life policies in the amount they desire. If this describes you, we recommend starting with a smaller whole life policy supplemented by a convertible term insurance policy.[34] With this type of policy, all or a portion of it can be converted to whole life later. (You'll want to verify that and make sure it doesn't convert to universal life.)

Although convertible policies don't build cash value and can't be borrowed against, they are affordable, provide a death benefit for a defined term, and lock insurability in place for years to come. And since term insurance is extremely likely to expire before the insured does, it is always best to pay a little more for convertible term. This keeps your option open to turn the policy into a permanent policy within a certain time frame. Just make sure the policy can be converted to a whole life policy (not universal life).

Contact Partners for Prosperity[35] or the advisor who referred this book to you for an illustration and assistance.

Universal Life.

Universal life (UL) was very popular in the 1980s and many people still own UL policies. We don't typically recommend UL policies as they have been proven to be problematic. Costs are not guaranteed, and the cost of insurance within the policy rises as the insured ages. Therefore, cash value can eventually be gobbled up to keep the policy alive.

There are also no guarantees on a minimum *amount* (not *rate*) of cash value. UL policies tend to be underfunded and they don't build cash value as well as whole life policies.

Although universal life is sold as permanent life insurance, we hesitate to call UL policies "permanent." Policies can fail if the cost of insurance within the policy rises to unsustainable levels. Policies lack guaranteed level premiums and (sometimes) a guaranteed death benefit, passing risk on to the policy owner. Sometimes policy owners are faced with large premium increases late in life—or else they will lose their insurance. UL policies also don't endow, so conceivably, you could outlive one. We recommend our article, "The Disadvantages of Universal Life"[36] for a better understanding.

Some UL policies perform fine, but we don't recommend them for Family Financing and Lending (saving and borrowing against). You want your savings to be "safe" and your death benefit to be guaranteed—no matter how long you live.

Variable Universal Life.

Variable policies allow the policy owner to literally "invest" their cash value into mutual funds or other types of investments. We don't recommend this as it turns your "safe and secure" money into a risky venture!

Equities and other asset classes can certainly be part of a balanced portfolio, but investing can be done more efficiently *outside* of a life insurance policy. VUL policies also have the same weaknesses as other universal life policies.

Indexed Universal Life.

Indexed universal life (IUL) has been popular the last couple of decades. These policies strive to combine some of the flexibility of UL with the investment component of variable life, but with less risk. They are sold as having "the upside of the market, without the risk!" Actually, the upside of an IUL policy is not comparable to investments, because of the market caps, fees and costs. And although an IUL won't lose cash value due to a drop in the stock market, cash value *can* be reduced by fees, expenses, loan interest, cost of insurance, premium loads, and many other charges.

IULs are often sold as one-stop financial product that combines life insurance, savings and investments. However, we don't recommend using life insurance for *investing*, because 1) you want your cash to be guaranteed to grow steadily and never decrease, and 2) you can do better investing outside of the life insurance environment. IULs can be problematic and there have been several lawsuits regarding misleading, overly optimistic illustrations. And as they are built on a flawed UL "chassis," we anticipate further issues as these policies age and internal policy costs continue to rise.

"No exam" and/or final expense policies.

For those who can't qualify for regular whole life insurance, these can be considered IF a person does not have other adequate assets. The rate of return won't be anything to brag about, but the policy can still act as a "forced savings account" that offers a death benefit, sometimes a savings component, too. You'll want to make sure it is a permanent whole life policy, not a policy guaranteed only to age 95 or 100, or one subject to premiums hikes.

Whole life insurance.

Whole life remains the gold standard of life insurance policies. Dividend-paying whole life offers guarantees that you won't find in other types of life insurance:

- A guaranteed death benefit—for life—no matter how long you live.
- A guaranteed level premium. Your premiums will never go up.
- A guaranteed minimum dollar amount of cash value, net of all costs.
- Guaranteed growth of cash value—even if no dividends are paid.
- A guaranteed mortality rate, which means the cost of your insurance is predetermined. No imploding policies and bad surprises.
- Guaranteed participation in the profits of the mutual company. Profits over and above expenses are distributed back to policyholders in the form of dividends. (Dividends are not guaranteed, but have been reliably paid by many companies for decades, even centuries.)
- Guaranteed ability to borrow against your cash value (usually up to 90 or 95%, depending on the policy provisions).
- Additional guarantees according to the policy riders you select.

Because of these guarantees, virtually any other kind of insurance will cost *less* than whole life insurance. It costs more because it provides more benefits! Mark Bertrang, our friend and long-time insurance professional, says, "Whenever an insurance company introduces a new policy design, the first question I ask myself is, 'What is the company taking away from their policy design to achieve its new competitive pricing advantage, and is it really in a client's best interest?' "

Of course, the premiums of a whole life insurance policy can fluctuate quite a bit depending on your age, your health, and also whether or not you maximize PUAs (paid-up additions) to build cash value faster. But you do tend to get what you pay for!

Policy Question Checklist

You may have many questions about life insurance. There are questions we get frequently, and questions that people probably *should* be asking, but don't know to ask! Below are some policy questions and resources where you will find answers:

You'll find the following in our article on ProsperityEconomics.org, "Questions You Must Ask BEFORE You Apply for Life Insurance."[37]

1. How do you choose the right life insurance company?
2. Is your death benefit guaranteed for life—regardless how long you live?
3. Do policy loans or changes in premium payments jeopardize the guaranteed death benefit?
4. Are the premiums guaranteed not to change?
5. Can you use your policy to store cash for as long as you wish?
6. Are policy guarantees based upon a guaranteed *rate* or a guaranteed *dollar amount*?
7. Are cash value returns tied to the stock market or non-correlated?
8. Does the type of insurance you're exploring have a history of stability or lawsuits?
9. Do you have the right help?

The next set of questions comes from a follow-up article, "Questions to Consider After You Apply for Life Insurance":[38]

1. How much life insurance should I get?
2. Will I qualify for life insurance?
3. Is the policy structured for maximum Cash Value or maximum Death Benefit?
4. Does the policy have a "Direct Recognition" or "Non-Direct Recognition" loan provision?
5. How does a policy loan affect the policy values?
6. What is the interest rate charged for a policy loan?
7. Is there a Waiver of Premium rider on the policy?
8. Is there a Terminal Illness rider available on the policy?
9. Is there a Long-Term Care benefit rider available on the policy?
10. Will you pay for the policy annually or monthly?
11. Should you backdate your life insurance policy?

You may have additional questions! Chances are, some of your questions are answered in our two other life insurance books (authored by Kim and edited by Kate). *Live Your Life Insurance* is a great introduction to whole life insurance and a handbook for how to build and protect wealth with it. *Busting the Life Insurance Lies* (co-written by Jack Burns and James Ranson) covers 38 myths and half-truths about life insurance, especially whole life. You can find them both on Amazon in paperback, Kindle and audiobook formats.

THE BOTTOM LINE

While the details might feel overwhelming, life insurance doesn't have to be complicated! We're providing you with LOTS of information as we are familiar with what people need to know, as well as what questions tend to arise! But you don't have to figure it out on your own (nor is there any savings or advantage to you if you did!)

Have questions? Unless you already have a trusted insurance agent or advisor you rely on, contact Partners for Prosperity[39] and we can help. No question is a dumb question… and we have answers! Send us an email at hello@Partners4Prosperity.com[40] or give us a call at (877) 889-3981 ext. 120.

We've been helping clients understand and obtain life insurance for more than 20 years and we love to do it. We can also provide an illustration which will estimate your premium and show you how your cash value and death benefit might grow and perform for you!

CHAPTER 8:
Inheritance Wisdom, Wealth and Warnings

It was breakfast time again at the Johnson household, and Carol uncharacteristically poured herself a second cup of coffee this morning after she had finished the first.

"Boy, I just didn't sleep well last night once I started thinking about this inheritance stuff."

"Yes? Tell me more," pressed John gently.

"Oh, I'm just overwhelmed. Last night, after you fell asleep, I still had 100 questions swimming in my head… 'How much should we leave our kids? How much might we need for ourselves? Should we give them their inheritances over time, after we die, or some of each? Should we tell them how much they might inherit, or not? And what about our church and the charities we support… should we include them as beneficiaries, or just the kids and grandkids!?' You know, simple little questions like that."

John chuckled, "Yes, those sound like simple little questions, dear. I'm surprised you got any sleep at all!"

"And then I got to thinking, if something happened to us, and the girls inherited it all, what do you think they'd do with it? I mean, if something happened now, so early in our retirement—and with the new policies—they would each inherit well into seven figures. That would be a lot of money for them!"

"Well then, I guess we've got to spend more money—and fast! I'm telling you, that new Mercedes would look good in the driveway." John was half-joking; he liked the new models, though he wasn't really in the market just yet.

"Yeah, but it wouldn't look as good as a trip to Italy!" Carol shot back mischievously. She was already starting to plan their third trip to Italy, this time, to Venice and Lake Como.

And suddenly, just before her mind drifted off into visions of singing gondolier's guiding them through the canals… Carol noticed the pattern. It wasn't terribly comfortable to discuss the inevitable, and they both had a tendency to avoid the topic at hand. For several years, they had started many such conversations, never finishing them.

Today, the topic could no longer be ignored. But how could they begin to make decisions? And what would the kids do if they suddenly inherited all they had? And as they put more policies in place, their inheritance would be even larger. How could they prepare their families to use it wisely?"

"In all seriousness," she said, continuing the conversation she had helped to derail, "I did some research about inheritances, and that's exactly the kind of stuff most beneficiaries spend money on… new cars and vacations abroad. As much as I'd like to think that they'd use it to save and invest for the future and for the boys, I don't honestly know how they'd handle it."

John's brow furrowed and he looked suddenly concerned, taking in Carol's words carefully. "I know we'll spend much of our nest egg down in time, but presently, it would make quite a windfall. They're barely established, and if they had a large sudden influx of money, well, I can't say they'd be ready for it. At least, not yet."

Carol nodded in agreement.

"We saw it at the bank all the time," continued John. "'Trustafarians,' we'd call them. When people don't earn the money themselves, sometimes it's not managed well, to say the least. It just isn't valued the same."

Now Carol was the one with the furrowed brow. "Well, what are the options? I know the money can be put in a trust, limitations can be set on its use... but is that the best solution? I mean, you and I have worked hard to be where we are, to be the first in our families with college degrees, to put our own kids through college, and to finally have the resources to enjoy ourselves and travel without scrimping. I'm glad our girls—or their boys—won't have to go through what we did. They've had a head start, and that's a good thing, right? But I don't want that head start to decrease their own motivation."

"Yes," John assured her, "The opportunity we've given our girls—and will give our grandsons—is a VERY good thing. I'm quite proud we're able to help them have a head start."

John came from a family of stellar character but very humble means. Carol knew that giving his girls opportunities he hadn't had himself was one of his great joys in life. They had been able to provide the girls with college tuition, and many small things along the way: soccer club, music lessons, a private tutor for Cyndi when she hit some snags in math, and support for Julie in her Thespian and drama club interests. They had also included the girls in some of their travel adventures, touring the cultural riches of Rome and Mayan ruins in Mexico, not to mention road trips to Yellowstone, the Grand Canyon, and the Smithsonian museums, a bit closer to home.

"But you see," John continued, "Our job's not finished yet. I said that 'sometimes' inherited wealth is mismanaged. Other times, beneficiaries take what they've been given and they multiply it! It's like the fishes and loaves in the Bible—I've seen even modest family gifts multiplied, utilized, invested and shared in amazing ways!"

John had spent his life working with people and their money and Carol respected his wisdom and perspective. He poured himself more coffee then continued. "You know the ball field where Sheldon coaches Little League? That was built with a gift from a community donor. No one even realized the guy had money— he was just a humble neighborhood guy living in an ordinary home. One day *his grandson takes an interest in baseball, and lo and behold, he plunks down the first $150k to break ground for the new baseball park! In cash!"*

"Oh good, I like success stories! But back up... what did you mean by, 'our job isn't finished yet'?"

"Well, usually when heirs are spendthrifts, it's because their families left them with just the money. When cash is inherited without wisdom, guidance and skills to go with it, the money doesn't usually last long. As a banker, I developed a sense of when this would happen. But when I met beneficiaries whose parents or grandparents had guided and mentored them to be ready for the gift, they were the ones who used their inheritance as a starting point for building their own legacies."

"Hmm, so some people see a gift of money as an end result—something for them to consume. Others see it as a seed to be planted and watered and cared for."

"Exactly!" nodded John. "It's all a matter of perspective."

"Well then, we do have a job cut out for us! We've grown and planted some dollars... now it sounds like we've got to train our family farmers to continue the work."

"AND," added John, "the questions that kept you up last night are important and need to be answered. Let's start setting aside some intentional time to tackle them. I know we'll want to update our estate planning as our Family Financing project evolves. I've got some ideas of how to approach this, and we're overdue for a meeting with Sylvia to update our estate plan."

"Thank-you, dear, I will sleep easier knowing we are handling these things," said Carol with genuine gratitude, adding with a sly smile, "Maybe we could spend a week or two hashing out Family Financing and inheritance decisions over espresso in Venice?"

. . . . .

Inheritance: To Give or Not to Give

One of the benefits of Family Financing with whole life insurance is that it typically increases the value of your family's estate. Rather than figuring out how to "divide up the pie" of your current assets between yourself and your intended beneficiaries, life insurance helps you make a bigger pie!

For some families, this is also one of the *challenges* of Family Financing. The prospect of an inheritance (or an ability to leave a larger-than-expected inheritance) may create a bit of a quandary. At the least, it raises a number of important questions:

"What determines if a beneficiary will use an inheritance wisely?"

"How can I know if my children or grandchildren are prepared for an inheritance?"

"How much should go to heirs, and how much to charity?"

"What will truly help my heirs and serve their best interests?"

"Should I even leave an inheritance at all?"

There is a strong cultural tradition of leaving an inheritance, assuming there are assets to be left. However, this tradition no longer represents "the way things are." Many working and middle-class folks already feel they have under-saved for retirement, never mind an inheritance. After all, an inheritance is a gift—not an obligation.

In spite of "the great wealth transfer" from Boomers to Millennials that is already underway, the percentage of retirees who say they will leave an inheritance is on the decline. A 2013 HSBC survey[41] of more than 16,000 people in 15 countries found American retirees were *less* likely to leave an inheritance than retirees from other countries: 56 percent of Americans vs. 69 percent of retirees around the world. (Interestingly, India topped the charts, with 86 percent of retirees surveyed planning to leave an inheritance.)

A more recent (2017) U.S. investor survey reported in a CNBC.com article[42] found that only 40 percent of baby boomers are planning to leave an inheritance. Unfortunately, 68 percent of their millennial children are *expecting* an inheritance, indicating our culture's inability to discuss money.

Apparently, the retiree shirts and slogans saying "I'm spending the kids' inheritance" aren't a joke after all.

Other parents question if their gift will be used wisely. This causes a majority of givers to remain silent on the details, fearing it could sabotage their children's ambitions or independence. Even the ultra-wealthy have been making headlines as they re-think how—and how much—to give.

When U.S. Trust surveyed individuals with more than $3 million in investable assets to find out how they are preparing the next generation for handling wealth, the reasons for the decline in inheritances became obvious. According to Chris Heilmann, U.S. Trust's chief fiduciary executive. "Looking at the numbers, 78% feel the next generation is not financially responsible enough to handle inheritance."

Additionally, 64 percent admitted they have been largely silent on the topic of money, leaving their children (adult and younger) in the dark—even if they will likely convey a sizable inheritance.

Inheritances can be difficult to talk about. Whether you are a giver or receiver, the topic of inheritance can push buttons in a way that few topics can. It brings up issues of wealth, trust, guilt and generosity. Some families worry their children could become lazy or entitled. Others are concerned about confidentiality. Discussing an inheritance may require you to reveal you've got more money than your kids realize. Or it may bring up regrets that you can't leave your children more. Either way, keeping kids in the dark is generally not the best strategy.

Will an inheritance be used wisely or wasted?

Some inheritances are slowly earned, yet quickly spent. That is usually the result when more effort is spent preparing *wealth* for heirs than preparing *heirs* for wealth.

"It takes an average of 19 days for the recipient of an inheritance to buy a new car," asserts Rhys McCarney Ph.D. when discussing the issues of sudden wealth. One study based on survey data from the Federal Reserve and a National Longitudinal Survey found that one-third of heirs had negative savings within two years[43] of the gift. For these beneficiaries—one in three—every penny is lost or spent.

"The vast majority of people blew through it quickly," says Jay Zagorsky, economist and research scientist at The Ohio State University and author of the study. "Americans who receive an inheritance save about half of what they get and spend, donate, or manage to lose the rest." Even when heirs invest with an inheritance, it can be lost on risky bets. (Apparently, it's much easier to gamble with money you didn't earn yourself.)

To be fair, the inheritances surveyed in Zagorsky's research were often quite small—under $10k. The larger the inheritance, the longer it lasted. For those who received $100k or more, only 18.7% spent or lost their inheritance.

How can you ensure an inheritance is well-received? How can you give successfully and increase the opportunity for your gift to be wisely used?

Whether you are planning to leave a modest gift or multiple millions, there is wisdom to be learned from the wealthiest among us. After all, those with more give must seriously consider the impact of generational wealth on their loved ones. Let's see what we can learn from these guides and mentors.

George Peabody: Generosity and Responsibility

You may have never heard of New England businessman and financier George Peabody, but his legacy lives on today, 150 years after his death. Sometimes referred to as "the Father of Modern Philanthropy," Peabody gave away over $8 million in his lifetime—the equivalent of over $1 billion in today's dollars. His gifts represented about two-thirds of his wealth and were mostly given during his retirement. He paved the way for philanthropists such as Carnegie and Vanderbilt and he mentored Junius Spencer Morgan—father of J.P. Morgan. Most importantly for our purposes, Peabody modeled ways to support family members in their needs and encourage heirs to succeed—without fostering dependency or entitlement.

As a philanthropist, Peabody's gifts provided the less fortunate with the means to improve themselves. Although George Peabody never completed his own schooling, he considered education "a debt due from present to future generations." It was a debt he paid in full, again and again. He funded many education initiatives, building prep schools, a music conservatory, libraries, lecture halls and museums in both the Northeast and the South, especially following the devastation of the Civil War.

A statue of George Peabody still stands in London, where his benefactions also made a tremendous impact. London was his adopted home the latter half of his life, where he founded the Peabody Trust in 1862 to fund affordable, sustainable housing for the working poor living in slums and on the street. Today, more than 70,000 Londoners live in homes built by the trust.

Peabody's generous life began life in the humblest of circumstances. Born in 1795 into a poor family in Massachusetts, the third child of eight, George left school and began working at age eleven lend support to the family. His father died when George was only 16, worsening their situation. Their home was so deeply mortgaged that George, his mother and his younger siblings were forced to move in with relatives.

George worked hard and was notoriously thrifty, saving all he could. At age 21, George repaid his father's old debts with money he had earned as a clerk, restoring his mother and siblings to their family home.

Although sometimes criticized as miserly for living simply and conducting business frugally, George supported his family in many ways throughout his life. As his success increased, he funded secondary school and college educations for younger siblings, cousins, nieces and nephews at fine institutions. He paid for the excellent care of his older sister who was often sick until she passed away at a young age. When George's younger sister's husband struggled in vain to farm a piece of unfertile land, Peabody bought them a new tract of land in more fertile location. In an age before insurance was widely available, George was the family member everyone turned to when disaster struck... when a young mother died, when a business burned down, when a dear sister was widowed.

Years of family correspondence reveals Peabody's generosity towards his family. In return, most—but not all—family members expressed unreserved gratitude. George was not an indiscriminate giver, nor did he give to all equally without regard to need or behavior. In return for his assistance, he insisted that those who received help exhibit integrity, accountability and a strong work ethic. Even in the low-income housing built by the Peabody Trust, while George was alive there were strict expectations such as a night-time curfew, a moral code and expectations of cleanliness.

George believed in second chances, but he refused to support self-destructive habits or those who would not help themselves. One of the companies Peabody co-founded hired three of his brothers—then fired two of them after they proved themselves unreliable, in spite of warnings. George settled debts for family members when he deemed it necessary. (A man of good reputation, George did not want his relations tarnishing the Peabody name.) However, when his elder brother David amassed significant gambling debts, Peabody wrote him out of his will—while *increasing* his legacy to his upstanding nephew, David's son.

George was closest to his sister Judith, who became his principle correspondent, family accountant, and sounding board for personal matters. Judith managed the finances disbursed to family members and kept her brother informed of each person's accounts and activities. She helped determine which family member needed money and which cause was worthy.

Gifts from George would be accompanied by a letter. In the letter, George would express his intention for the gift and instructions for its use. He would request a reply along with an accounting of how the money was used. This was to teach his beneficiaries prudent management, stewardship and responsibility. Financial gifts always came with guidance and required accountability. George required all family expenses to be vigilantly monitored, whether it was for clothing, educational costs, or other needs. Every expense was recorded and every gift was accounted for.

Additionally, many of his gifts to heirs were given during his lifetime, allowing George to advise and monitor his beneficiaries. By the time George Peabody passed away, his heirs were well-trained and well-trusted to use money wisely.

George never married or had children of his own, but as Judith wrote affectionately of his paternal love for his siblings, nieces and nephews, "...all the children are his children." He provided his heirs with more than mere financial assistance... he gave them his wisdom, mentorship, and when appropriate—tough love. He took care of genuine needs but never encouraged dependency or entitlement.

Rather than leaving his family his fortune, George Peabody left them something better—the means to succeed on their own. Rather than "waiting for an inheritance," many of his siblings, nieces and nephews used George's help to learn wisdom and discipline in financial matters, obtain an education, gain valuable experience and pursue a vocation.

Re-Thinking Inheritance with Buffett and Gates

"A very rich person should leave his kids enough to do anything, but not enough to do nothing," said Warren Buffett in a September 29, 1986 interview with[44] *Fortune*. As it turns out, that *Fortune* article influenced a young couple who began dating a year later. It shaped their philosophy of child-rearing long before they had children, a friendship with Buffet, or the world's largest private foundation in the world—in no small part thanks to Buffet. Bill Gates, sitting next to Melinda, echoed Warren's sentiments at a TED event: "We want to strike a balance where they have the freedom to do anything, but not a lot of money showered on them so they could go out and do nothing."

According to *Business Insider*, each of the Gates' kids will inherit about $10 million of their parents' $92.2 billion fortune—a mere drop from the Microsoft cash bucket. However, the couple supports the interests of their children in multiple other ways. For instance, they have supported their eldest daughter Jennifer on her journey to become a nationally ranked show jumper, attending competitions and funding horses and trainers, even purchasing a string of properties in Wellington, Florida—the equestrian capital of the US.

Jennifer Gates shows what having the ability to "do anything" looks like. Her dedication paid off with a national championship trophy (with a $100k purse) in 2017 and a prestigious award in 2018 from the United States Equestrian Team Foundation for sportsmanship and horsemanship. In addition to being a top-ranked equestrian athlete, Jennifer is a full-time Stanford student. She's studying Human Biology and focusing on issues surrounding the well-being of children. She has volunteered for a teen crisis clinic, traveled to rural Tanzania with her mother to study the barriers to education for girls, and is an ambassador for three organizations that advocate for equine welfare. She plans to proceed to medical school after graduating and perhaps a school break for more show jumping. She even fixes her own computer when troubles arise because, as she confessed in an interview with HorseNetwork.com, her dad is "not all that great at it."

The Gates family is passing on more than wealth—they are passing on their *mission*. In a "This Morning" TV interview and a TED conference event discussion,[45] Bill and Melinda both affirm that their kids are completely on board with their parents' charitable commitments to fight poverty and improve health and education outcomes for children worldwide. The conversations reveal that it is this *mission*—not mere money—that Bill and Melinda see as the *primary* legacy they are passing down to their children—and inspiring other business leaders to share. The Gates have given away $18 billion through their foundation, according to CNBC,[46] and they've helped Buffet give away $46 billion. Now hundreds of CEOs and founders have now accepted Buffet and the Gates' challenge to take The Giving Pledge[47] to donate more than half of their assets to charity. While Bill Gates has become a more controversial figure in 2020, the principles here are sound: aim to convey your *mission* to your heirs, not simply *money*.

Carnegie's Gospel of Wealth

Long before Gates and Buffett, steel tycoon Andrew Carnegie gave away an estimated $350 million[48] during his lifetime for the public good. The equivalent of about $5 billion in today's dollars, his gifts funded education, scientific research, peaces causes, and the establishment of over 2500 local libraries.

"The man who dies rich, dies disgraced," wrote Carnegie in an essay titled "The Gospel of Wealth,"[49] expressing his conviction that the wealthy had an obligation to give back to society. But while Carnegie gave much to society, he gave precious little to his descendants. He left his wife (per one of the first prenuptial agreements ever written) and children only small trusts and modest properties. He did not even leave his family a stake in the company he helped build.

So what do Carnegie's descendents think about this? A 2014 Forbes article, "The Gilded Age Family That Gave It All Away,"[50] sheds some insight. Linda Thorell Hills, one of Andrew Carnegie's great granddaughters, said her family has "lived conservatively and privately," noting that it is easier to blend in since they descend from his daughter and don't carry the Carnegie last name. Still, she said they're emboldened by his legacy.

"Making one's own way in life is a healthy way to be," says Linda. "Our family has been very much raised with the philosophy that our own individual lives are what we make of them."

Being a Rockefeller

Families such as the Rockefellers have taken a different route than Buffett, Gates and Carnegie. The Rockefellers have passed down great financial wealth, teaching subsequent generations to steward it with great care and generosity. Writes Eileen Rockefeller, great-granddaughter of John D. Rockefeller in *Being a Rockefeller, Becoming Myself*:

> *"We are free to spend our money as we wish, but we have inherited the values passed down from my great-grandfather: to give no less than a third of our income away annually, and to give our time to causes such as social*

justice, the arts, and land conservation. We have promoted innovations in medicine, education, and science. Philanthropy is the glue that has bound us through seven generations."

Indeed, the Rockefeller Foundation, whose mission is "promoting the well-being of humanity throughout the world," is now in its 105th year. It funds many projects, including bringing clean water and energy to off-grid communities, and sustaining New York arts programs, such as The Broadway Dance Lab and a Creative Arts Center.

Why Inheritances Succeed—or Fail

In spite of different approaches of Peabody, Buffett, Gates, Carnegie and Rockefeller, there is a common thread among these families: *they never saw money as the only or even primary gift they were leaving their children.* They all invested in what was most important to them—including their heirs. They modeled the ability to live and work for something larger than dollars alone. They passed on values as well as resources. And they made sure that their children would have opportunities to succeed and make their own contributions—not enticements to become unproductive spenders.

In contrast to the famous families profiled above, history is also filled with stories of heirs of great wealth who have descended into ruin, unable to maintain or manage the money, much less their own lives. The unfortunate fate of the Woolworth fortune is one such story.

Barbara Hutton, an heiress to the Woolworth fortune, blew nearly a billion dollars (with no small help from her seven husbands and her addiction to drugs and alcohol). She showered gifts on friends and even strangers until she found herself selling personal items to make ends meet. She died at age 66 in a New York hotel that had become her home with only $3500 remaining of her fortune, according to InvestorPlace.com.[51]

Yet Hutton's spendthrift behavior wasn't merely a financial failure; it was a symptom of the family's failures. Her ambitious father was both a workaholic and a philanderer, and her mother died (suspected suicide) when Barbara was young. With no parents present in her life, Barbara was shuffled around between family members or cared for by a governess. Meanwhile, she was ridiculed and hated by the public even as a child, seen as a spoiled debutante. Failed by parents, guardians and role models, Hutton's life became a fruitless spending spree—a desperate attempt to buy lasting love, approval and comfort elsewhere.

The Secrets of Successful Wealth Transfers

No amount of money will ever be enough for a child without values and self-discipline. Money won't "fix" character flaws and it only feeds addictions. Money can't replace an absence of love, acceptance and caring. And if a receiver is unprepared, money that arrives in large, sudden or unrestricted amounts can sabotage independence and motivation—or lead to even worse outcomes.

Fortunately, most inheritances have happier endings! Prepared heirs do not use inheritances to make grand purchases, meet emotional needs or subsidize a lifestyle they cannot afford. They may use legacy gifts to invest in themselves, perhaps financing a business or an education—formal or otherwise—for themselves or their children. Properly-mentored heirs may use money to purchase investment real estate or fund a foundation. Or they may simply save the inheritance to be prepared for future emergencies and opportunities.

Families that pass wealth successfully give their children *opportunities to succeed*, not enticements to watch from the sidelines. They recognize that "too much of a good thing" might end up being a not-so-good thing. They model the ability to live and work for a purpose larger than dollars alone.

TED conference organizer Chris Anderson asked Bill Gates if he planned to make his children all billionaires, noting that he had plenty of money to do so, despite his vast contributions to the foundation.

"Nope," answered Gates. "They need to have a sense that their own work is meaningful and important."

The significance of that last statement is tremendous: *Bill Gates sees his children's potential too valuable an asset to spoil with a billion dollars.* THIS is the essence of the *Perpetual Wealth* philosophy. It is the opportunity to help the next generation succeed through the transference of knowledge, education, love, encouragement, and yes—financial resources. It's helping heirs succeed on their own terms—with an extra helping of support. Generational wealth is *not* eliminating the need or motivation for heirs to earn their own way in the world—no matter who your parents are.

There are many ways to help cultivate the proper mindset and readiness so that an inheritance lands on fertile soil. It starts by raising responsible children, nipping entitlement in the bud, and encouraging productivity. It continues with open communication about money, and teaching children how to participate in family finances and manage their own. (We've dedicated a later chapter—Chapter 13—to "Raising Financially Responsible Children.")

Finally, successful giving must be built on a foundation of long-term thinking. It is better to give an *orchard* than a *harvest*. Even a handful of seeds and loving instruction can make a profound impact for generations.

Leaving a legacy is one of the most loving things a parent, grandparent, aunt or uncle can do. Wise mentorship, unconditional love, and resources to invest in oneself and in assets—*not* unconditional, unlimited financial subsidies—allow heirs the best opportunity for a rich, successful life.

Should You Expect an Inheritance?

Regardless of your family's financial position, we believe it is wise not to *expect* an inheritance—rather, to be *prepared* for one. Even if you have been told you are receiving an inheritance, things can change.

Regardless of a parent's intention or promise, many would-be inheritances are gobbled up by unexpected medical expenses in a person's later years. A recent report from Fidelity estimates an average retired couple age 65 in 2018 may need approximately $280,000 saved (after tax) to cover health care expenses in retirement. According to a 2015 report from the Employee Benefits Research Institute, a 65-year-old couple should put aside $392,000 to have a 90% chance of covering their health care and possible long term care costs in retirement. We have seen people close to us with memory loss require much more than that for care expenses in just a few short years.

Then there are living expenses to consider... taxes to pay, and money to travel, enjoy hobbies and spoil grandchildren! And with more people living to and beyond 100... there is less to leave. We have also seen retirees lose sums of money through poor investments. Some who intend to leave an inheritance don't, or the amount may be far less than they anticipated.

You may have parents with a level of wealth or assets that virtually assures an inheritance. We would still advise you to keep expectations to a minimum. Even if your parents or grandparents have permanent life insurance, they could sell the policy for cash in their later years, annuitize it for income, or utilize an acceleration clause. (For instance, with a terminal illness or a long-term care rider, some or all of the final benefit could be "accelerated" and paid to the insured with an appropriate diagnosis. And that's a very good thing—even if it does disrupt an inheritance!)

Perhaps the *best* reason NOT to expect an inheritance is that it can lead to a false sense of security. If you believe you will inherit a million dollars—or ten million—it could reduce the pressure to save and invest as diligently as you might have otherwise. Instead, seek your own financial independence with no expectations of outside help. If you inherit money that you don't "need," you can supplement your investments, pass along the gift to another generation, or use the money to support the causes you care about. It's better to end up with an abundance of money than a shortage!

If you believe you may receive an inheritance, prepare yourself to manage it well and wisely. It can be quite personally devastating to receive a large financial gift only to fritter it away. I (Kate) have heard the concept, "You can only keep the amount of money you believe you could have earned yourself." I believe there is truth to that. Sudden wealth can bring up all kinds of emotions, including shame, even resentment—especially if money has been used as a tool for control.

If you are receiving an inheritance, we recommend an article we wrote: "Sudden Money: What to do with an Inheritance or Windfall."[52] That is a good place to start. Of course, you can also reach out to us at Partners4Prosperity.com/contact.[53] You might benefit from a complimentary consultation.

If you wish to *leave* a legacy, following the advice in this book is the best way to do it! There is a saying, "The best way to predict the future is to create it." We think the best way to predict a legacy of *Perpetual Wealth* is to *create* that legacy—with Family Financing!

THE BOTTOM LINE

The key to a successful inheritance is this: *founders must pass on a legacy of more than money.* When money is passed generationally devoid of mission, purpose, values and love—without the human, social, intellectual and spiritual capital that shaped the founders' legacy—it can lead to poor, even disastrous results.

However, when money is passed down with know-how, guidance, wisdom, purpose and values to well-nurtured recipients—heirs can become the best possible stewards of wealth. Rather than spending and disposing of capital, wise heirs use capital to invest in their future and the future of their family.

When it come to receiving an inheritance, don't count your chickens before they are hatched. Life is unpredictable and so are inheritances. No matter how wealthy your parents are or what their current will stipulates, you must be prepared to take 100% financial responsibility for yourself and your family. If you lack self-discipline with money, work to develop it. Focus on growing your own golden goose that can produce golden eggs for years—or generations—to come.

CHAPTER 9:
The Rockefellers' Secret Weapon

"Did you know that the Rockefellers began the concept of the family retreat?"

John peered over his Sunday paper, "You don't say? Well then, that will be one thing we have in common!"

Taking a sip of coffee, John continued, "You know, I was reading about how some families fly in coaches and advisors and financial psychologists... book a conference room in a nice destination hotel, have it catered, but wow, that adds up fast... if we drop $35k every summer on a fancy family retreat, well, we're going to drain the Family Fund!"

"Well, I know we don't have a Rockefeller budget, but I think you're going to be pleased... I checked out big homes and cabins the whole family can rent on AirBnB.com... We can rent this big house on a lake on the edge of Rocky Mountain National Park in Colorado. It has a big family room to meet in, and it sleeps 16—Paul and Phyllis could even join us, potentially—for less than $1500 for all 3 nights... taxes included!"

"Seriously!? You're a miracle worker," said John, taking Carol's offer to scroll through the pictures of the vacation home on her smart phone. "I like it... homey and comfortable with a dash of mountain rustic... works for me!"

Carol beamed, pleased with John's reaction.

"And I hear you... the idea was to have a Family Fund primarily for GROWING wealth—not SPENDING! But I like what Jerry Lee said about starting small. We've got tremendous resources right in our own family. Yes, we may decide to hire a professional to help at some point in time, but I have a feeling the Invincible Johnsons can pull this thing off with some brainstorming, white boards, delegation and teamwork."

"And Play-doh...didn't you tell me when all else failed with those middle schoolers, you'd get out the Play-Doh?"

"Already on the packing list!"

John smiled. They hadn't even proposed the retreat to the kids yet, but Carol was already planning the details as she scoped out locations and did what she referred to as her "family retreat feasibility study." Carol was one of those people who truly did think of everything. John liked to say to her, "What would I do without you?" To which Carol always replied, "Don't ever find out!"

They had agreed to pitch this first family retreat to the kids as a "reward" for getting the life insurance policies set. John and Carol hoped it went well enough that the family would wish to make it an annual event, but that—like many other things in this Family Financing project—would ideally be a family decision.

· · · · ·

Why Family Retreats?

While most families fragment and lose their wealth in two generations or less, the Rockefellers have thrived, not only financially, but in maintaining their family identity, culture and values. Their secret? Family retreats. John D. Rockefeller Jr. began the tradition of annual family retreats, and although the family is enormous now, the youngest being six generations removed from John Sr., the family still gathers together—now twice each year.

Eileen Rockefeller, the great-granddaughter of John D. Rockefeller Sr., discusses the retreats in her memoir, *Being a Rockefeller, Becoming Myself.* Eileen credits the family retreats as the force that perpetuates the family mission, values and identity. They provide a structured opportunity for the family to discuss family matters and maintain their bond among themselves and across generations. The retreats are also a time when members help each other, exchanging and sharing the intellectual capital of the family.

Even before the retreats, the Rockefeller family was passing financial education and discipline from generation to generation. Great-grandfather John D. Rockefeller Sr. starting keeping a ledger of his daily expenses when he was a young boy, working for pennies wherever he could, and marking every expenditure (including a 10% tithe to his church; he was Baptist).

As a parent, John Sr. taught his children the same habit of scrupulous ledger keeping. According to NewYorkSocialDiary.com, "They earned allowances and noted inflow and outflow line by line in their own ledgers. Luxuries were not in evidence. John D. Jr., the youngest of five and the only son, wore his sisters' remade hand-me-downs until he was eight."

When John D. Rockefeller Jr. became a father, he taught the third generation to be ledger keepers. This tradition was passed down to his son, and together he and his son taught the next generation a philosophy of philanthropy that continues to this day.

Eileen writes: "Though most of us in my extended family no longer keep ledgers, we still practice philanthropy and service, balancing questions of worth and relationship with opportunities and responsibilities. We are free to spend our money as we wish, but we have inherited the values passed down from my great-grandfather: to give *no less than a third* of our income away annually, and to *give our time to causes such as social justice, the arts, and land conservation.*"

Family Financial retreats have risen in popularity as more families cross the threshold into 7, 8, and 9-figure wealth with the realization that the younger generations often need a lot of training to become capable stewards. However, a family does not need to be uber-wealthy to benefit from such retreats. With only 37% of adults saying they talk openly with loved ones about money, a retreat can be the perfect way to tackle some important topics that too often get pushed to the back burner. Courtney Pullen, a counselor who has facilitated many family financial gatherings, says, "Most families live such harried lives that they don't take time to work on themselves *as a family*... The advantage of a retreat is that a family can step back—invest in themselves."

The most important reason to consider a Family Retreat (or a series of family dinners or meetings, for those who aren't quite ready to scale) is that being together is the best way to build bonds of trust and healthy communication. As we've seen, if the family doesn't last, the money won't either! So make sure you've got a structure to strengthen relationships and communication in your family.

And for families with a Family Fund, Family Office, Donor-Advised Fund or foundation, a Family Retreat is very helpful. It provides an opportunity for the Council or Board of Directors to meet, make decisions and go over finances. Which leads us to the OTHER secret weapon of the Rockefellers...

The Family Office

Rockefellers don't call up Morgan Stanley or Wells Fargo for investment advice or to open an account. They have their own dedicated team that handles their affairs—and their finances—for them. The trusted team dedicated to managing matters for a family is known as a "family office."

The Rockefeller family office was founded in 1882 and today reportedly manages tens of billions of dollars worth of assets for the Rockefellers and related entities. An unspecified number of other families (estimated in the thousands) now also have family offices. Many of these families have investments of $100 million or more, operating at average estimated cost of approximately 1% of assets annually.

There are two main types of family offices:

1. **The Single Family Office** (SFO) is a private company that manages investments and affairs for a single family. The SFO may be governed by a board of directors consisting of both family members and outsiders. In addition to handling investments and trusts, an SFO is likely to manage:

   - rental properties (or property management staff)
   - household staff
   - bookkeeping
   - accounting and payroll
   - travel arrangements
   - lifestyle services
   - legal advisors
   - family retreats
   - and philanthropic giving

   Typically family offices consist of a team, although occasionally they will begin with a single staff member or dedicated advisor.

2. **A Multi-Family Office** (MFO) manages the finances and sometimes other matters for multiple families. Multi-family offices are often simply an extension of traditional wealth management models, though they can take many forms.

While the purpose and principles of a Family Retreat are scalable to families with a wide range of net worth, family offices have a hefty price tag that make them too expensive or impractical to anyone not considered an "ultra high net worth" family. Typically the net worth of a family utilizing such services would be well into 8 figures—if not more.

Because of the expense of the family office environment and the fact that there are already many other books and resources on the topic, we are only skimming this topic here. While some reading this book may participate in a multi-family office, our focus is on strategies and practices that can be used or adapted by a wider range of investors, such as Family Financing and Family Retreats. However, if you are looking for a comprehensive management team such as a single or multi-family office, we are happy to recommend people we have worked closely with who provide such services. Just send us an email at hello@Partners4Prosperity.com[54] and we'll point you in the right direction.

Planning Your Family Retreat

First, define your goals of the Family Retreat so you can begin with the end in mind. You can definitely add whatever elements fit your family, but we recommend beginning with the following as a starting place:

- **Define and support the Family Mission and Values.** The family creates the Family Mission and Values, which in turn shape the family's culture and identity becomes part of the legacy that is passed down to future generations.
- **Deepen inter-family and inter-generational relationships.** A combination of guided questions, simple exercises and just being together can help extended family members get to know each other in new ways.
- **Support each family member in developing their unique ability.** To create a space where members share their wins and the challenges and can benefit from a "Family Mastermind" that supports their success.
- **To grow and develop the human capital of the family.** Retreats nurture the intellectual, emotional, social and spiritual capital of the family for the benefit of all. Elders have an opportunity to provide wisdom and guidance, while participants of all ages can try on leadership roles, develop presentation skills and exercise their self-expression.
- **Build bonds and make memories.** Family meetings are a place to share love and have fun! A balance of free time and coordinated activities (sports, recreational, educational, artistic or cultural activities) is ideal. "Open mic" talent shows that allow family

members to perform or tell stories work well in some families. And don't be afraid to try new things! A family retreat is a perfect opportunity to leave comfort zones behind.

- **Forward the financial work of the family.** A Family Fund has its own mission and purpose, which may be to:
  - Preserve wealth and keep it in the family by eliminating unnecessary transfers to the government, financial institutions, creditors, predators and unchecked spending.
  - Educate and mentor beneficiaries to grow, develop, preserve and pass on generational wealth.
  - Use the financial capital of the family to invest in individual or corporate goals and projects in alignment with the Family Mission.
  - Further the Family Mission in the world through gifts and philanthropy.

As you'll see with John and Carol's family, you can create your own curriculum. In our family retreats (Kim's), we typically bring in a resource from the outside, which could be a video (TED talks are great), a book such as Steven Covey's *The 8th Habit*, a profiling tool such as the Kolbe profile (Kolbe.com), etc. You can also bring in a counselor or coach trained to facilitate family retreats, or a speaker, advisor or estate planner. The benefit of outside resources is that it's not always easy to be "the expert" in your own family. Plus, there are simply so many great resources you can tap into!

A hint of what *not* to do: A Family Retreat or Family Meeting should *not* primarily consist of the Founders giving long speeches to the rest of the family. Family members tend to be "hearing impaired" when it comes to learning from elders or a spouse—even if they're right! However, with or without a speech, there are many practical ways Founders can help foster an environment for learning, belonging, and success. Dan Coyle's *The Culture Code* gives suggestions for doing this in groups and organizations that are relevant to the family. Practices that lead to a healthy group culture in which the members want to participate and contribute include:

- Be present and give people your full attention when you are communicating.
- Let people have a hand in making decisions or choosing how resources are used.
- Vulnerability is key to developing trust. Build the vulnerability habit by sharing weaknesses. Lead by example, showing that it's safe to tell the truth.
- If correction or constructive criticism is called for, aim for warm candor, not brutal honesty.
- Craft your purpose through frequently signaling your priorities and values. Share stories and goals, reiterate your top values.
- Ask questions. Communication scientist Robert Bales discovered that although questions comprise only 6 percent of verbal interactions, they create 60 percent of ensuing discussions.

We believe that annual retreats with additional (perhaps virtual) meetings between are the best structure to support the aims of Family Financing. It could be a three-day weekend, a couple of day retreats, or a longer vacation with a day or two dedicated to Family Meetings.

When necessary, meetings can happen online on Zoom. In spite of 2020 complications, there's a special dynamic that happens when the family can be together, so do make an effort to gather face-to-face when possible! However, online meetings can be a great way to fill in gaps between retreats, hold Council meetings with those in different locations, or allow a family member who is unable to travel to be "present" for portions of the retreat. If a retreat isn't workable, a series of dinners can also suffice, if everyone lives close enough. Of course, you can create whatever structure seems to works for you; just start somewhere and build from there.

As far as how to pull off a Family Retreat, logistically and financially, there are an unlimited range of options for a Family Retreat that fits YOUR family. You can go to a five-star resort with a private conference room, or you can take a camping trip and hold your meetings at an amphitheater in the woods or around a campfire.

You can "go Dutch," the Founders can pick up the tab, or you might consider picking up the accommodations and letting each family or adult plan and pay for their own travel. Just make sure it works for everyone, and don't be afraid to ask for financial participation from the adults, perhaps by taking responsibility for some of the meals.

The setting can be anything that will be conducive to family meetings. We suggest getting clear on your budget and proposing a few options, and let the family have input to help shape it from there. Unless necessary for budgeting reasons, it's preferable not to use your own home, even if it's large enough to manage the crew. A "neutral" location is best.

A good option is to make it a "destination" trip, perhaps vote on locations. (Hint: letting the kids have some influence on location can increase enthusiasm!) And if you travel to a "destination location" you can integrate a vacation into the trip. Before or after the family meetings, you can do whatever your family likes to do—hike, ski, watch movies, ride horses, enjoy art or sandy beaches. If your family is spread out across the country, maybe trade off locations so that not everyone has to travel each year. Or if there are family members who may have a difficult time travelling due to health or other reasons, consider gathering at a location near them.

As far as feeding the family, there are many options, and some might take planning. If you have the budget to have it catered or to use resort facilities (perhaps a banquet room at the hotel or restaurant near the resort), that makes it easy for the family to keep focused on the topics at hand. Or someone can purchase ready-made fresh items from a store or pick up take-out food. If you rent a facility with a large kitchen, planning and cooking your own meals can be part of the "together" time and much more budget-friendly. Just take care that everyone will be fully present during the Family Meeting time. Consider bringing along a "helper," a friend of the family to be in charge of shopping and cooking.

Oh—and don't be afraid to delegate! Like Family Financing, a Family Retreat should be something you do WITH your family, not TO them. The more input and participation, the better. Everyone should have a "job," even the kids. Your job is to instigate and guide the process and make sure it has the "structure" it needs to succeed. Involve others, use their gifts, and keep everyone focused on the main goals of your Family Retreat.

. . . . .

After a few more weeks, the policies were all set. A family meeting was called to share the details and celebrate this major step in the Family Financing project! Arrangements had been made for dinner at Carol and John's house, as they had the best living room for the family discussion. After they were updated on all the personal family and school news and the dinner plates were approaching empty, John said he had a special announcement.

"First of all, I want to thank all of your for working together on this goal to get every family member insured."

"Project 'No Johnson left behind' is complete!" interrupted Carol with delight, as a cheer went up.

"Now, I know applying for life insurance is not the most fun thing you've done this year—at least I hope not!—but it may be the most important. I owe a big thanks to my wife for helping to make it happen. I know I am sleeping better already just knowing that we have our 'ducks in a row.'"

A few "quacks" erupted from the grandsons.

"Thank-YOU," said Cyndi, addressing both of her parents. "I'm thrilled that our ducks are lined up, too, so to speak. It feels really good to have a structure for saving regularly. And I can't tell you how grateful Sam and I are to feel so supported. I know we've got big financial challenges ahead—there's college, then retirement—"

"And don't forget my Ferrari!" said Sheldon, which cracked everyone up.

John continued, addressing the grandsons specifically. "Now, you boys all know that your parents have just started life insurance policies on you, which might seem a little strange. The reason for doing this is that these policies are beginning a savings plan you will have for the rest of your lives.

"A lot of people try to play the 'get rich quick' game. When you see people buying lottery tickets in check-out lines, they are putting their hard-earned dollars on a one-in-a-million chance that they'll have the winning ticket. Of course,

the great majority of people don't win the lottery—they just lose their hard-earned money!

"The stock market has much better odds than lottery tickets, but it is still very risky. We didn't feel good about putting essential family money for college and other important things where it would be at risk."

Carol added, "Life insurance is the exact opposite of buying a lottery ticket, because these policies are guaranteed to grow and build wealth. Now it takes a lot longer than winning the lottery—but it's guaranteed. And it will help your parents—then you—become geniuses at saving!"

Carol could tell James liked the idea of being a genius.

"When people ask me what my favorite part of retirement is, that's easy," said John. "It's spending time with the people who are most important to me, the family sitting around this table. These family dinners have been fun as well as rewarding. But I think it's time we took things to the next level."

Everyone at the table looked at John with wide eyes, wondering what he meant.

"I know you have your family vacations planned this coming summer, but we also want to treat the family to a long weekend together—A Family Retreat! We'll take a day to do some work on the Family Financing project—but we'll also get out for some serious fun. Carol?"

Carol proceeded to give them some options, showing pictures on her tablet of the potential places they could stay and the main attractions nearby. Pretty quickly, it became clear that the rustic mountain lodge in Colorado, near a lake and beautiful hiking trails, was the winner! Soon the whole family was buzzing with excitement. Carol and John were pleased, and much gratitude was expressed.

The stage was set... the Johnson clan was going to Colorado!

$$\cdots\cdots$$

THE BOTTOM LINE

Pioneered and still embraced by the Rockefellers, Family Retreats are a highly recommended practice for any family who wants to create *Perpetual*

Wealth. Retreats help families communicate effectively, build trust and deepen bonds. They provide opportunities for education and mentorship and create a place for "family business" to be done together. (They can also be tax-deductible in many circumstances. Consult your tax specialist for guidelines.)

Families with more significant assets may wish to consider a Family Office of some kind—another structure utilized by the Rockefeller family. There are many ways to do this to "scale" appropriately.

Family Retreats can be scaled to virtually any budget, taste, location or circumstance. Virtual meetings and dinners can be good starting places. With multi-day events, families can hire facilitators or go the "Do-it-yourself" route. Best of all, retreats can be incredible fun, creating memories that will become part of the founders' legacy. A great way to get the kids on board is to include them in some of the decision-making, such as choosing a location.

CHAPTER 10:
The First Family Retreat

"And we're off!" exclaimed John, as he loaded the suitcases into the car, preparing for the drive to the airport.

Carol was still double checking her checklist to make sure they had not forgotten anything. They had each packed a small suitcase for clothes and personal items, and there was a larger suitcase with notebooks for each participant, art supplies, a "sticky note" flip chart, and yes... Play-doh. Satisfied that she couldn't be forgetting anything too crucial, she stepped into the waiting car and said, "Ready or not, Family Retreat, here we come!"

It had been seven months since their first family meeting dinner, and a three-day retreat was a big leap for the Johnsons. Although he didn't show it to Carol, John had his moments of apprehension. "A Family Retreat!? What have I gotten myself into... and can we pull this off!?" he had thought to himself more than once.

Carol seemed to know what he was thinking. "Five kids, four generations, three days, and one big idea," she said. They both understood these next three days would be important, even pivotal days in their family: the formal christening of the family legacy they would leave behind.

Five hours later, John and Carol pulled into the driveway with the big cabin in Colorado. On their way to the airport, they had picked up Ellie and her daughter, Tessa.

Ellie, who was in her early 30s, had been an honorary family member for the last few years, attending every Thanksgiving and Christmas celebration, and more than a few Sunday dinners. Formerly John and Carol's next-door neighbor, Carol had taken Ellie under her wing when her husband had been killed in an accident, leaving Ellie to raise their young daughter by herself.

Carol thought back to the conversation she had had with John a few months back...

"What about Ellie? I mean, I don't see her as a participating member in the Family Fund, but... in many ways, she IS part of our family."

"Hmm, you raise a good point... I know you've been trying to figure out how we're going to pull off feeding this brood while still focusing on the other things we have planned... Doesn't Ellie make a mean beef stew and apple pie?"

"Brilliant!" said Carol, dropping a kiss on John's check to let him know how much she appreciated his willingness to include Ellie. "Plus, we need a Family Retreat photographer! If Ellie's not already booked for a wedding or catering event, why don't we hire her for the weekend?"

"Well, we could use the support alright," said John. "And maybe the Family Fund could make a contribution towards Tessa's education."

It was a triple win. The Johnsons had a support person who could help with meals and other important details. Ellie got to spend time with her "adopted" family and even earn a little money for doing so. And as she learned more about what the Johnsons were doing with Family Financing, Ellie decided to use the money she was paid for being the Family Retreat assistant towards her own life insurance policy. Tessa had just turned six, and it would have plenty of time to grow. And now that her photography and catering business had taken off, Ellie could use the discipline of saving regularly. She knew it was time to leave behind the excuse of, "Single motherhood is hard," and start building towards her own prosperous legacy.

. . . . .

By 6 PM, the entire family was there, eagerly awaiting the stew, spinach salad and apple pie that filled the cabin with irresistible aromas. There was no agenda for this first night other than to be together and enjoy each other. Carol was pleased that the boys had left their gaming computers behind, and seemed to have fun playing Monopoly (brothers James and Jeffrey teamed up and won the day) and a particularly hilarious round of Pictionary with the rest of the family.

Saturday morning, John's mother, Phyllis, and brother, Paul, arrived. They had chosen Colorado for the retreat to make it easier for Paul and Phyllis to participate. In her 90s, Phyllis lived in assisted living and no longer travelled. However, John and Paul convinced her to "escape" for a day with the family.

After the breakfast dishes were put away, the work began. John and Carol's daughter, Cyndi, had planned the first exercise. A marriage and family counselor, Cyndi was adept at getting people to communicate.

"Everybody partner up with someone in the room who is not in your immediate family, and not in your generation," instructed Cyndi. "Pick an A and a B. Got it? Okay... B's go first!"

The pairs were given some simple questions to create a "vulnerability loop," which is a shared exchange of openness, a building block of trust. (The following questions are adapted from Dan Coyle's The Culture Code. They become more personal as they go, encouraging deeper sharing. They can also create a degree of awkwardness, which helps partners to see each other's vulnerability and create a trusting bond.)

Cyndi had Ellie use a timer to make sure both partners shared and they moved onto the next question in a timely manner.

"What was the best gift you ever received, and why did you appreciate it?"

"Where would you most like to travel—someplace you've never been—and who would you take?"

"If you could pick an expert, author or public figure to learn from, who would you choose and what would you learn?"

Now they switched partners for a new set of questions.

"If a crystal ball could tell you the truth about yourself, your life, the future or anything else, what would you want to know?"

"Is there something that you've dreamed of doing for a long time? Why haven't you done it?"

"What is the greatest accomplishment of your life so far?"

They gathered back in a circle, then Cyndi asked, *"What's one new or surprising thing you learned about your partner?"*

As observations were shared, Carol observed how this simple exercise had taken them into deep sharing, easily and effortlessly. The tone for the day had been set.

(Another technique that can be effective in creating personal reflection that leads to dialogue in a group: Ask participants questions, and have them write their answers in a journal. Next, have them share in pairs or a small group. Finally, ask for feedback in the larger group or circle for summaries or notable answers.)

Next, each family member was asked to share with the group about:

- their biggest "win" over the last year,
- the biggest challenge they encountered, and
- their biggest or most important goal for the coming year.

These questions had been sent out to the group a couple weeks in advance, so they had some time to consider it. John and Carol usually heard about the "wins," they hadn't heard about all of the big goals!

Cyndi's husband Sam planned to add a triathlon to his list of accomplishments. Sheldon, Cyndi and Sam's eldest son, would join his father training on weekends. Julie, the drama teacher at the high school, had been secretly working on a script for what she hoped would be her first produced play. James, following in his mother Julie's footsteps, set his sights on getting a role in the school musical. Meanwhile, Jeffrey—the "baby" of the cousins—lived for Little League games and was hoping to start pitching. Phyllis had taken up painting, and now that he was retired, Paul was preparing to hike a portion of the Appalachian Trail with an old buddy from his college days! Carol found herself tearing up, thinking, *"I never would've known half of these things if we had not set up this retreat and asked the questions!"*

Each family member had six minutes to share, and they were encouraged to leave at least a couple of minutes' time at the end for other family members to ask questions or suggest resources to help them move towards their dreams. It was similar to a Mastermind structure, and as the sharing and the suggestions got deeper, it became apparent that they could have allotted more time to this exercise.

John noticed a nice balance of wisdom and innovation in the questions and suggestions. More mature family members offered advice that came from years of wisdom experience. And when it came to technology, the younger members seemed to know at least one "app" that could solve virtually any problem! Soon the phrase "There's an app for that!" became the running joke of the morning.

The sharing of ideas continued through lunch, and into the afternoon of free time. Sam and Sheldon went trail running, while James and Jeffrey followed their Aunt Cyndi and Uncle Paul down the trail at more leisurely pace. John, Carol and Julie spent the afternoon visiting with John's mother, Phyllis, while Jackson relaxed on the porch with a book.

That evening, the family gathered around the table for "Thanksgiving in June." Ellie had roasted a turkey and served it with the family's favorite salads and trimmings. Meanwhile, Carol asked everyone to share Gratitudes that related to the family. As they went around the table, each family member could finish one or more of the following sentences, which had been posted so all could see:

- *"What I appreciate most about this family is..."*
- *"I was especially grateful for this family when..."*
- *"I'm thankful for this family retreat because..."*
- *"The family memory I treasure the most is..."*
- *"The person in this room I'm most grateful for right now is..."*

Julie took notes as people shared. She had volunteered to be the family "scribe" and thought the dinner conversation might give them a few helpful nuggets when it came time to writing the Family Mission statement.

By the time the pumpkin pie disappeared, everyone around the table was stuffed to the brim with good food and gratitude! Sam patted his tummy and declared, "This was SOOO delicious! Ellie, you're amazing! Remind me, somebody... why do we only celebrate Thanksgiving once a year?" Everyone nodded in agreement.

"More Thanksgivings!" declared James. "Can the Family Council pass a rule that we have to have Thanksgiving at least twice a year?"

"I'll see to it," said John.

After a time for coffee and clean up, tonight they would gather in the family room for the very first meeting of the new Family Council. The basics of how the Council would operate would be discussed as well as some family financial business.

All of the adults would attend the full meeting. The boys were invited to attend just the first 30 minutes when John and Carol planned to explain some basics of how they thought family governance might operate—at least until the Council had better ideas! Then they'd be free to go while additional business was discussed. (You'll learn more about governance and the Family Council in a future chapter.)

The next morning, after breakfast, it was time to continue with the business of brainstorming the Family Mission Statement. This work had already been started at the family dinner six weeks ago, and Julie refreshed everyone's memory and caught up Phyllis and Paul by reading some of the answers to the worksheets they had filled out.

Now it was time to brainstorm values together. They were asked to get in a group with those from their own generation. Armed with colored markers and enormous "sticky notes" that functioned as temporary white boards, each generation was asked to list both the values they saw represented in their family, and the important personal values that they would like to see integrated more intentionally into the family as a whole.

As each generation came back to the family room and presented their list of values, Carol made a new list with the words that popped up on multiple boards:

- Kindness
- Generosity
- Sustainability
- Encouragement

- *Gratitude*
- *Stewardship*
- *Resourcefulness*
- *Productivity*
- *Learning/growing/expanding.*

Guided by additional questions from Carol, a robust dialogue ensued about the meaning of family and the identity of their particular family—what was unique about it? What did it stand for?

There was one value that surfaced on everyone's boards, but in different words... "Can-do attitude." "Perseverance." "Grit." "Johnsons don't give up... Until we succeed!" Plus there were several references to a favorite family movie: The Invincibles.

Julie helped wordsmith the ideas and the words on the board into a more encap-sulated Family Mission Statement—a draft to be sure, but a starting place. She asked Carol to read it aloud:

We are the Invincible Johnsons!

We are unstoppable and we don't give up.

We believe in each other and help each other be our best.

We nurture each other's talents, strengths and super-powers!

We are strongest and most powerful when we work together.

We treat each other with love and kindness.

We invest in ourselves to expand our potential.

We help each other grow wealth for a prosperous future.

We give and act generously to make the world a better place!

Carol looked extremely pleased, while John declared, "Great job, everyone! Now THAT is a family I am proud to be a part of!"

They all gathered for lunch, after which a group headed to the lake to rent stand-up paddleboards and kayaks. A wonderful time was had by all, meanwhile,

Phyllis watched from shore using her watercolors to capture her impression of the beautiful day.

· · · · ·

Your Family Mission Statement

What exactly is a family mission statement, and why should you have one? Stephen Covey defines a family mission statement as "a combined, unified expression from all family members of what your family is all about—what it is you really want to do and be—and the principles you choose to govern your family life."

You might say that your family mission statement describes the IDENTITY of your family—your "family self-image." As an individual, your self-image is how you define yourself. In *Psycho-Cybernetics*, Dr. Maxwell Maltz states, "You will act like the sort of person you conceive yourself to be." What's important to you? What is possible for you?

Similarly, a family mission statement helps a family to define itself. What sort of family does yours conceive itself to be? What values does your family embrace? How do family members interact with each other and the world? What are your unifying goals? The answers to these questions can shape a family—especially when the mission statement is displayed, repeated and discussed frequently.

While you don't have to have a Family Mission Statement to participate in Family Financing, it can be very helpful to have a cohesive family identity that can be easily communicated. It can be a meaningful part of your family's legacy and a great way to nurture a desirable family culture. It can even act as a guiding light for Family Lending, Giving, and other decisions.

Guidelines for Crafting a Family Mission Statement:

Include the entire family (anyone old enough to understand the concept). You might not have luck with your two-year-old, but school-aged children should participate. You want everyone to have an investment in the mission statement.

Ask questions. This will get the conversation flowing. There is a helpful list of questions at TheArtofManliness.com[55] including the following:

- What is the purpose of our family?
- What kind of family do we want to be?
- What kind of home would you like to invite your friends to?
- What do we want to be remembered by?
- What kind of relationships do we want to have with one another?
- What are our responsibilities as family members?
- What families inspire us and why do we admire them?

Write things down. A white board, journal, or worksheets can come in handy. Older children can play "scribe" to compile ideas.

Identify your family's core values. You can start from scratch, or you can use worksheets that list values as a starting place, asking family members to circle values they identify with the family.

Brainstorm phrases or memes that your family identifies with. These could be quotes, books, movies, poems or speeches, or they can be original.

Decide on 6-12 "big ideas" that can be encapsulated in a phrase or sentence. You can vote on ideas to narrow them down or select the ones that resonate best.

Write the mission statement. Whether you have a designated "word-smith" or do it collaboratively, you'll want to arrive at a definitive written statement. However, there is no rush and it doesn't have to be "done" in one sitting.

Hang it where family members will see it regularly. Print it, post it, perhaps even have a graphic artist (or artistically inclined family member) create a visually pleasing, "suitable for framing," version.

Use it! Look for opportunities and teachable moments to refer to your family mission statement often. Grandparents might even consider offering small gifts (perhaps a $5 bill or a silver dollar) to grandchildren who memorize it!

Expect the mission statement to evolve. Even when it feels "complete," as your family grows, it is worth revisiting as new generations rise through the ranks.

Examples of Family Mission Statements

A family mission statement can be long or short, eloquent or simple. Below are three diverse examples.

From *The 7 Habits of Highly Effective Families:*

> **Our Family Mission Statement:**
>
> Our family mission is to:
>
> Value honesty with ourselves and others.
>
> Create an environment where each of us can find support and encouragement in achieving our life's goals. Respect and accept each person's unique personality and talents.
>
> Promote a loving, kind, and happy atmosphere.
>
> Support family endeavors that better society.
>
> Maintain patience through understanding.
>
> Always resolve conflicts with each other rather than harboring anger.
>
> Promote the realization of life's treasures.

> **Bruce Feiler's family mission statement, drafted with input from his five-year-old:**
>
> May our first word be adventure and our last word be love.
> We live lives of passion.
> We dream undreamable dreams.
> We are travelers not tourists.
> We help others to fly.
> We love to learn.
> We don't like dilemmas, we like solutions.
> We push through. We believe!
> We know it's okay to make mistakes.

We bring people together.

We are joy, rapture, yay!

(Bruce Feiler, author of The Secrets of Happy Families)

And this example from home-school-coach.com[56] is quite beautiful:

[Last name]'s Family Mission Statement

We are compassionate and kind.

We are committed to family.

We will be caring in our relationships with our family and friends. We want to be role models and guides for our children.

We will encourage creative expression in each other.

We will lovingly support each other as we strive to reach our individual potentials.

We will grow old and wise together.

Our home will be filled with love and laughter.

Our sanctuary will inspire and renew us, enabling us to contribute our best to the world.

Our home will be a haven for our family and friends to gather and share life's ups and downs.

Our home will be a nurturing place for children and animals.

Our home will be a safe and comfortable place for self-expression.

We enjoy helping others in our daily lives.

We strive to work with passion and discipline.

We want to bring the love and positive energy from our relationship into our careers and the world around us.

We will live our lives in a manner that is free from harm to other living beings.

Kim's most recent Family Mission Statement:

Our home is the center though not the circumference of our love for each other. We strive to make it a "house of both," where choices don't end with either/or. We thrive by living in a complaint free world where our principles reign. We give first. And we choose our words wisely.

Family Mission Statement Resources:

Some further resources to explore to help you craft your family mission statement include:

7 Habits of Highly Effective Families[57] by Stephen R. Covey

The Secrets of Happy Families[58] by Bruce Feiler

What Would the Rockefellers Do?[59] by our friends Garrett Gunderson and Michael Isom

The Art of Manliness blog post: "Creating a Positive Family Culture: How and Why to Create a Family Mission Statement."[60]

. . . . .

Tonight was the last formal piece of the Family Retreat, although Cyndi and Julie's families were both going on a trail ride tomorrow. "Long-term wealth" had been named as the theme of this retreat. Wanting to involve everyone, each family member had been asked to bring a 5-10 minute talk or presentation on that theme. Carol had chosen the theme because she knew that the family had to start thinking long-term about money or any inheritances wouldn't last long!

The boys had looked less than thrilled when their assignments were given. Carol worried if she was expecting too much from the younger family members, although they had participated well so far. But what did fifth, sixth, and seventh graders know about long-term wealth!? They were all about to find out.

"I'll kick this thing off," said John. "After all, I got you all into this!"

"Aside from my dear mother Phyllis—and I'm so happy you could join us," John said, nodding at his mother, "I'm the oldest person in the room."

"And with the exception of my mother, nobody here knew me during 'the difficult years,'" John said. "And by the way, my parents lived through The Depression and they had their own 'difficult years.'

"So you see us now, doing well, taking vacations, having a little extra money to help with tuition, put on a family retreat, even plan a legacy. But it wasn't always this way—not by a long shot.

"I've done a few things right—I've saved money, nearly every month since I began working at the age of 17, bagging groceries at the store down the street. I scrapped and saved and put myself through college while working nearly full time. I worked two jobs for seven years, which meant I only had a day off every other Sunday. For six years.

"I bought my first house, then, fortunately," and now he smiled at Carol, "this amazing woman came along, and I started to realize that a little work-life balance might be in order. I cut back my second job to two days per week, and I took every Sunday off," he laughed.

Carol nodded, recalling her husband's sometimes taxing work ethic.

"Then some beautiful little girls came along, and I quit the second job to spend more time with them and be more helpful around the house.

"So I didn't inherit family wealth… But I did inherit the values of honesty, hard work and a belief in myself. And if these values were all that I could pass on now to each of you, I'd consider us to be a very rich family."

"Along the way, I've made some poor decisions as well as good ones," John continued. "I spent too many hours at work; I missed too many piano recitals. And sometimes, I did dumb things with money. Let's just say that when the dot com bubble popped, so did my investments. If it wasn't for the money I've been saving and our whole life policies, I'm not sure we could have put you girls through college."

"The rental houses helped us get back on track, and so did the promotion to branch manager, but in my experience, success isn't a straight line. It's a series of decisions, and you've got to make more good choices than bad choices.

"As far as my missteps, this retreat is part of some changes I'm making. Sometimes, I was better at making money for my family than I was at being there for my family, especially for my favorite three girls. Sometimes, I blew it, and my daughters let me know when I did. Fortunately, you haven't kicked me out of the family yet, and in the years I have left—and I hope that there are a lot of them—my commitment is to be there for each of you and if I can, to help you make more good choices than bad ones.

"Secondly, I used to feel that the burden for the family finances was on my shoulders. And while I've been the primary breadwinner, I can tell you, no one is more capable with numbers or money management than Carol. As I have relinquished control and we have transitioned into a true partnership, we have made better decisions together. We've protected more of our wealth from risk. Without Carol, there might not be a Family Financing project.

"Thanks Mom!" said Julie, while Carol nodded in acknowledgement. "And you, too, Dad."

"And now, I realize it's time to relinquish control again. Carol and I plan on being around for a long time to come. But it's high time that we start thinking about how our money—what Carol and I have saved—can serve the larger family and become 'our' asset—a Family Fund that can support us all."

"Finally, I haven't always been very good at talking about financial things with the rest of you. It's 'taboo' to talk about it. But you know what? If we want the family—and whatever wealth we may have—to last, we've got to break that pattern. This weekend, it feels like we already have, and I'm grateful to each of you for being here for what I hope will be the first of many Family Retreats!"

As applause broke out, John settled into a comfortable chair, relieved he could now relax and eager to hear what the rest of the family would present.

"That's a hard act to follow, but I'll go next," volunteered Jackson. The accountant in the family, Jackson owned a small tax preparation and accounting office. "In the 15 years I've been in the business, I've made some observations about those who build wealth, and those who don't," he began. "Everyone thinks they just need to make more money... A higher income can indeed be helpful, but I have observed that long-term wealth is all about how much you keep!"

Jackson went on to describe how those who lived in the biggest homes and pulled up to his office in the fanciest cars wearing the nicest clothes were rarely 'rich' at all. Though they looked like they had plenty of money by the way they spent it, these were usually the people who struggled with debt and rarely accumulated much on their balance sheet. They were often doctors, lawyers and salesman with healthy six-figure incomes. They just didn't keep any of the money they made.

Then Jackson described his wealthiest clients. Business owners, farmers, a school teacher couple who fixed up and bought a new rental house every summer... they were the long term thinkers. Some of them earned large incomes, some of them very modest incomes. But they all paid attention to their balance sheets! They used what they had to build long-term assets. They reduced their taxes and they saved for both emergencies and opportunities. Oh—and they almost never bought new cars!

"Do you know what my wealthiest client drives?" asked Jackson.

"A Ferrari?" asked Sheldon.

"An old Ford pick-up truck!" answered Jackson with a smile, almost anticipating the response. "He could purchase two Ferraris with cash tomorrow... but you see, he'd rather have the cash!"

Sheldon looked a tad disappointed. Maybe he would have to settle for a used Jaguar.

Julie went next, sharing research and ideas on how to raise money-savvy kids. "I'm warning you kids... This is the type of thing us adults sometimes talk about behind your back! But I thought, what better opportunity than a Family Wealth Retreat to start discussing this as a family?"

James, Julie's son and budding thespian, was the first of the grandsons to volunteer. James shared how famous people have LOST their fortunes! He told the cautionary tales of Warren Sapp, an NFL player who went bankrupt only five years after retiring from his $82 million career; Willie Nelson, who ended up owing the IRS $30k in back taxes; and Barbara Hutton Woolworth, the heiress who spent a fortune worth hundreds of millions in today's dollars, reportedly passing with only $3,500 left to her name.

"If you're taking notes," said John, "remember, this is what NOT to do!"

"Besides," added Carol, "if you spend like those people, YOUR inheritance will only last three or four days!"

Cameron, Sheldon's younger brother, stepped up next. He had gotten curious about life insurance after he knew his parents had taken out policies on him and his brother. His Prezi slideshow was well-researched and explained the history of life insurance. "At first," said Cameron, "life insurance didn't make sense to me. But it does now… It's all about people pooling their resources to share risk. And I learned that Mutual Life Insurance Companies are owned by policyholders, not shareholders, and have traditionally been used to save money."

"Yup," affirmed Carol, who was pleased. "It fixed the roof of our first house, put your mother through college, and provided the down payment for one of the rental homes."

John noted that the other cousins were paying close attention, as he realized that none of the adults had thought to explain life insurance to the kids in a way that they could understand.

Cyndi played a video from Shawn Achor, a positive psychologist who had studied the relationship between happiness and success. She even brought laminated reminder cards that outlined the five daily practices Achor recommended for a happy brain and a prosperous life:

- *Write three things you're grateful for every day.*
- *Spend a couple additional minutes writing about a positive experience that happened in the last 24 hours.*
- *Meditate daily.*
- *Exercise daily.*
- *Every day, thank or compliment somebody who has made a difference for you.*

Sam, who was a physical therapist, a basketball coach and a marathon runner, gave an inspiring speech about the relationship between health and wealth. He shared research about how poor health was literally bankrupting many retired people as they watched a lifetime of savings devoured by medical bills, while others were competing in marathons, dance competitions, or hiking the

Appalachian Trial—like his uncle would be doing soon! Sam was adamant— "It's largely up to you if you want to be healthy or not in your old age. We have way more control than we think."

At the close of his presentation, Sam shared, "I know that I've got a lot of work to do to get my own family in shape financially. And I also know I have tremendous knowledge about what makes and keeps people healthy. And I just want to say to all of you—I'm here for you as your personal family health coach! Part of our long-term thinking about growing and keeping wealth in the family has to involve each of us staying fit and healthy for as long as possible."

It was becoming obvious that each member of the family had something of tremendous value to contribute to the discussion on long-term wealth. Sam's eldest, Sheldon, was up next.

"Why are the Swiss a wealthy society?" began Sheldon. It wasn't a question anyone else in the family had ever contemplated, and Carol couldn't wait to see where her eldest grandson was going with this presentation. Showing slides from various countries around the world, Sheldon went on to explain a theory that people who lived in harsh weather have been forced to develop long-term thinking and problem-solving. In places such as Switzerland, where the winters were brutally cold and farmlands were covered with feet of snow, if you did not learn to conserve and save resources through the winter, you did not survive until spring! In contrast, other societies did not have the need to save and store because they could grow or hunt food year-round. And none of those cultures became as prosperous as the Swiss.

"Wow," said Jackson, visibly impressed. "That makes sense! Nature forced the Swiss into long-term thinking, planning and saving."

Carol shared about the importance of a Growth Mindset, a concept developed by Carol Dweck, who had made significant contributions to the field of education.

"There's an important correlation with wealth," observed Carol. "If you THINK you're 'not good with money' or 'no good at math,' you're going to sabotage your ability to get better. But when you have the mindset that you can learn and get better at something, it turns out, you're right about that, too! So when you find managing money or learning about investments frustrating, just keep

a Growth Mindset about it. It will get easier if you do. I can tell you, I'm 70 and STILL learning about so many things!"

Now it was Jeffrey's's turn. Only 8, Carol had worried that perhaps it wasn't fair to ask him to make a presentation on long-term wealth! But she was about to be surprised...

Jeffrey used six-year-old Tessa to help him. Tessa distributed marshmallows to each family member, with explicit instructions... "Don't eat the marshmallow!"

Jeffrey had Googled to find out what determined if a child would become successful, and he ran across what is sometimes called The Great Marshmallow Experiment. Conducted by a Stanford researcher, the study tested to see if children could resist eating a marshmallow for 15 minutes, holding out instead for the promise of a second marshmallow. In follow up studies, it was determined that the kids who held out for the second marshmallow went on to have better SAT scores and more successful lives than the children who had gobbled down their only marshmallow. The ability to delay gratification for longer-term goals was a key to success.

"I'll bet the Swiss are good at saving marshmallows," said Sheldon.

"Yes they are! That's why there are marshmallows in the Swiss Miss Hot Chocolate!" added Cyndi, as laughter broke out.

Everyone had gone now except Phyllis. John wasn't sure if his mom had prepared anything, or if a 90-something woman should be held accountable for "homework." Yet Phyllis motioned for John to help her up and escort her to the front of the room. She then passed around a photo of a quilt. It was a beautiful quilt, stitched together from floral fabrics of blues, greens, rose and white. Phyllis had made it nearly three decades earlier, and it was still the focal piece of her bedroom.

"This quilt represents for me the most precious thing I have: Family," began Phyllis. "We all bring different colors—different gifts—to the whole. We each are beautiful alone, but together we are spectacular! And when we come together, we provide warmth and shelter. We are stronger and better together. Without any of you, our Family Quilt would not be complete."

You could hear a pin drop, and Carol noted that some eyes around the room were filling with tears as the Kleenex box was passed.

"Thank-you so much for including me, for travelling so far to make it easier for me to come. I'm thrilled that my sons have been so successful, and I commend John and Carol for taking such leadership in creating this retreat and their generational wealth project. It's a gift that should never, ever be taken for granted.

"You are each precious and I hope you know that there is nothing more valuable than each other. You are my greatest treasures. You are the true wealth of the Family. Use your resources wisely and you will thrive long after I am gone. Look after each other. Take care of one another. Don't bicker about silly things that won't matter in the long haul. And don't forget to save all you can, because you've got to plan on living to at least 100! I didn't think I'd live as long as I have, but I'm glad I get to watch this beautiful family grow. Thank you, sincerely, and I can't wait to see you all next year!"

John gave his mother the longest hug he thought he had ever given her. And when he turned around, there was a line of grandchildren and great grandchildren waiting to get in on hugging Phyllis.

"Let me sit down, for heaven's sake!" the matriarch said, as Ellie announced to everyone, "S'Mores by the campfire in five minutes! And you can EAT the marshmallows now!"

Carol knew she'd have plenty to put in her gratitude journal tonight: the First Annual Family Retreat was a resounding success! She squeezed John's hand and he held her tight.

"Thank you, Sweetheart," he spoke softly in her ear. "There is no way I could have pulled this off without you... and I'm so glad we did!"

. . . . .

THE BOTTOM LINE

Family Retreats are a fun and rewarding way to build bonds and reinforce family values. Creating a Family Mission Statement together is an impactful activity that helps forge a family identity. Family gatherings and retreats are worthwhile, meaningful events that can lay the groundwork for successful Family Financing traditions.

How you define your "family" is up to you. When you can include extended family members (even if you are not "banking" with them) it can be a gift. Look for ways to involve each family member in age-appropriate ways that works for them.

Put some thought and structure into your retreat so that you fulfill the goals you have for it. Perhaps you wish for family members who live far away to be able to bond with each other. Maybe you want to nurture leadership or public speaking skills. You might have a key topic, theme, or piece of business you wish to cover. And remember: questions can be more valuable than answers. Leave room for all to participate. Have fun... and most of all, love and enjoy each other!

CHAPTER 11:
The Beauty of Borrowing

John and Carol settled down to breakfast, enjoying a "John's special" Saturday brunch of a smoked salmon, cream cheese, green onion omelet with blueberry muffins from their favorite bakery on the side.

"You know," he mused as he buttered the blueberry muffin, "when I started in banking decades ago at that little local bank, I envisioned us a bit like Jimmy Stewart's fictional Savings and Loan in It's a Wonderful Life. *We often had the power to make our own decisions, sometimes even based on our relationship with that person. I used my gut, and things usually worked out."*

"I remember," Carol reflected. "You felt really good when you could really help someone, as long as they paid back the loan, of course!"

"Well, times have changed. As the years have progressed and as I moved to the larger bank, we became forced to automatically turn down all loans that didn't fit the bank's lending 'formula.' A person could even have good credit, a great business idea, or a genuine emergency—it didn't matter. If the borrower or the purpose for the money didn't fit the rules in any way, we'd have to say no. I can't tell you how many times things crossed my desk that I wished I could have done something about."

"And? Are you thinking about our own Family Financing project?"

"You got me!" John replied with a twinkle in his eye.

"You know, the pay isn't nearly as good as your last banking job," Carol added with a wink.

"It's definitely a volunteer position. Heck—I pay to do it! However, there may be some pretty good benefits—for the whole family."

Carol smiled and nodded affirmatively.

"I think of all the good that it could do to give the kids and grandkids access to capital," continued John. "Maybe it can help the girls get the grandsons through school, or start building some additional assets, like rental homes of their own."

"And it's not just the money," added Carol, "it's the financial education as well. I'll bet we can use Family Lending to teach about evaluating opportunities, and the process of applying for financing, borrowing and paying things back. And we can help steer them right if they get off course.

"Now that we've got the Family Financing project launched… it's time to think about rules and guidelines!" said John. "Obviously, it's going to take time for the brand new policies to build up any meaningful cash to borrow. But we have quite a bit in our older policies. It's not too soon to start thinking about how we want Family Lending to work."

· · · · ·

Lending vs. Giving Money to Children

What is freely given is often undervalued. What is *earned* is appreciated and treasured. We observe these truths in business, in life, and in family finances.

If you give your children all the money they want, it will never be enough. Show them how to care for and manage money, and they will not waste yours—or theirs. Lump sum inheritances given without accountability are a recipe for disaster. During your lifetime, lending can be an effective way to teach children to use money wisely.

In chapter five, we described how the Vanderbilt family spent the largest fortune that had ever been seen in the United States in just a few generations. We contrasted that to how the Rothschild family has continued to grow their fortunes over *many* generations.

The big difference between the Vanderbilts and the Rothschilds was that Cornelius Vanderbilt's heirs treated the family fortune like a personal bank to be spent at will, while the Rothschild sons used money productively. Rather than draining the family's wealth, they multiplied it by building more banks. The Rothschilds have persisted as a family of wealth because they have used money to make money... *for hundreds of years.*

Think of a traditional bank, such as your local neighborhood bank. The son or daughter of the bank manager can't just walk into the bank and "demand" money to purchase a new car or take a Hawaiian vacation. If they want money, they will have to earn it, make it or borrow it—perhaps through a loan, mortgage or credit card—like anyone else! Even Warren Buffet gave this advice to his daughter when she asked for $41k to renovate her kitchen: "Go to the bank and do it like everyone else."

Now, it probably doesn't hurt to be Warren Buffet's daughter—or a bank manager's son. But responsible parents don't hand out blank checks. They teach their children how to manage money. And an essential part of effective money management is the ability to borrow money strategically and pay it back honestly.

There is a huge benefit to the parents/grandparents as well. By lending rather than giving money, they can keep *control* of assets they might possibly need in the future—while still helping family. This is a huge win-win, since the future is unpredictable. You can never know with any certainty what expenses may arise or what sort of care or help you might require in the future.

By using policy *loans* rather than withdrawals, there is also more cash value left in the policy—which means a larger policy! When money is *withdrawn* from a whole life policy, it reduces the size of the policy and the size of the future death benefit. But when money is *borrowed against* a whole life policy (and repaid), the policy keeps growing. That not only leaves more for heirs, it leaves more money in the policy for potential living benefits. If you have a terminal or chronic illness rider and/or a long-term care benefits rider on your policy, you'll keep growing those benefits.

Why borrow against a life insurance policy?

So you want to borrow money—or perhaps lend money to invest in the success of your family. Why use life insurance? Why not use your bank or credit union? Why not use a credit card, a line of credit, or other financing? Here are 10 reasons we believe life insurance is one of the best ways to borrow:

1. **Life Insurance loans put you in control—not the bank!**

    Who determines if you can obtain a credit card, bank or mortgage loan? The lender, of course! There is a saying, "A bank is a business that lends money to people who do not need it," and there is truth to that! Lending institutions will not only require a certain credit score, proof of income, and possibly other qualifying factors, they can even determine if you are borrowing money for an acceptable purpose.

    Unsecured loans (aside from education loans) are quite difficult to obtain approval for. And even then, the bank decides what constitutes acceptable "collateral." For example, if you want to borrow money to purchase a brand new car, that is fairly easy to do, often at a competitive rate. But what if your teenage grandson wants to buy an old VW bug to restore? The new car will only depreciate, while you can put sweat equity into a vintage bus and resell it for a profit. Unfortunately, no bank is going to lend on an old car—especially to a teenager!

    Education loans may be readily available to some, but what if your granddaughter has a brilliant business idea and the talent and drive to make it happen? Or your grandson is well-suited for a non-traditional apprenticeship? Perhaps someone in the family already has a business that could be improved with the right coaching and mentorship. Kim has been a part of Strategic Coach for many years, both as an Associate Coach and a participant. Tuition plus travel may add up to five figures a year. The returns can be exponential, yet if someone wants to *finance* this smart business investment, they'd likely have to use an unsecured credit card with high interest.

With life insurance policies, *you* control the lending. A policy owner can request a loan and have money in their hands in about a week. No muss, no fuss. (Of course, you may have a family approval process—that's a different matter we'll discuss a bit later.)

2.   No qualification required.

Only the most qualified need apply for a bank loan. You'll need a good credit score, a positive lending history, proof of income, and often, proof of assets. If you are a business owner, qualifying for a loan or mortgage can be brutal, as you'll have to prove YEARS of profitability. And if you are young and don't yet have credit established... good luck!

You might think, "Of course I don't have to qualify, it's 'my' money," but that's not exactly true. A policy owner borrows *against* the policy, not *from* the policy. When you take a policy loan, you borrow from the insurance company (it's their money, not yours) using your policy's cash value as collateral. The quality of the collateral makes it easy to borrow against your policy—generally up to 90 or 95 percent of cash value.

This is significant because—even if you have significant assets—many assets are difficult to borrow against! Have home equity? Great! You'll need to qualify for a HELOC (home equity line of credit) or second mortgage. If you have a sudden interruption or decrease in income (a common reason you might want to tap your equity), you will likely be turned down. Already have a HELOC? If the real estate market has a downturn, your limit could be reduced or the line of credit could be halted altogether.

Other assets such as gold, collectibles, and mutual funds can be extremely problematic to borrow against. (Read more in "The Leverage Test: Borrowing Against Assets."[61])

Even with an excellent credit score and borrowing history, if you lack collateral and/or have a temporary interruption in income, it can be difficult to qualify for financing.

3.   Borrow for any reason.

You can use a policy loan for an emergency, investment, business purpose, wedding and honeymoon, or *anything* else. We've known of people who have borrowed against their policies to:

- Launch or expand a business.
- Renovate a kitchen or remodel a home.
- Fund a down payment on a rental property.
- Invest in bridge loans or other income investments.
- Pay for education, coaching or mentorship.
- Purchase an asset at a significant "discount" to resell later.
- Fund a honeymoon or once-in-a-lifetime trip—including a trip to space!
- Take time off from work during the illness or death of a loved one.
- Buy a vehicle or other asset during a period of unemployment.

There are *no limits* on what you can use the money for. Now, that doesn't mean you don't want *guidelines* on what types of loans the family will—and won't—fund. You do! Since borrowing against a life insurance policy provides you much greater flexibility than leveraging other popular assets, you can develop your own criteria for a worthy loan.

With many assets, such decisions are made *for* you. If you wish to take an IRA withdrawal without paying taxes and penalty (if you are under 59-1/2) your situation will have to fit strict criteria. For instance, you can withdraw up to $10,000 if you are a first-time homebuyer. If unemployed, you can use IRA withdrawals to pay health insurance premiums. Most other reasons are a no-go.

Likewise, the rules about borrowing from or withdrawing from a 401(k) tax-and-penalty-free are quite restrictive. Some plans don't allow loans at all. Many allow them only to pay for education expenses, prevent an eviction, pay for un-reimbursed medical expenses, or buy a first-time residence.

Additionally, there's a BIG catch to borrowing from your 401(k): you'll have to repay the loan with *after-tax dollars!* If you are in a 24% tax bracket, for example, you'll have to pay back $1,000 of pre-tax dollars with about $1300 of after-tax dollars. *Ouch!*

4. Privacy: it's nobody else's business!

When you obtain a mortgage, a car loan or other bank loan, use store credit or use a credit card, the debt is reported to the credit bureau. Anyone who runs your credit or views your credit report will see the amount of the debt, your payment amount, and any late payments made in the last seven years. (Bankruptcies report for ten years.)

Debt and credit usage reported to the credit bureau can determine whether or not you qualify for other credit. For instance: car loans and credit card debt affect the size of mortgage you can qualify for, because those debts count towards your allowable "debt ratio." The credit card debt may only be short term, yet it could still prevent you from making an offer on your dream home! Even *unused* available credit can affect whether or not you can qualify for new credit, such as a credit card with a "0 interest for 12 months" feature.

As a policy owner, loans between your life insurance company and you are *private*. They are not reported to the credit bureaus. Since policy loans are not taxable, they are also not reported to the IRS. The amount of cash value you can borrow against, the amount actually borrowed, and the payments you make are nobody's business but yours!

5. Competitive rates.

It is common for unsecured debt interest rates to be in the "high teens" or well into the 20-percent rates, even 30 percent for people with fair-to-poor credit. Debt at such high rates can be very expensive—and difficult to repay! High-interest debt is a trap that costs many people peace of mind as well as wasted dollars.

In contrast, life insurance loan interest rates tend to range between 5 and 8%, although they can be lower or higher. The exact rate is determined by policy.

Most companies offer either *fixed rate* OR an *adjustable rate* policy loans. If you already have a whole life policy, your policy determines which you have. Currently, *fixed rate* policy loans are about 6 to 8 percent at the present time, depending on the company and when policy was originated. *Adjustable rates* may be a little lower than fixed rates at the moment, but of course they are subject to change. Similar to many adjustable rate mortgages, a policy loan interest rate is typically declared annually or bi-annually based on a pre-determined index and margin.

Sometimes you can get an even BETTER rate by using your cash value as collateral at a bank for even better rates. We wrote about this in "Collateral Assignment: Banking on Your Life Insurance Policy."[62]

Partners4prosperity.com//collateral

6. **Flexibility of repayment.**

With most types of loans, the repayment schedule is pre-determined and often monthly. If you do an IRA rollover, the money must be paid back (or rather, put into a new IRA) within 60 days!

With whole life policy loans, *you* decide the repayment schedule. You can pay back the loan on any schedule you like, and you can even change it if necessary. Some options:

- Interest-only payments (until you have funds to repay principal).
- Principal plus interest. If the policy loan is taking the place of a higher interest "loan" such as credit card debt or equipment lease, we suggest you pay back your policy loan with the same (or even higher) payments.
- Monthly income from investments. If you use your policy to purchase a rental property or other income-producing asset, you

can use monthly cash flow to repay the loan. In time, you'll repay the loan and still have the asset!

- Lump sum payments. This can work well for investors who use their policies to fund real estate rehabs or other investment projects that produce a lump sum profit when a project is complete.

7. Life insurance can make your investments better!

Those who say "the returns of whole life are lousy" don't understand how to use whole life. And there are two things the critics often miss.

First, cash value is NOT an *investment* strategy; it is a *savings* vehicle. And when compared long-term with other *savings* strategies—savings accounts, bank CDs and money market accounts, etc.—life insurance tends to earn far more—often several times more! (While savings accounts are paying one to two percent, internal rates of return for whole life policies are currently around 4 percent—*net*—tax-deferred or even tax-free.)

Second, you can generate impressive profits by leveraging your cash value to pursue opportunities, make investments, and expand assets. That's where the real gains are.

Many businesses have been started or assisted with money from whole life insurance, including Disneyland, J.C. Penney's, Foster Farms, and Pampered Chef. (Learn more in "The Surprising Business Financing Secret of Top Entrepreneurs."[63])

Cash value life insurance is also very powerful when paired with real estate investing. There is a case study my husband, Todd Langford, shares that shows how using a policy loan can make a good real estate deal even better! By using the leverage of a mortgage plus a policy loan, you can actually increase your rate of return. You can read it here: "How do I tell if my real estate deal is a good one?"[64] or watch a presentation on the Truth Concepts YouTube channel.[65] (It's titled, "Truth Concepts: Real Estate—7 of 8.")

8.   **Lending is a learning opportunity.**

Through loans, the Family Financing model can offer valuable financial skills such as:

- Getting comfortable with talking about money.
- Learning to apply for and obtain loans.
- Writing a business plan or doing investment analysis (when applicable).
- Understanding the value and reasons for lending guidelines established by the Family Council.
- Having the experience of paying off loans successfully.

The goal isn't to shield family members from ever using commercial lending sources. (There are good reasons to do so—including building a positive credit score and profile!) Rather, by utilizing Family Lending, you can give children or grandchildren a head start. They can become money-wise beyond their years, learning how to utilize finance—even if they cannot qualify for a bank loan. And if you choose, you can provide funding for educational and business opportunities that don't fit traditional lending rules. (Be aware that contracts with minors are not legal... but certainly parents and teens can "negotiate" whatever informal agreements they want.)

9.   **One step removed.**

When you use a policy loan for a family member, it's not "your" money (or even money from a family trust, if the policy is owned by a trust) that is being loaned—it's a loan from the life insurance company. We think there are advantages to this!

We may have all heard about a situation in which money is borrowed from a family member and never paid back. Intentional or not, it happens. And such situations can cause conflicts and awkwardness, even family rifts.

Using the Family Financing model, the agreement is made with the Family Council—not just an individual. And technically, the money comes from the insurance company—not an individual. Should a borrower fall behind on payments, this helps the situation be less "personal." No one is going to miss a mortgage payment because someone else didn't pay them back!

Now, if a loan takes longer to pay back, the borrower will pay more interest to the life insurance company. But what if the loan cannot be repaid? In that situation, there's a built-in "stop gap." If necessary, money *can* be *withdrawn* from the policy to pay off the loan. While that is not our preferred strategy, it is an option. Then, if gifts (via withdrawals) are made to one child rather than loans, their future inheritance or other benefits can be adjusted to maintain fairness.

We see withdrawals as more of a last resort because they "shrink" the policy permanently. Once removed as a withdrawal, money cannot be put back in the policy. (Those are just the rules of life insurance. You add dollars through premiums and paid-up additions, but when dollars are withdrawn rather than borrowed against, premiums and PUAs—if allowed—are still your only avenues to put dollars back into the policy.)

Again, long-term thinking is all-important here! Life insurance is a long-term product, not a checking account you go to every time you need cash. With loans, as long as they are repaid, Family Funds are always growing and being replenished, rather than being consumed.

10. The underlying collateral (cash value) keeps growing!

This is a BIG benefit to Family Financing, and one reason why whole life insurance is so efficient as the foundation of a family's personal economy. When you borrow against your cash value (not withdraw), *the money stays in the policy and grows, even while it is being used as collateral.*

You aren't "starting from scratch" every time you need access to money. The importance of this cannot be underestimated!

What happens when you borrow against a credit card, a bank line of credit, or take an installment loan? You pay it off, with interest. You go from "in debt" back to "zero" again.

Need money again? Great, go re-qualify and start from scratch. Borrow, then repay. Borrow, then repay.

You *pay* interest, but you never get around to EARNING any interest! The borrower is stuck at zero. Everyone loves the idea of being "debt-free," but if you're not building assets, "debt free" just keeps taking you back to zero. Unfortunately, it takes some people years, even *decades* to move past this stage.

Those who save up to pay CASH for things are almost in the same boat! They save in a bank account (for virtually no interest)—sometimes for years. They buy the car (or other major purchase); then they're back at zero. Soon it's time to save for the next car, vacation or college tuition bill. Then they're back at zero once more. Savers avoid an interest *payment*, but because they are not *earning* interest, you could say they still have an interest *cost*.

The problem is this: *your own cash has a cost*. This is the economic principle of "opportunity cost." When you save up money in places where it earns virtually nothing, your dollars aren't working very hard. With "lazy assets," you pay the opportunity cost of NOT earning interest!

This is why there is a BIG advantage to borrowing against cash value or other forms of collateral that keep GROWING. You want the wonder of uninterrupted compounded growth *working in your favor*. While you could leverage money in a bank account as collateral, whole life cash value will grow faster than dollars in a savings account, CD or money market fund over time. So when you borrow against a life insurance policy and pay the loan back—you end up with *more than you started with*. You're never just getting "back to zero." You're building wealth!

Now you know why borrowing against a life insurance policy can be very beneficial. However, perhaps you would prefer to never borrow at all! There are advantages to being debt-free... but is it really the best strategy? We'll go back to the Johnsons for some insight on this.

· · · · ·

Carol had decided to book a call with Jerry so they could all discuss some questions Cyndi had brought up the previous week. Today's "coffee shop meeting" was being held at Cyndi's home so they could put Jerry on speaker phone.

Cyndi had some specific questions about the idea of borrowing against policies. Her best friend had been to a financial workshop at their church and had shared about it with Cyndi. Cyndi wasn't sure how to process two of the ideas her friend shared: First, the most important thing is to be debt-free. No mortgage, no car loan, no credit card debt. And second, to buy cheap term insurance rather than obtaining whole life insurance.

Carol introduced the questions Cyndi had asked her, summarizing the concerns that she had relayed to her about using whole life and borrowing against policies. "Did I summarize that correctly, Cyndi?"

"Yes, that's a fair representation. I feel good about what we're doing with Family Financing, but I didn't really know how to respond to my friend."

"I definitely have some ways to answer those questions," said Jerry over the speakerphone. However, I'm curious what Carol might have to say first!"

"Well, I know that whole life insurance gives us some important living benefits you're never going to get from a term policy. John and I were interested in the long-term care benefit care rider and the terminal illness rider. We hope we will never need either, but if we do, we can turn our own death benefit into a living benefit. We also have found whole life to be the best way to save. The life insurance bill shows up and it gets paid! To be honest, we didn't have much success using the 'we'll save what we have left over at the end of the month' approach. We had to make it a priority!"

Cyndi nodded, knowing that she and Sam had also tried and failed at saving successfully multiple times.

"Now Jerry, maybe you can speak to the question of debt. But my response to the idea of being 'debt free' is initially this—isn't there such a thing as 'good debt' and 'bad debt'?"

"That's a great point," said Jerry, "and you are correct! Could you and John have purchased your home without a mortgage?"

"Well, definitely not when we did. If we had to buy our home with cash... well, we couldn't have... we would have had to save much longer and purchase a much smaller home. Same with our two rental properties. We couldn't—or wouldn't—have purchased them with cash. Maybe we would have saved money on mortgages, but isn't it good that we have the homes now?"

"I'll answer that with another question," said Jerry. "Are you better off now, in terms of your wealth, because of the mortgages you took advantage of?"

Carol ran some quick figures in her head for a few moments. "Absolutely! I'm guessing our net worth is almost a million dollars more today thanks to our ability to use mortgages. And I doubt we would have purchased the rental properties at all, which now contribute to our cash flow."

Julie and Cyndi nodded thoughtfully while Jerry continued.

"So the ability to use debt helped you get ahead—in the long run."

"Absolutely," Carol nodded.

"Now think about the most successful companies in the world. Let's use Apple as an example. Of course, Apple is a publicly-traded company. Many people are invested in the company as shareholders. Now, do you know what all those shareholders also represent?"

Carol and the girls looked at each other for a minute, stumped.

"Well, shareholders are essentially investors in the company... so they provided Apple with capital, right?" asked Carol.

"Exactly. Now, company shares are technically equity, not debt, although of course shareholders invest for a positive return on their dollars. Most companies also have debt of various kinds, from mortgages on properties to lines of credit that allow them to expand their locations, services or inventory. So... why do you think companies take on shareholders and/or debt?"

Now Cyndi saw the light. "So they can grow faster!"

"Exactly!" said Jerry. "Would Apple be a huge company if they had only grown as fast as they could with no additional capital... no investors, shareholders, or debt?"

"Of course not," Carol smiled. *"We would probably not even know the name 'Apple,' except as a crunchy round fruit!"*

They all laughed, while Cyndi exclaimed, "And I wouldn't have my iPhone!"

"Probably not!" said Jerry. "Smartphones might not even exist. And you can look at your personal economies in a similar way. As a matter of fact, I hope you do! Sometimes it pays to expand your family's personal economy. And sometimes that means using debt—borrowing money to acquire new assets. Does that make sense?"

"Yes," replied the girls.

"Great. Let's go one step further now with good debt and bad debt. Mortgage debt—as long as you can afford it and it's a sound property—is good debt. Can you guess what 'bad debt' might be?"

After a pause, Cyndi spoke up, "Credit card debt? Especially high-interest debt, I'm sure." Cyndi saw Carol nod affirmatively then continued. "Or even low-interest debt on things you don't need in the first place—like the extra TV Sam brought home for our bedroom, right before we concluded we didn't even want a TV in our bedroom!"

"Exactly! If you're paying high interest—or paying for something you don't need—that's definitely not good debt."

Carol spoke up again now. "I think what I've learned is that the best kind of life insurance loan is one that allows us to grow our family's wealth. Like investing in education or training that allows a family member to earn more. Maybe we use a loan to fund the down payment on a rental property—and the cash flow repays the loan. Or maybe Sheldon finds a vintage car to rehab with Grandpa John!"

"Yes—that's 'good debt'; using loans to create cash flow or future income. As a general rule, you don't want to be simply 'spending' with policy loans, you want to be investing in something that will pay you back.

"Now, your cash value is also the perfect emergency fund. Let's say you didn't have adequate savings. Let's say your extra cash has been going into investments, such as mutual funds. What happens if you need a new roof on the house?"

Now Julie spoke up. "Well, we'd have to either rack up some high-interest debt by maxing out our credit cards—or else we'd have to sell mutual funds to replace the roof. Which would NOT make Jackson happy!"

"And what if the stock market was down that year... and your roof was leaking?"

"Yikes... I guess we'd be forced to sell mutual funds at a loss."

"And pay taxes on the sale, and if the funds are in a retirement account—a penalty!"

"Or what if one of the family breadwinners was out of work for a spell, and you needed cash? Do you think a bank would loan it to you if you couldn't prove you had income to pay it back?"

Now the girls were groaning at the thought. "Ok, Ok, we get it... a life insurance loan would be a WAY better solution!"

"Yes it would," said Jerry, sounding pleased that they understood the value of having a sizable emergency/opportunity fund. "Borrowing against life insurance isn't always the best choice for every situation, but it's a very valuable option to have available!"

"Now, Cyndi," Jerry continued, "were you the iPhone fan?" he inquired.

"Yup—that's me."

"You know, whole life policies have been compared to smartphones. That's because they can do so many things! Not that many years ago, I had a flip phone for calls, a pager for work, a GPS for my car, a digital camera for family outings and a walkman CD player for music. That was before the iPhone, obviously! But that's still how a lot of people manage their money. They save for college in a 529 plan, retirement in a 401(k), they have life insurance that is just life insurance, with long-term care insurance elsewhere, plus a separate savings account.

"Ultimately, that's just not very efficient! You've got your dollars all split up in different places, so it's hard to put very many dollars together in any one place. Yet you don't really know how you're going to need those dollars in the future! If your roof leaks and your dollars are socked away in a 529 plan and a 401(k), that's a bummer."

"That makes a lot of sense," said Cyndi.

"Now let's talk more about your other question. The concept of 'buy term and invest the difference' has been around for some time. It was a slogan used by a big company that sold mutual funds. Of course, the cheaper your life insurance, the more you can spend on mutual funds! But as you can see now, mutual funds aren't the same thing as savings. And they don't provide any protection if you die. And you want all three—savings, investments, and protection. Life insurance isn't so much an 'investment' as a savings vehicle and a risk management tool that helps keep your investments safe."

The daughters gave satisfied nods and thanked Jerry for his explanation. Carol added, "Jerry, I think a couple of light bulbs have been turned on today. We sure appreciate your time."

"My pleasure. And if there's anything else I can help you with, any of you—feel free to shoot me an email or give me a call. And Cyndi and Julie—your parents know more about financial matters than they let on—but know that I'm always here for you, too."

"Thanks Jerry!" they exclaimed almost in unison as Carol said the final goodbye.

· · · · ·

To Borrow or Not to Borrow

We see many people with whole life policies making one of two mistakes. This first mistake is being so cautious in borrowing that it *restricts* wealth. Some people resist utilizing debt even when it could *expand* their assets, cash flow, and/or earning capability. This comes from the flawed notion that it is always best to be "debt free." We prefer growing assets and income—and sometimes that is best done by leveraging an asset by borrowing against it. You must consider the "big picture" of your personal economy. Sometimes, debt makes financial sense!

The second mistake is the opposite. People borrow "too much, too soon, and too often." The flexibility of policy loans can be a real blessing. It can also be dangerous if you are prone to over-spending! A primary purpose of your Family Fund is to establish *liquidity*. Borrowing against a policy reduces liquidity, so define your financial priorities carefully. Some general rules of thumb to help you decide whether or not to borrow:

First and foremost, your policy should act as your *emergency fund*. Therefore, you should not borrow an amount that would decrease your liquidity below that level—unless it truly is an emergency. Keeping enough cash for a minimum of 6 to 12 months of living expenses is common. If you are a business owner or work in sales, you might want a bigger emergency fund. If you have an extremely reliable income and/or a lot of other assets, saving a year's worth of expenses might be overkill.

Beyond the emergency fund, the next purpose of your cash value should be for *opportunities*. This could be an investment property down payment, a business expansion or a cash-flowing investment (which may require a lump sum).

If you borrow against life insurance dollars to invest—be cautious. Do your due diligence. Work the numbers. Don't speculate. The *last* thing you want to do is borrow money for an investment that can't pay you back. And of course—you want the investment to pay back the life insurance loan—including interest—plus produce a profit for you. If the numbers don't work, or if there is any significant risk, don't do it.

Last and least—a policy *can* be used for consumer purchases such as cars or vacations, or to fund a home remodel. This does not always make financial sense, as there might be better places to borrow. Car loans are typically at lower interest rates, and often home equity lines can be used for home remodels—often at lower rates and sometimes even tax deductible.

When might it make sense to use a policy loan for a purchase?

- When you cannot qualify for a lower-interest car or home equity loan.
- If you need to keep purchases off of your credit report (perhaps you are home shopping or trying to raise your credit score).
- In instances where your other option is a credit card. In most cases, a policy loan will have significantly lower interest.

Of course, oftentimes it's best *not* to spend the money at all! So make sure the purchase is important enough to make even though it will cost interest. If you are constantly borrowing for vacations, you are probably over-spending. If it takes several months to pay off a trip, look for ways to enjoy time off within your budget.

We prefer to use policies to:

- expand assets
- grow a business
- increase cash flow
- invest in yourself and your family
- and protect loved ones from emergencies and loss.

If you are using your policy for consumer purchases or for necessities when there's no emergency situation—it's time to rethink!

Important Facts about Life Insurance Loans

Direct or Non-Direct Recognition? (It doesn't really matter.)

A question many people have when purchasing a whole life policy is, "Does the policy have a 'Direct Recognition' or 'Non-Direct Recognition' loan provision?" Some advisors believe the answer to this question is a big deal that should determine what policy you buy. However, that just isn't so!

First, let's explain what direct and non-direct recognition policies are. In a nutshell: direct recognition policies adjust the dividends paid on a policy when there is an outstanding policy loan, non-direct recognition policies do not. Owning a direct recognition policy can affect your dividends either positively or negatively, though only by a tiny amount—literally pocket change. And while there are pros and cons to either, they are fairly minor. We agree with TheInsuranceProBlog.com's conclusion:[66] "When it comes down to it, one is not superior to the other. All this talk... is a game of smoke and mirrors used to keep your focus away from the really important stuff."

The bottom line: direct or non-direct, you'll be fine as long as you follow our advice about choosing the best life insurance company[67] AND choose an advisor to help you.

You should (almost always) pay policy loans back in a timely manner.

When you borrow against your policy, you will have a policy loan to pay off—with interest. You can pay it off on your own time schedule, fast or slow. The interest on a life insurance loan is WAY lower than credit card rates, which makes it easier to pay off. (Rates are about 6-7% right now, depending on your policy, with bank rates—using your policy as collateral—running around 5%. And remember—the underlying cash value is still growing—one reason we love life insurance!)

If loans are never paid off, the health of the policy can be threatened. If the loan is neglected and allowed to keep growing with interest until it exceeds the cash value, the policy can collapse—with ugly consequences. (More about that in a moment.)

If you are unable to pay back loans from your income and/or policy dividends, take a *withdrawal* from the policy and pay back the loan with that. This will permanently reduce the size of your policy, but it will eliminate the loan and keep the policy in force!

Now, since whole life policies are built to last, you don't need to worry needlessly. Just pay back your loans within a few years and you'll be in good shape.

Don't treat loans like "tax free income."

A policy loan isn't "free money!" There is an idea out in the marketplace being sold as "tax-free income." It involves getting policy loans and using them as income with no attempt to pay back the loans. This is poor advice that could backfire.

Try to avoid taking out big policy loans and allowing the interest to just accumulate, year after year. Unless you have a lot of equity in your policy or are very elderly, this is a dangerous strategy. If you leverage all of the cash value and let interest accumulate until it bankrupts the policy, you can end up with a big tax bill. (This is why we don't recommend using policy loans for income.)

The exception to this rule would be near the end of life. If your life expectancy is very short, perhaps just a few years or less, it is possible to borrow a reasonable portion of your cash value and let the interest come out of the future death benefit.

If your goal is to increase your income, it could be a better strategy to *annuitize* the policy, turning cash value into a permanent income stream. Another strategy for cash is to *sell* a policy, often to a life settlement company that purchases them, although a family member or any private party could also be a purchaser. (You can only sell a policy commercially if you are elderly—typically in your 80s or beyond—and not in good health.) Or you can take a withdrawal of cash, as mentioned above, rather than a loan.

Policy loans are not typically taxable or tax-deductible

Funds from policy loans are generally not taxable as they are *loans*, not *income*. They are also generally not tax-deductible. However, there are few important exceptions.

First, if your policy is a MEC—a Modified Endowment Contract—loans become taxable. (Be aware that Single Premium Whole Life policies, or SPWL, are MECs by definition.) Traditional whole life policies can also *become* a MEC if you overfund the paid-up additions. (The company will alert you if you have done so and it can be corrected—if corrected soon enough.)

Second, as mentioned above, money borrowed against your policy can be classified as income and taxed if you do not keep any policy in force. So if you borrow to the hilt and then your policy lapses—whether through unpaid policy loans or by repeatedly failing to make premium payments—you might be left with a "tax bomb."

When a life insurance policy is surrendered or lapses, the remaining cash value is used to repay the loan. If a policy's cash value is completely used up to repay a life insurance loan, that doesn't erase the taxes due on the gain of the policy. If the policy lapses without any remaining net cash value due to a loan repayment, you could end up with an income tax liability based on the policy's gains.

Potential taxes on loans are a *non-issue* with policies that remain in force since the death benefit is not taxed. Any loans would be repaid from the tax-free death benefit with the remainder paid to heirs.

If you seem to have continuing cash crunches, contact the insurance company. There are actually several possible solutions to keep a policy in force for a lower premium—sometimes no out-of-pocket premium at all. See "Reduce or Stop Premiums... and Keep Your Whole Life Policy!"[68] on ProsperityEconomics.org.

Lastly, be aware that interest on a policy loan is rarely tax-deductible. However, if you are borrowing for a business purpose, it may be possible to set it up that way. (Consult your tax advisor on this.)

No, you don't "pay yourself interest" when repaying a policy loan.

You might have heard that you "recapture" all your finance charges or "pay interest to yourself" when you utilize life insurance loans. This is not accurate and is a major misconception in some "pro-whole life" circles. At best, the language is misleading.

It's true that you don't pay interest to a *bank* as you might for a credit card, car loan or mortgage. But you still pay interest when you borrow against your policy. You pay it to the life insurance company—not yourself! You may pay LESS interest than you would with a credit card, therefore allowing yourself to save the difference... but the interest charged on a policy loan doesn't go into your pocket.

You don't "pay interest to yourself" with a policy loan any more than you "pay taxes to yourself" when your tax dollars fund roads, schools or parks that you use. (I.e., there may be some truth in each case, but the wording is not helpful.) You could say a portion of your payment goes to yourself as additional savings. But thinking of it as "paying interest to yourself" can lead to poor financial decisions.

Sometimes confusion arises when agents or advisors advocate paying back *more* to the policies than the interest rate charged by the life insurance company. For example, if the credit card was going to charge you 21 percent, you might be encouraged to repay your life insurance at the same 21 percent rate. You'd end up repaying the principle, paying the interest, plus paying—or rather, saving—"extra" that could be added to your policy as PUAs (paid-up additions), increasing your cash value and death benefit.

However, if you are already maximizing your PUAs as we recommend, "repaying a loan at a higher rate" can be problematic. Not all companies will allow you to raise or lower your PUAs at will. And if you pay too MUCH into the policy, it would become a MEC, or Modified Endowment Contract, which would turn loans into taxable events! (You can also simply *withdraw* cash value, though once removed, dollars can't be "put back." So borrowing is the better choice to keep your cash value keeps growing.)

Always keep in mind that funding and growing your policy and paying back your loans are *two different transactions*. They're not entirely unrelated, but they are *separate*. Your cash value is going to grow whether or not you borrow against the policy. So *always take the loan that makes the most financial sense*... whether that's from the life insurance company or from a different source.

If you keep these transactions separate in your mind when making decisions, it will lead to the right decisions. And since you're NOT "paying yourself interest," you want to pay the least amount interest possible on any loan!

Best Practices for Family Lending

First, evaluate the best lending source on a case-by-case basis.

When someone in the family desires financing, don't assume a policy loan is the best option. You may have other choices available for a particular loan, such as store financing, a mortgage, student loan, or bank loan.

You'll want to assess which has the lowest cost, along with other possible pros and cons.

Sometimes, it might be advantageous to use your policy as collateral to borrow from a bank. Other times, it may make more sense to utilize a no-or-low-interest loan (perhaps a car loan from a credit union) than your policy. Let's look at a few examples.

Interest rate example 1:

Your adult child may have a choice between buying furniture for their first house with:

    A. Store financing of 25.9 percent.
    B. A credit card charging 18.9 percent interest.
    C. A peer lending loan at 15 percent interest.
    D. A life insurance loan at a rate of 7 percent (your policy may be higher or lower).
    E. A bank loan at 6 percent using cash value for collateral.

D, the life insurance loan or E, bank loan would be the best choices. The life insurance loan would be more flexible in terms of repayment, and the bank loan in this example has slightly lower interest.

Interest rate example 2:

Same scenario as #1, but in this case, the furniture store offered "6 months same as cash!" financing at no additional cost. (*Always* run the numbers to check that no finance charges have been added in! Often there is a cash discount you don't get if you finance.)

IF the store offers a true no-interest option with no additional fees or costs *and* IF there was high confidence the furniture can be paid off (or refinanced) within 6 months, then the "same as cash" store financing would be the best option.

Interest rate example 3:

You would like to finance a new car. You have a choice between:

    A. Borrowing against your policy at 7 percent to finance a car (your policy may be higher or lower).

B. Borrowing from a HELOC (home equity line of credit) at 6 percent.

C. Borrowing from a credit union at 2.99 percent to finance the car.

D. Letting the dealer finance the car, also at 2.99 percent.

Take C, the credit union loan! It's a better rate, and it leaves your policy cash value in place, growing and awaiting an opportunity. A newer car is excellent collateral and auto financing options can be excellent. And by lining up your own bank or credit union financing, you can take advantage of any cash rebates from the dealer.

Interest rate example 4:

You would like to remodel your kitchen. Your choices are:

A. Obtaining a loan from a peer lending site (such as Lending Club) at 13 percent.

B. Borrowing against your policy at 7 percent (your policy may be higher or lower).

C. Obtaining a HELOC (home equity line of credit) from your bank for 6 percent.

In this case, C, the HELOC probably makes the most sense. Not only is it the best rate, but if you use your HELOC for capital improvements such as remodeling your home, it may be tax-deductible! (Consult your tax advisor.)

Have a defined process for applying for a loan.

While asking for money from parents or grandparents often happens informally in a single nuclear family, there are big advantages to having an application process and a written agreement. Putting financial agreements in writing clarifies expectations, responsibilities and consequences. Applying for the loan is also great training for the borrower as they will one day want to apply for a mortgage or perhaps a business loan.

With Family Lending, you'll find it helpful to have a process and an application in writing (perhaps in something like a Google document, to keep it easily accessible and updatable). These can be very detailed or quite simple. At the least, the process should cover the basics of "how to apply." A simple example:

"Family Lending Process"

Loans are to be granted only to family members, either immediate family or their spouses or children. Family members must meet qualifications as determined by the Family Council.

1. Fill out the Family Lending Application form (This could be a Google doc form or page with questions such as the ones listed below.)
2. Submit by email to (name/email).
3. Expect a response within (time frame—such as 30 days).
4. If approved, an agreement will sent to you outlining your responsibilities, to be signed by you and the policy owner who will supply the funds.
5. Loans will be funded within (time frame—such as two weeks from approval).
6. The Family Council secretary will start and maintain a file for all approved, active, and repaid loans.
7. Repayment of the loan. (A very important step!) Payments are to be made by the first of the month, with a 7-day grace period before any penalties are assessed. Payments to be submitted to (define how and to whom, which may be the secretary or the policy owner). After the tenth day, a penalty of (per diem to a pre-defined limit) will be assessed.
8. Report back in quarterly emails and/or at the next Family Retreat about the loan, including how it is being used, and the end result, when complete.

A set of questions can comprise an application in a Google doc or editable PDF, such as:

"Family Lending Application"

1. What size loan are you applying for? (A dollar amount or a range.)
2. What will the money be used for? (Be specific).
3. Why is this important to you?

4. How will this loan help you meet your goals or fulfill your (or the family's) mission statement?

5. When is the money requested? (A minimum of 45 days please.)

6. How and when will it be repaid? (Be specific; submit a repayment schedule for approval.)

7. Please list your household's current income and liabilities, including debt payments, rent or mortgage and insurance premiums.

8. What gives you confidence in your ability to borrow and replay this money? (Skills, income, repayment history, commitment.)

9. Besides or in addition to this loan, how else can the family support you with this project?

10. Besides monetary repayment, is there anything else of value offered in exchange for the loan?

11. What will you do next if this loan is not approved?

12. What steps will you take (specifically) if the loan is approved?

13. Is there anything else you'd like us to know or consider?

14. Please attach any relevant documents, spreadsheets, or photos. (You may wish to require proof of income or even credit, as a bank would, or you might find that unnecessary or even undesirable for young borrowers.)

15. Submit to (appropriate parties/process for submission).

These examples are plain and simple. Alternatively—or in addition—your family can infuse whatever practices fit your family's personality. Money is often such a heavy subject… but there is no reason your family can't make it fun!

For instance, if your family is entrepreneurial (or if you wish to nurture that spirit), presentations could be made "Shark Tank" style, complete with family "judges" to grill the contestants! Or a "GoFundMe" model could be used, with applicants submitting a video presentation and short description to "sell" the loan or investment opportunity, as one would on a crowdfunding site. Such presentations can be done in addition to—or perhaps as part of—a written application process. Would-be borrowers could be coached how to improve their presentations and/or applications.

There's no "right way" to do it, as long as it "fits" your family and those approving the loan agree.

Develop criteria and a process for approving loans.

Just as you want a defined process for loan applications, you'll want consistent criteria for loan approval. With a simple Family Lending arrangement, the policyowner (typically the patriarch, matriarch or 'grandparents' in a family) can approve a loan. With a larger, more established Family Fund, founders or board members can evaluate:

- If it is a loan predicted to help the applicant succeed.
- Whether or not a life insurance loan is the best source of funding.
- If the application is strong, compelling, and complete.
- The ability of the family member to repay the loan.
- If it aligns with the Family Mission and values. (Some loans may be worth making, but might not fit guidelines for Family Lending.)
- The availability of funds in the amount requested. (Always leave ample liquidity in a policy; we never recommend "borrowing to the hilt.")
- Whether or not it is a loan the Family Council (or policy owner) would like to make.

The Council may decide the guidelines for loan approval, and/or the family can vote for approvals. Voting can be fun and educational, and board members may argue their reasoning. Founders or board members can come up with a grading or ranking system, or it can be subjective. And the process may start out subjective, then as applications are reviewed, decision-makers can develop and articulate criteria for approval. It is easier for the applicants if they understand the criteria for an approvable family loan.

Preference might be given to family members who have not yet utilized a loan, or to those who have a successful track record of repaying family loans. Certain needs may rank higher than others, such as borrowing for a down payment on a first home rather than a third rental property.

And remember—the Family Council doesn't have to approve every loan request! And it doesn't have to be a "Yes" or "No"—the response may be a compromise, such as "Not yet," or "Yes, but"—perhaps approved for a lesser amount or under different terms. Ultimately, the policy owner makes the decision or has "veto" power, so they must feel it is a loan worth making. Usually that is the parent or grandparent, perhaps the founder of the Family Fund, although there's no reason someone else in the family (aunt, uncle, sibling) couldn't choose to make a loan.

Family Lending creates opportunities for learning and mentorship.

Family Financing gets families TALKING about money, and allows the experienced wealth-builders in the family to mentor the next generation. We've even heard of a family that gives the kids money to *invest* for the year—then compares results at the next Family Retreat!

Now, some families use family funds for investing, many do not. There's no right or wrong—that's up to you and your family. The policyholders, founders and decision-makers for the Family Funds get to set the criteria for lending. (But if you do use policies to invest, stick to solid investments with cash flow that can pay off the insurance loans!)

Those with financial savvy can educate younger or less experienced family members as to what constitutes a worthy, necessary and approvable loan. If a family member asks for a loan because they wish to roll the dice on crypto-currencies, that's the perfect time to have a conversation about the difference between saving, investing and speculation.

Define and communicate the consequences of a failure to repay.

This may be the most difficult piece of family lending, but it can also be a rewarding and important learning experience. When you allow for success, you also allow the possibility of people failing to follow through on what was agreed upon.

Some rules of thumb:

- **Don't let a borrower off the hook at the first sign of trouble.** Keep the borrower accountable, offering support or coaching as needed. Ask questions and help them find solutions if requested.

- **Define consequences in advance.** Family Lending is not a game of Monopoly, and the money is real! Therefore, the policyholders or Board also have to prepare for "what happens" if (or when) a loan is not repaid as agreed. For instance, the agreement signed before the loan is funded should stipulate, "Late payments or default on loan procedures," such as:

    - *"For late payments, the Family Board will apply a penalty of $20 per day for each day the payment is late, past the 10th of the month, up to a maximum of $100 or 10% of the payment due, whichever is greater.*

    - *"In instance of a loan default, the Family Board will remove the amount of the loan, plus (X percent) annualized interest, from the Borrower's stated inheritance. If cash value of life insurance is the source of funds, and the Borrower doesn't pay the loan back, a certain portion of the death benefit can be removed from that Borrower's inheritance as 'payback.'*

    - *Alternatively, the policy owner who funds the loan reserves the right to 'call the loan due' plus (late fees and/or X percent interest) after 90 days of non-payment. Notice of such intent must be delivered in writing and the borrower will have 60 days to repay the amount owed or propose another acceptable solution in writing."*

- **Sometimes extreme circumstances require flexibility.** Unlike many banks and commercial lenders, the maker of a family loan has flexibility to change terms as they wish to account for extreme hardship. (For instance: it won't help to keep assessing late fees if someone is hospitalized after an accident that interrupts their life and income.)

"In extreme circumstances or hardship, the policy owner can change the terms of the agreement."

- **Value relationships over money with integrity.** It is possible to forgive a *person* for failing to follow through as planned without forgiving the *financial debt* they owe—the balance and interest.

  When people owe money or get behind, they may start to avoid others—especially anyone they owe money to. Strive for open lines of communication and teach that—even if people are struggling financially—they do not need to hide or live in shame. Embarrassment or fear of being shunned does make any financial problem better, but support and understanding—along with clear communication and expectations—can help someone overcome a challenging situation.

At the end of the day, money is never as valuable as the love of family. *And* (because it's not either/or, it's both/and) you can and should still make adjustments in inheritances for an unpaid loan. That is only fair to the heirs who have repaid their loans!

Again, there's no "right way" to do it. (Although if your Family Financing project is causing division rather than bonding, learning and mentorship, you might be doing it wrong!) And some family members can be more challenging than others.

As noted in earlier chapters, a family's ability to communicate is one of the most important factors of successful generational wealth. So consider that even working through difficult financial conversations with love can prove worthwhile and can be an important piece of Family Financing.

THE BOTTOM LINE

Borrowing is an age-old way to expand assets, create wealth, and finance purchases as well. There are significant advantages to borrowing from a life insurance company, although a policy loan is not the best solution for every financing need. Understanding how to use life insurance loans (and what not to use them for, such as speculative investments and long-term income) is helpful.

When it comes to making loans to family members, families will benefit from processes, criteria and structure. Define your application process and your criteria for approving a loan. Even if you are the only decision maker, it can provide a foundation upon which the family can build to provide future multi-generational financing.

There is no one-size-fits all. You can start small and simple, and you can get creative with processes that fit *your* family best. You may encounter learning curves and late payments, but focus on the big goals: investing in your loved ones and having a structure that allows more experienced family members to mentor younger ones in money matters—including borrowing and lending.

Note: The examples in this chapter of family documents are provided for informational and educational purposes only. They are not to be construed as legal advice or legally binding language in any way. We advise you to consult your own legal counsel to write or review any legal agreements or contracts.

CHAPTER 12:
Family Financing, Governance and Leadership

"Do you realize it's been one year since we first proposed the idea of Family Financing to the kids over dinner?" said Carol, as John sipped his morning cup of coffee.

"You don't say! And not a single loan request yet."

"Well, I'm not surprised. It's really only been a few months since we ironed out the application process."

John replied with a smile, "Maybe no one wants to run the risk of being turned down!"

"Well, I suspect we'll see some action when the boys are old enough to drive… and certainly when college comes around."

"No doubt! And who could resist our special FDIC funds?"

"Oh!?" replied Carol with a puzzled look.

"Yes, FDIC… Family-Derived Investment Capital!"

The Johnsons had started their Family Financing project quite simply. John and Carol both had long-established life insurance policies and initially, the two of them came up with the application process, application questions and requirements. (After all, the Family Fund would be money from their own policies, at least until other policies were adequately funded.)

However, remembering what Jerry said about Family Financing—it should be done "with" your family, not just "for" your family—they brought their ideas to the Family Council for feedback and input. A rich and productive discussion followed and quite a few improvements were made. An updated version was voted on at the next Council meeting and unanimously passed.

Presently, the Family Council consisted of the family adults—John, Carol, Julie, Jackson, Cyndi and Sam. John was the president, at the insistence of the rest. Cyndi was the Secretary and kept the meeting minutes. Jackson was the Treasurer. He tracked the progress of Family Fund policies and would track loans and payments in the future.

Carol, Sam and Julie were all voting members, and each had moved into unofficial roles of sorts. Carol was "the elder" who offered wisdom and perspective. She could be counted on to smooth things over, if necessary, or remind people of the family's mission and values when they started to drift away. Julie was the wordsmith and she helped craft communications for the wider family that went beyond what Cyndi did as Secretary. Sam, the resident athlete and sports enthusiast, offered motivation when needed. Carol would smile when he did so. His years of participation and coaching with sports teams had given him a knack for knowing when a little encouragement could go a long way.

The council met quarterly, usually after a meal while the boys watched a movie or played outside. John and Carol were grateful to have their assistance, though in future years, perhaps just one representative from each family would be sufficient representation. It was agreed that after the first year, Council members would be free to rotate out for a year or two, as long as their immediate family was represented on the Council.

As the months went by, Carol had noticed greater understanding and participation from their daughters and their husbands. The Family Fund was no longer "John and Carol's project"—it was something in which they all had ownership.

On this particular morning, Carol pondered this as she gathered the breakfast dishes.

"You know," said Carol, as John put down the morning paper to give her his full attention, "I see now, Family Financing isn't just about growing and developing the financial wealth of the family. It's just as much about growing and developing the leadership of the family!"

John smiled and nodded. "I've noticed that, too. We're growing the true wealth of our family—the human capital!"

"Yes," nodded Carol. "And I believe we are honing our own leadership abilities in the process. That's a pretty nice side benefit of this project... I think we have a greater ability to serve, guide and influence this clan than ever before. Plus... I'm learning plenty from the kids!"

"We really do have a wonderful family."

"Yes we do!"

. . . . .

Servant Leadership

> *"A leader is best when people barely know he exists, when his work is done, his aim fulfilled, they will say: we did it ourselves."*   —Lao Tzu

"Servant Leadership" is a concept that has made its way from ancient leaders and Biblical teachings into the corporate world in recent years. From the legendary Chinese philosophers and New Testament depictions of Jesus washing the feet of his disciples, the message is simple: to be truly great, you must serve others.

Leadership does not imply a dominant position or your ability to dictate your terms per your wishes and whims. Nor does it mean that a leader should be submissive and weak. You "serve" as a leader. Leadership goes beyond your own selfish goals, and it has nothing to do with being a "boss."

Servant Leadership flips the pyramid of power. It shows that those who truly help those "beneath" them—in rank, status or ability—are the true leaders. Servant leaders are those who develop skills of listening, empathy, awareness and persuasion. They lead through understanding, not force, and they have an ability to rally people around a unifying cause and motivate them to action.

"Good leaders must first become good servants," said Robert K. Greenleaf, who popularized Servant Leadership in the 1970s and beyond. Mother Teresa and Mahatma Gandhi were among those who served while leading. In modern corporate culture, Servant Leadership means "putting people [employees] ahead of profits through shared values like authenticity... freedom and ownership, community, and collaboration," said a 2017 Inc. com article.

Titled "The World's 10 Top CEOs (They Lead in a Totally Unique Way)," the article details examples of corporate cultures where profit-sharing, recognition, personal growth and positive social impact are the norm. It notes that this new model of leadership provides "the only sustainable model for the future of work."

As we explore generational wealth and how to break the three generation "curse," models of sustainability cannot be ignored. After all, sustainable wealth is what we're after. Servant Leadership is the essence of Family Financing. It's a model that:

- invests in the future
- motivates people to action
- recognizes and raises up the value of each participant
- and allows leaders to serve.

The members of a Family Council are the ones who get to make the rules. Yet ultimately, they are those who simply serve the rest, putting structures into place to encourage the growth and success of all. Let's take a deeper look.

Family Governance

You do *not* need a Governing Body structure to start a Family Fund or utilize policy loans effectively. It can, however, be instrumental with cultivating leadership within the family. It also builds relationships and bonds. So consider building your structure for family leadership. It is especially important when Family Financing projects span multiple generations and/or make decisions on significant sums of money.

A Governing Body (Family Council or Board of Directors) can be elected as a steering committee or decision-making body. The Council typically consists of Officers and directors. Officers have specific roles and responsibilities (President, etc.) and are usually elected after volunteering for or being nominated for the role. Directors (board members with "non-specific" roles) may also serve on the Council through election, appointment, or volunteer opportunity. Directors provide feedback, wisdom, and votes on decisions.

Each adult family member (18 years or older) may be required to serve one or more terms as Officer or Director. Alternatively, in a small family, the board may also be comprised of all adults within the family.

If the matriarch and/or patriarch are the exclusive funders of the bank, which may be the case if their children are minors or just beginning careers, they may serve as the decision-making board. There are benefits to having others involved, as it develops leadership, allows family members to "take ownership" and ensures continuity of Family Financing and Governance from generation to generation.

Council members should think like the life insurance companies do—in 100 year increments. Decisions must balance present needs with what will be best for future generations. The growth of the money should always be more than the amount borrowed to ensure sustainability. Tasks of Council or Board may include:

- Choosing guiding values, which are to be aligned with the Family Mission Statement.
- Keeping account of family assets, loans and gifts.
- Guidance/planning of Family Retreats.

- Directing Family Giving.
- Disbursing assets to family members (according the instructions of a trust, if applicable).
- Managing any family properties or assets.
- Authoring a Family Constitution, which lays out the rules and guidelines for family governance, processes, and code of ethics.

At its annual meeting, the governing body will evaluate if the Family Financing project is adequately achieving goals and expectations as determined by the steering committee. Policies and other assets should be healthy and sustainable. Members should be gaining and reporting value from lending opportunities. Family Retreats or other events should be productive and well-attended. Essential council positions should be filled and a majority of family members should participate in voting. If these measures and other goals are not being achieved, the Family Council should submit ideas for improvement.

Family Council Roles

The following are guidelines and ideas only. Of course, you should do what makes sense for your family, which may mean simplifying or combining roles.

President

The President is typically the founder or the visionary who started the Family Fund. A President could also be the leader to whom the President delegates this role after relinquishing it.

Vice President

A Vice President is optional and can be helpful if it is a larger board or if the President is not fully available. The President finds it helpful or necessary to share the leadership role for reasons of health, travel or other obligations.

The Secretary

The Secretary is responsible for meeting minutes and communication within the Family Council. In smaller Councils, the Secretary might also serve as the Treasurer, for simplicity's sake.

Pertaining to Family Lending, the Secretary will also create a file for each borrower and his or her specific loan. This file will contain any and all paperwork regarding the loan, including the application, the amortization and the payment record and any notes from council meetings pertaining to the loan. The Secretary also records payments and any loan defaults and resulting procedures.

The Treasurer may maintain hard copies as well as electronic copies of policies, trusts and other important documents using a system such as DropBox.com.

The Treasurer

The Treasurer keeps track of family resources, such as policies used for Family Lending and/or other assets or properties that may be part of a Family Fund or Trust. This serves multiple purposes:

To ensure that family members are *saving*—a requirement for participation in Family Financing—and not simply borrowing.

To track the progress and health of the various policies, avoiding overfunding (which would turn the policy into a Modified Endowment Contract, or MEC) or depleting the policy through unpaid loans.

Other Roles in the Family

Members

Members are family members and participants in Family Financing. Members can be defined however a family chooses. In our example, we decided that Members are those who are 15 years and older and who meet eligibility requirements (described later in the letter to a grandchild later in this chapter). These are the voting participants of the Family Financing system.

Elders

An Elder brings valuable wisdom and perspective to a family. They are often grandparents, aunts or uncles, perhaps great aunts and uncles or great-grandparents. They may or may not serve on the Family Council or Board of Directors. They are not generally named as Elders in an official capacity, but they fulfill a valuable role.

Elders, in many ways, are advocates for the family vision and values. They remind family members of their history, their Mission Statement, and who they aspire to be. Elders are often useful to resolve family disputes or misunderstandings. They remind others what is truly important—and what family members have committed to.

Aunts and Uncles

Often children listen and learn more easily from adults who are not their parents! Sometimes being one step removed can make it easier for aunts and uncles to advise minors or give them feedback that will be well-received.

Grandparents and Great-Grandparents

Grandparents are often one of the first trusted adults in the lives of a child. They also have the benefit of experience. One of the big advantages of Family Financing is that it gives grandparents and great-grandparents a way to convey hard-won wisdom.

Older grandparents and great-grandparents can sometimes be effective mentors when it comes to generosity and philanthropy. Older generations are more likely to be retired and focused on volunteering and giving back and less focused on earning. They can also provide a depth of family history that children can benefit from.

Children

Children are the future of the family! While they may not be earning, saving, voting or fulfilling roles in Family Governance, they inspire those who are. Resist seeing Family Financing as an "adult activity" and include children whenever you can. Not only will they bring joy and laughter to the occasion, but it is never too early for them to be exposed to financial management.

Family Financing Questions to Consider

If each family only utilizes their own policies, nuclear families can simply make their own rules. If you have a Family Financing project with multiple generations or related families, you'll want to consider some of these points. Complexity and possibility both increase with more families, family members, and generations.

Who is eligible to participate in the Family Financing project?

Is it for blood relatives and adopted children only? Spouses? Unmarried significant others? Is there an age limit for voting, for loans, or other benefits or responsibilities?

Are there requirements such as saving/having their own policy in place, attending retreats or council meetings? (We believe saving should be a prerequisite for borrowing, though exceptions can be made for members who are not currently working, such as students, stay-at-home parents, etc.)

If adult children do not participate in saving through Family Financing policies, will they have any responsibilities (for instance, to serve on the Council), or access to any of the benefits of the Family Fund? (We suggest that Family Retreats and events be for ALL—but you probably want requirements for access to Family Financing.)

Who is eligible to serve on the Family Council? Are members required to serve on the council? How are officers elected? What roles are necessary?

Keeping things simple is always best, but it may be necessary to spell out expectations in order to ensure you have an adequate participation for decision-making, planning retreats and so on. Consider:

- How long will someone serve on the council... are there minimums? Maximums?

- How will officers be nominated and elected?
- Will there be any compensation or reimbursement of travel expenses?
- How will procedures and processes be determined for future board members and officers?

How often will the members of the family meet to discuss loans and the status of the Family Fund?

Meetings should be often enough to handle business without becoming burdensome. Consider video conferencing if it is not practical to meet in person.

What will the Council be responsible for? Do they handle financial matters only, or do they also plan Family Retreats? Is Family Philanthropy a part of your Family Financing project?

Family members should be able to use their skills and participate in the things that interest them the most. Before beginning a new project, make sure you have volunteers and leadership in place.

Who will determine the goals, structures, rules and guidelines for Family Financing loans?

This may be the Family Council or Governance, although it could be as simple as the policyowner of the policy that would be borrowed against. There is no right or wrong answer as to who the decision makers are, but it should not be a mystery. Ideally, there should be a pathway for any family member to become a decision maker (even if that pathway is saving in their own policy).

What purposes or goals constitute allowable loan applications?

Criteria should be defined for an acceptable loan, understanding that the guidelines may be a moving target for awhile. No matter who determines the guidelines, care should be taken that they align with the Family Mission Statement.

What procedures will be followed for Family Financing loans?

Make sure there is an application available and clear communication about the application process. You want all eligible family members to feel they have access.

Additional questions for Family Financing loans and processes:

- If an application is not approved, is there a process for reconsideration if the goal of the loan is acceptable but the proposed amount or timing is not?
- What will be required of the borrower, once the loan has been approved?
- How will interest be calculated on the loan, if different from the interest rate the insurance company charges? (Some families may wish to charge more, or if policy loans within the family have different rates, perhaps select the highest rate.)
- What will be the process for bringing a loan current if it is not repaid as agreed? What will be the penalty or result of a loan in default?
- Is there an advantage (such as a reduction of interest) if the loan is prepaid or paid faster than the proposed schedule?

Not all decisions must be made ahead of time, as it takes a few years until the cash value feels substantial enough for any major loan. It is still helpful if there is a cohesive vision or at least some basic values and guidelines from the beginning about how such loans could be used. (See chapter 11, "The Beauty of Borrowing" for more.)

A Family Financing Letter to a Grandchild

Carol and Julie were working on a project together for the next council meeting. Carol had proposed there should be some kind of simple "rite of passage" or invitation for each of the children when they were old enough to participate in Family Financing. The Council liked the idea. Carol and Julie began drafting a template letter that could be given a child when they became eligible to participate in the Family Fund.

An appropriate age for receiving this letter was debated… 16? Later? Earlier? Eventually they settled on 15 as the age the boys would be formally invited to participate. The letter would be personalized for each child and delivered on their 15th birthday. It would lay out Family Financing basics: the goals, benefits, values and expectations. It would also provide an overview of Family Financing governance and additional resources. It would be both a personal communication and a reference document that could be referred to again and again.

To a Grandchild on His or Her Birthday

Dear Sheldon,

Happy Birthday!

On your 15th birthday, I want to say how proud your grandfather and I are of you and all your accomplishments, to date. I know they are mere precursors to the greatness that lies ahead of you. Yet I also want to acknowledge the uncertainty that might be setting in, as you contemplate your future, your responsibilities and expectations that may be coming your way. I felt the same way, when I was your age. And we would like to give you an advantage that I did not have myself when growing up. Count this as your "coming of age" present.

This is your official invitation to be a participating member of our Family Financing project. Although you are already familiar with it, we wanted to give you some background, context, and also next steps for you.

Your grandfather and I came from very humble families, where love was plenty and financial resources just covered the essentials. We were both the first in our families to go to college, and we both paid most of our own way. (Of course, college was a little cheaper then!) After graduation, were both savers from the time we had our first full-time jobs. We have never stopped saving and investing.

Now, our needs are met, our children are grown, and we are able to spend our time as we please. We would like to think we have done well for ourselves. And we want to share—and even help you improve upon—whatever wisdom, experience and systems we have benefitted from.

Over the years, we have put money into stocks, bonds, life insurance and real estate. Now we want to be able to help you grow your own wealth, beginning with the financial foundation that served us so well. We also want to "invest" in your dreams and help you create opportunities to fulfill those dreams. **That's why we created the Family Fund—to give you a head start towards your success.**

As you grow older, the dreams you have now may come into focus or may change altogether. But you will always be moving towards dreams and goals. Those dreams may benefit from guidance, support, mentorship, and sometimes, an investment of capital. (That's another way of saying money, although capital comes in other forms, too.)

To be clear, you do not *need* **family money to reach your goals.** You—along with your dreams, talent and commitment—*are enough*. But sometimes, having access to a little money can decrease the time it takes to succeed by lessening the obstacles in your way.

We implemented Family Financing to have a *simple* **and** *repeatable* **system for saving money and financing dreams.** Just as you have to walk before you can run, you have to save before you can invest. That's why we started a life insurance policy for you years ago. Someday, the policy will be yours and you can pick up where we left off. It will provide you with stability during stormy weather. It will guarantee that you have a system for saving safely and steadily—no matter the circumstances of the stock market or the economy.

It is a *permanent* **life insurance policy.** One day when you have loved ones to look after, it will offer them protection and security, should something happen to you. And should you thrive into old age, it will guarantee an inheritance you can pass on.

The Family Financing system is also something you can pass on to your own children. It will help them build their own wealth and security.

And it will continue to make our larger family wealth sustainable for generations.

It may be hard to think about what may happen many decades into the future, so let's start with today. As an educator, I want to make sure you don't have to choose between working full-time through college or saddling yourself with a mountain of student loan debt. We also want you to be able to choose the *type* of learning that suits your dreams best, whether that ends up being a college, a trade school, an apprenticeship, mentorship, studying abroad, or a combination of options.

As a banker, your grandfather wants to make sure your dreams aren't dependent on the current interest rates, lending atmosphere or your ability to convince a bank you are a worthy borrower. (We know you're worthy, which is why we are making this invitation!)

Family Financing Goals

Our Family Financing project has 7 goals. Allow me to explain them:

1. **Create long-term "safe and sure" wealth.**

   The center of our Family Financing project is the Family Fund we are building in a trust put in place for the benefit of our family. It holds our life insurance policies and someday it may hold other assets including life insurance proceeds paid from these policies. (Don't worry if you don't fully understand this now... it will become more clear as you get older and start funding your own policies.)

   There are many ways to grow wealth that leave it open to risk, loss, unnecessary taxation, fees and other dangers. For this reason, we structured our Family Fund using permanent life insurance policies. Whole life insurance is a traditional way of saving money that's been around for hundreds of years. It's safe and guaranteed.

   This isn't money for vacations, risky investments or "wants." It's our financial foundation. It's the money we save for emergencies and opportunities. It's "rain or shine" money that we can count on. It's for leaky roofs, home down payments and wise investments in the success of family members.

These policies provide the *foundation* of our family's wealth. By "foundation," we imply that it is the safe and secure starting point that supports all that comes after. Just as we have additional investments for cash flow and growth, so will you. And remember: the ability to build wealth all comes back to the simple act of *saving*. Spend less than you earn and have a systematic way to protect your savings from loss. That's how wealth begins.

2. **Protect against loss and provide for a family in ANY circumstance.**

   When we grow the policies in our Family Fund, it is more than just a savings plan. It's also life insurance with both living benefits and (eventually) death benefits.

   These policies guarantee that whether your Grandfather or I had died at an early age or we both live to 100, our loved ones will be taken care of. The policies also protect us—and you—in case of a chronic or terminal illness. It guarantees that, no matter what happens, we will have the resources we need.

3. **Cultivate long-term thinking and an enlightened view of wealth.**

   Family Financing is about developing the most valuable assets of our family: our family members! Never believe that money is the most valuable part of Family Financing. It's not! Our family values, connections, love and support for each other, the talents each of you possess and the collective wisdom and experiences of our family are more valuable than any "investment" we could make.

   Our Family Fund exists to serve the human capital—the people in the family. Family Financing can help you develop your value—skills, knowledge, experience and discipline—to create your own wealth.

4. **Implement strategies for generational wealth creation.**

We've saved for you. Soon, you'll be saving for yourself. And some-day, you'll save for a new generation. Our aim is to help you grow your own wealth—and to one day teach your children to do the same. Family Financing is our primary system for doing that.

5. **Raise children—and adults—who are financially responsible.**

We will continue to help you understand money, use it wisely, and not take it for granted. Family Financing provides a structure to help you save money and use it wisely. It's a system with built-in accountability and mentorship.

6. **Use wealth to support the people and causes we care about.**

We started the Family Fund to have a system for investing in our most valuable assets—our grandchildren! That was our dream.

We know you have dreams and goals, too, some which will change over the years. Family Financing allows all of us to invest in your dreams. Nothing will give us greater fulfillment than seeing you realize your potential and offer your unique contributions to the world.

We are also looking at ways to use our family's assets to fund Family Giving—a project we hope you'll help us with!

7. **Create a legacy of more than money.**

Our Family Financing vision goes far beyond financial assets. It includes the following:

- Family Mission Statement
- Family Retreats
- Family Council
- Family Giving
- The Family Fund (the trust that holds your grandfather's and my whole life policies)
- Family Lending (access to family capital through borrowing and replenishing).

Most of all, our Family Financing vision embraces and is defined by who we are as a Family! Our family is the place where you can share your stories, dreams and contributions, knowing you are loved and supported. We truly believe: "We are strongest and most powerful when we work together!" We consider this family to be our greatest legacy.

Perhaps the seven goals of Family Financing can be summed up: "to build financial assets to support, protect, and invest in the success of our family." Some of the goals may not mean much to you now, but as you come back and re-read this letter every year or so, your understanding will deepen and evolve.

Our Family Financing Values

These are our guiding principles. Allow me to explain our four principles and why they are important.

Stewardship is our first value.

This is not a word you commonly hear, but according to Merriam-Webster, it is "the activity or job of protecting and being responsible for something." By Stewardship, we mean protecting and taking responsibility not only for the family assets, but for other family members as well. Owning this responsibility is an approach to life that will reap great rewards, as well as give others great value.

Stewardship is infused in our Family Mission as well as in our money management. Family Financing works because we are all—and each—responsible for it. We will ask you to fulfill certain responsibilities, which you'll find in this letter. For our family's wealth to continue to grow and flourish, each person must fulfill their role. Those in future generations will do the same, which leads to our next value...

Sustainability is our second value.

When approached with a commitment to Stewardship, family wealth will be Sustainable throughout generations.

Did you know that the Vanderbilts—a family that was once the wealthiest family in the United States—lost the majority of their great wealth in less than two generations? Our family's wealth is very modest and could be quickly mismanaged and spent. Managed sustainably, however, it could theoretically last forever!

Your grandfather and I founded the Family Fund by contributing to it for many years. Your parents are also participants and contributors to it. Our entire family can benefit for lifetimes to come, as long as we keep contributing and maintaining it.

Productivity is our third value.

By productivity, we mean that Family Financing exists to allow each of us the ability to be more productive. There are many things that can enhance our ability to be productive, such as a good education, valuable experience, mentorship and following solid business and financial principles.

Money invested in skills, careers, homes and income-producing assets tends to offer a good return. Adult children who have access to funds to help them purchase a home, further their education or training, or become investors in cash-flowing businesses tend to do well in life. However, adult children who are simply *given* money to spend as they wish do not fare well. They end up becoming dependant on others rather than independent, productive people.

We established the Family Fund to give you the ability to be productive, and to create or build whatever you wish in your life. This is to foster independence, never dependence, on family money. Family Financing requires *inter-dependence* in the form of cooperation and communication. That's why we ask family members to contribute gifts back to the family by offering their talents, skills and leadership in service of the family.

Generosity is our fourth value.

We want to provide a means for our family to think and act beyond ourselves—to give back. This value was recently added and it is one we are still growing into. Our Family Fund is small now, with many "young" policies that are just starting to build savings. Someday, there will be healthy dividends, as well as substantial proceeds paid out as death benefits to the trust. A portion of these profits and proceeds will go into a Family Giving Fund. Family members will select and vote on non-profits that will receive donations.

The 4 Cornerstones of Family Financing

What we call the 4 Cornerstones is a visual representation of the Family Financing project that the Family Council put together recently. We share it again here because it is a wonderful reminder of the essential components:

Legacy	Leadership
Passing on money + knowledge	The Family Council
Family mission and values	Learning and growing
Traditions and memories	Serving and nurturing

Family Financing

Financial Foundation	Family Lending
The Family Fund	Borrowing and replenishing
Savings and protection	Funding for opportunities
Positive money habits	Investing in human capital

Financial Foundation: Your grandfather and I established this foundation by saving in our life insurance policies. Now we have a Family Fund—which is the trust that holds the policies. The Family Financing system ensures that this wealth is regenerated by teaching each generation to replicate what we have done. We have already started *your* policies... and someday, you will continue them!

Family Lending: This is our way of investing in your success. You can now apply for loans to fund opportunities. These might be opportunities to develop yourself—such as training and education—or opportunities to invest in your own home or business. (Of course, these opportunities must be productive so you can repay what you borrow!)

Leadership: Our Family Financing project grows people as well as dollars! Everything is designed to be a learning experience. You will continue to grow your confidence, knowledge and skills as you participate and serve through Family Retreats, the Council and other opportunities.

Legacy: If we only left you dollars in a trust fund, we would not be very good grandparents! Our hope is that we are leaving you with much more—with the knowledge and values to put dollars to their highest and best use.

Participation in Family Lending

You will have the ability to borrow against (and repay!) monies from the Family Fund. This capability is available to you, your siblings and cousins, as well as future generations. What do we mean by "participation"?

First, you are now welcome to attend Family Council meetings. We encourage you to do so! There's something to be learned in every meeting. You are eligible to vote on Council decisions starting now, if you feel ready to do so.

Secondly, after completing some simple requirements, you will be able to apply for Family Financing loans. This privilege comes with requirements, as anything of value comes with investment. The expectations are as follows:

- **Attend a minimum of one council meeting per year.** We always meet at the Family Retreat and at least two other times per year. (Virtual attendance is also possible if necessary.)
- **Read *The Richest Man in Babylon* by George S. Clason.** (There's no "quiz," but we will have some friendly questions afterwards as we will want to hear what you gleaned from the book!)
- **Read *Live Your Life Insurance* by Kim Butler.** This will give you a nice, concise overview of whole life insurance. (Again, we will want to know your takeaways.)
- **At eighteen or earlier, you will read *Perpetual Wealth* by Kim Butler and Kate Phillips.** This is a longer book that goes into detail about Family Financing. It's a good reference book that we have used to guide us many times.
- **Save a minimum of ten percent of your income.** That applies to odd jobs and all future employment. Right now, that will be in a joint savings account. Once you have obtained your first steady, full-time job, we will either set up a new whole life policy for saving (the premiums turn into cash value savings), or you may contribute towards the premiums for the existing policy we purchased for you. (Eventually, you will be gifted this policy and it will become yours.)

A few things to know about Family Lending:

1. **Loans are granted only to qualified family members, either immediate family or their spouses or children. Qualified members are 15 years or older, have read required books/ resources and are committed to saving 10 percent or more of income (if employed).**

2. **Family Lending provides a means for our family's savings to be leveraged by making loans to family members at reasonable interest rates. This might include such things as:**

   - Business loans, including loans for equipment, mentors, or specialized training.

- Loans for down payments on a first home or a cash-flowing investment property.
- First car loans for grandchildren without established credit.
- Loans for higher education, trade or certification programs.
- Anything that funds your dreams, honors our values and "makes sense" financially.

3. **Loans are not for lifestyle enhancements such as luxury or recreational vehicles, boats or vacations outside of any designated Family Retreats.**

4. **You'll find the process and application in our Family Documents (listed below).**

Family Lending is not an obligation... it is an *opportunity*. Even if for some reason you cannot participate in our Family Financing system, as family member, we hope you will always attend our Family Retreats. You can always vote on the next Family Retreat location and our future Family Giving Fund recipients! And... you'll *always* have our unconditional love and support—no matter what!

Family Lending Resources

The procedures for applying for Family Lending are outlined in an attached document. You will also receive an email with a link to a Google doc, as we periodically update procedures. *(Reader: See Chapter 11 for sample ideas on best practices for loans.)*

In addition to the books listed above, you will also find these and other Family Financing resources in our Family Google documents:

- "Family Lending Process" *(Chapter 11)*
- "Family Lending Application" *(Chapter 11)*
- "The Johnson Family Mission Statement" (although we know you have a framed copy in your room at the moment!) *(Chapter 10)*
- "The 7 Phases of Prosperity" *(Chapter 14)*

Family Financing Governance

Let me share with you the structure of the Family Council, so you have an understanding of how it helps to fulfill our values. This is information you will need when you wish to apply for a Family Financing loan, or when you fill your role on the Family Council, which is the decision-making body for our Family Financing project.

The Family Council meets quarterly (or as necessary) to discuss current loans, projects that are in line with the values and goals of our Family Financing vision.

Some specific guidelines for The Governing Body:

1. **The Governing Body will include: a President, a Secretary and Treasurer, along with a minimum of 2 additional qualified family members. We currently have a President (Grandpa John), Secretary (Cyndi) and Treasurer (Jackson) in addition to three Board members (myself, Julie and Sam).**

2. **The terms will be for two years. Choosing who fills the roles each year is determined, along with any other decision regarding the Governing Body, by a simple majority vote of all members of the family, age 15 and older.**

3. **Each family member age 21 and older is required to serve a term at least once every five years (more frequently if they wish and if there is a position to be filled**

4. **No compensation is provided for Officers or Directors other than food, travel, lodging or other expenses necessitated by Family Financing business.**

5. **At its annual meeting, the Governing Body will report to the entire family how it is achieving its goals.**

The Council also directs a separate Retreat Committee that plans the annual Family Retreat. Committee members need not be council members. The Retreat Committee works with the Council's budget and reports back to the Council. Retreat locations are nominated by the committee and decided by popular vote of family members age 10 and up.

Beginning next year, one-tenth of all policy dividends and life insurance benefits, if applicable, will be paid into a Family Giving Fund. A Giving Committee will be elected which will propose recipients for the funds. Family members age 10 and up will vote for the organization(s) to receive funds. A portion of the funds will be available as Family Grants for extended mission or volunteer work or sabbaticals with a proposed and approved purpose.

A lot love and effort has gone into the Family Financing project. We want the opportunities of financial capital, service and leadership to be available to all within the family for generations to come. We also wanted to reward those who were willing to put some "skin in the game," by purchasing their own life insurance, creating good habits in spending, and honoring our families values of Stewardship, Sustainability, Productivity and Generosity.

As you can see, there's a lot to digest! You will gain confidence about financial matters as you grow older and begin to progress through the 7 Phases of Prosperity. (See attached document.) *(Reader—next chapter.)*

Please don't hesitate to ask us questions, dear. We wish to pass on whatever knowledge or experience we have gained to you. We hope you will assist us in passing this knowledge and experience—along with your own wisdom—to future generations.

> Much love to you and your promising future,
> Grandma Carol

Our sample letter is written from a grandmother's point of view. It could just as well be written by one or both parents. The letter could even be an invitation signed by the entire Family Council. While each letter should be personalized, much of a letter like this can be used as a "template" to convey your family values and rules for participation.

Another idea could be to use *your* Family Mission Statement in its entirety as a way to discuss family values and how they relate to your Family Fund.

And of course, the age and all of the details are up to you. Feel free to borrow what is helpful and use your imagination and the wisdom of *your* Family Council to create the rest!

THE BOTTOM LINE

Family Governance exists to both help a family grow and develop its financial resources and its human capital. The structure for such governance can take many forms and can be simple or complicated.

Family Council officers and unofficial roles such as that of "Elder" can each fulfill a role and offer tremendous value to the rest of the family. Consider what structures and guidelines will best fit your family. Know that it will evolve in time.

Consider using a written document or letter as a formal welcome when children are old enough to participate more fully in Family Financing, such as attending council meetings and/or applying for loans. It can be personalized and updated as necessary.

It always helps to keep the important things top of mind: Family Mission and Values, Family Financing goals, Servant Leadership, and most of all— the precious people in your family.

CHAPTER 13:
Raising Financially Responsible Children

The Family Financing project had been a tremendous success in its first year. Every family member was now insured and every family had a system for saving. The first Family Retreat had been a hit! And the Family Council was off to an excellent start.

It gave Carol and John a lot of satisfaction to be able to invest in the success of their children and grandchildren. They also began to see positive changes in how the girls and their husbands managed their own finances as they started saving in their own cash value policies.

Still, they wondered if they were doing enough to help prepare the kids for their inheritances. How could they be sure that such gifts would be used wisely and not wasted? How could they be confident that inheritances would be helpful, not counterproductive or even harmful? After all, they had seen what had happened with their neighbors, the Jones family.

When both Mr. and Mrs. Jones passed away within a year of each other, they left millions to their adult daughter. Unfortunately, she did not seem to have any idea of how to manage this money for her own good. They watched as she quit her former job, purchased a fancy new car, and moved into the much larger family home her parents had left to her. She remodeled the master suite and kitchen with high-end finishes and added a big pool in the backyard. She took the kids on shopping sprees for clothes, new tech gadgets, or whatever they wanted. The family also went on 5-star vacations to Germany, France, the Bahamas, Singapore, and Hawaii… even a month-long Mediterranean cruise!

Unfortunately, there was no cash flow to sustain such spending habits. Even as her assets dwindled, she couldn't bear to tell her kids "no" if they wanted something. Predictably, it all came crashing down. The fourth year following her inheritance, the house with the fancy new kitchen, master suite and pool was in foreclosure. The woman ended up in an apartment and returned to her old job.

Even worse, John and Carol observed that as her children matured, they resented their mother for not thinking long-term with the inheritance! One graduated with a medical degree and a hefty six-figure student loan debt, while her other child struggled in his business, short on start-up capital and proper training. The fancy vacations, cars and sunny days by the pool had been nice at the time, but it really wasn't what they most needed to pursue their dreams and goals.

John and Carol didn't want their own family to make the same mistakes! They wanted their legacy to last generations. And thanks to the Jones family, they understood that no matter how much is given, if the receiver is not ready, it will be wasted!

John and Carol's daughters had never been spoiled. To tell the truth, when the girls were small, John and Carol didn't have much money to spoil them with! They had been very resourceful, babysitting and working odd jobs in high school, and earning their own spending money and even paying for their own (well-used) cars in college. However, now that they were grown with families of their own, they had greater capability. And while their boys weren't exactly entitled, it concerned John and Carol a bit to see how they expected their parents to spend money, which seemed to be part of cultural trends.

"Mom," Carol had heard her grandson James, ask her daughter, "I dropped my iPhone at Robby's house, and the screen is all cracked now! Can I just get the new iPhone? Robby has one and it's really cool!"

"I suppose we could do that," Julie had replied. "Though I do wish you'd be more careful with your phones! I think this will be your third phone in three years!"

"Thanks, Mom. I promise; I'll be more careful."

The grandsons were all between ages 8 and 13. They were all wonderful boys, but Carol recognized that there was room for improvement with their level of financial responsibility. And after watching what had happened with their next-door neighbors, the Johnsons, Carol wanted to nip all signs of entitlement in the bud.

John agreed—family wealth was not something to take lightly. It had great capacity for good, but if parents were used as piggy banks for every whim, the kids would never learn to "do for themselves"!

John and Carol began to discuss financial maturity and how to nurture it. How could they ensure the money they saved would be used wisely? What can a family do to cultivate financial responsibility? They could not assume that their daughters would automatically know how to encourage this quality. They examined what had worked for themselves and other families. Carol took notes on the best ideas she found and John offered his wisdom and feedback. They decided to plan a special mini-session for their daughters and husbands at the next retreat to share strategies that could help shape how their grandsons related to money.

Both families lived in very well-to-do neighborhoods, and some of their grandsons' friends came from families that seemed to have money for anything and everything. They drove brand new cars and spent school vacations at 5-star hotels and resorts. Yet, Carol noted, it didn't seem that their friends were expected to work or contribute. Housekeepers, landscapers and handymen did all the work around these neighborhoods, and the kids seemed to take a lot for granted.

"You know," John said to Carol, "I never want our family to forget the value of honest work. I'd still rather do my own gardening than pay someone else to do it."

"I know, honey," replied Carol. "I think it's high time we started discussing these things. Sometimes I wonder what expectations our grandsons might be

developing, or if they are being handed too much on the proverbial silver platter. We don't want to undermine their ability to be resourceful and independent."

"I found a good article on 'Raising Kids to be Financially Responsible,'" Carol added. *"I'm going to send it to the girls to get them thinking. At the next retreat, we can discuss the ideas and brainstorm together when we have our session for the 'adults.'"*

"Excellent idea," said John. *"I've been reading the whole series by* The Millionaire Next Door *co-author Stanley Danko. The books have some powerful warnings about doing 'too much' for your kids. Thankfully, our daughters have always been self-supporting, but I worry about what kind of moms they could be—they just give those boys anything they want!"*

"Now I realize, it's not enough to just give money to heirs… you have to prepare them to RECEIVE it!"

"Well put!" Carol said. *"I think I'll go print out that article now, and I'll print a copy for you, too."*

· · · · ·

Raising Kids to be Financially Responsible

> *"It is not what you do for your children, but what you have taught them to do for themselves that will make them successful human beings."*
> —Ann Landers

There is a saying attributed by some to Abraham Lincoln, *"You have to do your own growing no matter how tall your grandfather was."* This is especially true when it comes to money!

As we addressed earlier in the book, multi-generational wealth often fails within a generation or two, no matter how much money is transferred to future generations. It fails when the children—even if they are middle aged "children"—haven't done their own growing. Money given to someone not ready to hold it is like water poured into a leaky bucket.

Passing on assets successfully depends on the receiver's ability to manage and maintain those assets. And there are steps you can take to help prepare a child (grandchild, or great-grandchild) to be a good steward of money. Educating beneficiaries is one important step, as we'll discuss in a future chapter. But even the best estate planning attorney can only do much. This readiness is something that takes a lifetime to cultivate.

It's every parent's nightmare to raise a child who grows into a spoiled, dependent adult. Maybe you are willing and able to pay for your child's first car and college, or assist them in starting a business or buying their first home. But how do you ensure that your support doesn't stunt their financial ability and confidence? And if you are a "parent of means," how can you take measures to inoculate children from attitudes of entitlement?

Fortunately, there are many things parents (or grandparents) can do to help *prevent* children from growing up entitled. Let's look at thirteen ways to AVOID this problem and nurture self-reliant, money-savvy kids.

1. Talk about Money.

In *The Opposite of Spoiled: Raising Kids Who Are Grounded, Generous, and Smart About Money*, Ron Lieber says, "Every conversation about money is also about values. Allowance is also about patience. Giving is about generosity. Work is about perseverance."

Money isn't dirty, it's not shameful and you're not greedy if you discuss it! Yet if you DON'T discuss it, don't teach your kids about it, don't communicate about your intentions to transfer (or not to transfer) wealth to heirs, you're setting your children up to fail financially. (You also might be laying the ground for a family feud!)

A family is rarely served well by the old taboo, "It's not polite to talk about money." Discuss your own financial decisions and priorities. Discuss decisions you made in the past, when perhaps you had much less money than you have now. Talk about your giving, your budgeting, and your long-term intentions and goals with money.

You don't have to discuss dollar amounts of inheritances—it may be better if you don't, suggests Rick Randall of the National Network of Estate Planning Attorneys.[69] It's the *concepts* and the *conversation* that are important. These conversations help you prepare your children mentally and emotionally for an inheritance.

2. **Expose Them to Money Management.**

As Kim discusses in a Prosperity Podcast Episode, "Talking With Your Kids About Money,"[70] opportunities arise early to teach children about money, such as when they see something they want in a store. When our children ask us to buy them something, it can be an opportunity for us to educate them about:

Saving. Is there something that they want that is modestly priced? Give them an allowance (whether automatic or as a reward for extra chores), and teach them that they can save towards it. Ron Lieber suggests in his excellent book, *The Opposite of Spoiled*, to start with small allowances and give a "raise" each year on their birthdays. With children under 10, 50 cents to $ 1 a week per year of age is a good place to start.

Values and Priorities. Perhaps you don't personally choose to spend money on certain items, such as health-sabotaging junk food, violence-based games, or luxury apparel brands that cost five times more than comparable items without the label. Our spending is an important expression of our values, and it's instructive to let your kids know why you don't spend money on certain things.

Try not to default to "We can't afford it." That's an over-used phrase based in scarcity thinking. If an expense just isn't important enough to spend money on, say so!

Budgets/Spending plans. Educate children that adults don't spend "whatever they want." Rather, they have guidelines to ensure that they live within their means. Lieber suggests teaching the concepts of budgeting with younger children by having them split their money into three clear plastic containers: one each for spending, giving, and saving. This is, in effect, a first budget. With older children, perhaps envelopes or even different bank accounts can be used for different things.

Math. If they are old enough to do some shopping for themselves, let them add the cost of items and tax together to ensure they have money to pay for what they want.

Choosing Priorities. Let children make their own choices with limited amounts of spending money. Kate's daughter has managed her own spending since grade school, when Kate expanded her allowance to cover school clothes as well as lunches. The money still came from Mom, but she had to learn to prioritize lunches and other priorities before shopping.

Shopping for Deals. Kate: When my daughter started to pay for her own clothes, I was amazed at the deals she found! When I paid directly for the clothes, she would just ask for what she wanted with without looking at the price tags. When I gave her money to shop with, she made it stretch. She quickly learned to find discounts—even designer dresses—on sales racks. It built her confidence and also showed her a practical application for math.

Find opportunities for your kids to practice shopping for discounts. Perhaps they can help with grocery coupons or help you price something online.

Concepts of "No" or "Not Now." Just because a child wants something does not mean we should buy it! We can teach them to work towards what they want. Studies such as the famous Stanford Marshmallow study have proven that kids who can delay gratification will be measurably more successful in life.

3. **The Importance of Building Character.**

We need go beyond financial education. Financial responsibility isn't just about numbers or even about money; it's about *character* and personal *responsibility*.

A few years ago, the story of a 22-year-old college student who had blown through her college fund too early[71] was in the news. Her grandparents had gifted her a $90,000 education fund, and her parents had stressed it was for "classes only." But after spending a good chunk of money on shopping sprees and a trip to Europe, she had no way to pay for her senior year of college.

The young woman expected her parents would simply pony up more money for her, but they refused. That's when the young woman took her complaints to the airwaves in Atlanta, calling a radio show to complain about her stingy parents!

Although she admitted she saw the shortfall coming, she systematically shot down suggestions of how she might take responsibility to turn the situation around. Getting a part time job would be "embarrassing" and a school loan would be a hassle. Her parents told her they didn't have the money to help her—but she didn't believe that was true. "They're not being honest with me... my dad has worked for like a million years and they have a retirement account," she said.

Callers to the show called her a "spoiled brat." She was belittled on Twitter for giving millennials a bad name. Many listeners also blamed her parents... for raising such an entitled daughter!

Eventually, she came to an agreement with her parents: They'd co-sign a loan, but only if she got a respectable job.

"I know they're trying to teach me a lesson and blah-blah-blah and character-building, but I hope they realize that this could have such a negative effect on my grades and as a person," she said. "I won't be focused on my studies."

Perhaps she was majoring in entitlement?

Dr. Keith Ablow says the parents of the entitled college student who blew her college fund are also responsible for the situation, not because they didn't teach her accounting, but for not teaching her character! "When your child is behaving like this, you've got to look in the mirror and wonder why you could not pass your values along."

With some sympathy, Dr. Ablow acknowledges that it's tougher in this social media world for parents to impart the values they hold dear. Sometimes friends—who may have more money for vacations and clothes—are a greater influence than parents.

So how do you combat the influence of the culture on a child's character and sense of responsibility? Be a good role model and look for chances to impart important life lessons as well as financial lessons.

Our friend Patrick Donohoe is very successful in business, yet he is careful not to spoil his children. Patrick's wife grew up in Mexico in a cinder block home with a dirt floor. Patrick emphasizes, "She doesn't want her kids to go through what she went through, but she wants them to be contributing citizens, contributing people, as opposed to being entitled."

He believes the worst thing you can do with your kids is to give them anything they want—"stuff"—without asking them to earn it. And the best thing you can do is give them wisdom. "I try to instill values; I strive to be an example. I want to teach them so they can understand who they are and they can discover how they can improve not just their lives, but improve others' lives. If you are driven to improve other people's lives, your life is going to be improved."

4.   Give Them Responsibility.

Make sure that you are not "doing" too much for your kids, but encouraging them to do for themselves. Kim's sister has had her kids doing their own laundry since they were in grade school! (Taking responsibility for their own laundry also solved the problem of ruined and lost clothes.) Given the chance—or sometimes a little "push"—kids can do more than you think.

My (Kim's) kids are anything but spoiled, and have helped on the farm and been responsible for chores for a long time. They came home from college and helped us at home with a big landscaping project. Recently, my daughter spent several days working hard and cheerfully, helping her grandfather on home projects.

We've covered their college expenses, yet they truly do earn our support! I (Kim) don't tell my son or daughter that they "deserve" college tuition or other financial help—I say they have *earned* it! And that's because they have. They have always contributed to the household cheerfully, whether that meant helping with farm chores, working jobs to pay a portion of their own college costs, or pitching in wholeheartedly when another family member needed assistance.

5. Start Them Saving!

Wells Fargo found "71% of adults surveyed learned the importance of saving from their own parents. Despite this, only a third (36%) of today's parents report discussing the importance of saving money with their children on a frequent basis, with 64% indicating they talk about savings with their kids less than weekly or never."

When children want something that won't be covered by their allowance, such as a vehicle or a trip, teach them to save for it. Depending on their age and the saving project, this could include: giving them extra allowance for extra work, matching funds, assisting them with a mini-business (from lemonade stand to lawn mowing), encouraging them to get a part-time or summer job, or starting a fundraising campaign.

Saving money is its own reward, but it's also a habit that impacts a child's thinking in essential ways. Saving money teaches:

- Patience and perseverance: Good things come to those who wait—and save!
- Priorities: "Would you rather buy the $5 toy or put $5 towards the new bike?"
- Financial self-control: Discipline and delayed gratification translates directly into success.
- Resourcefulness: "Want the bike or a new iPhone faster? What could you do to earn money/save more?"

Family Financing should also be part of your family's saving strategy. We don't use policy loans for small things that we can save separately for, but policies are great for long-term savings. And for short-term savings (a bicycle, new phone), consider a money jar, envelope, or even a separate savings account (just make sure it doesn't have monthly fees that will siphon off your child's savings!)

6.   **Educate and Serve Outside the Classroom.**

As valuable as reading, writing and arithmetic are, no education is complete without exposure to those less fortunate and participation in service work. Whether volunteering in a soup kitchen or shelter, viewing documentaries about the third world, or taking a "vacation with a purpose," there are many opportunities to learn service, gratitude, and the bigger picture of the world.

My kids have learned both the importance of helping others and the inherent value of work... even when it is not connected to an hourly wage, such as through chores and volunteering.

In high school, my daughter Kaylea had an opportunity to travel to an impoverished part of South Africa with a non-profit organization, The Simuyne Project. This was a life-changing trip for her, one that gave her a completely new look at the world.

We don't do our kids a favor by keeping them sheltered—they need to experience the world for themselves and have a chance to understand the challenges, meet mentors, learn teamwork, develop compassion and make a difference.

7.   **Teachable Moments: Is Anything Really "Free"?**

When my daughter said that she would get a "free Gym membership" at college, I corrected her thinking so she understood it was not "free," rather, it was "included" as part of her rather pricey tuition package! Teaching children to think critically about costs and also advertising is an important part of parenting. And when they get offers for "0% credit cards" in the mail, they need to understand there is no such thing as free money.

The news headlines can also provide good topics for discussion. Is there such a thing as "free" healthcare and college? What could the impact be of dramatically raising the minimum wage or continually inflating the national debt? What kind of public policy leads to thriving businesses, and where do you notice businesses contributing to the public good? For this type of conversation with older children, you'll find some good resources at FEE.org,[72] the website for the Foundation for Financial Education.

8. **Encourage Earning.**

Some parents don't want their children to have to work until after college, yet that doesn't help children build the financial confidence that comes from earning. Start them as young as you can, whether hiring them in your work (which is also a good tax strategy) or encouraging them to help others—whether through a formal job, babysitting, lawn care—and receive pay in return.

Kate saw her daughter, Maddie, journey towards independence smoothly after holding part-time jobs since the age of 15 in her father's catering business and local farms or restaurants. While her friends were racking up big college debts, Maddie paid for her own living expenses while her family covered her college costs. Later her daughter earned her own money, then transitioned rather seamlessly into paying for her own rent, car expenses, and food when she moved out.

Kim's kids are grown and her son, her eldest, has graduated from college. He now works in fundraising, earning money through helping others make meaningful gifts. At an age where many young adults are spending every penny, he is saving steadily for his future through two whole life policies of his own.

Another of our team members, Mimi, home schools her children and includes them in her business. They help out as virtual assistants, and one of Mimi's daughters has helped at our annual event for advisors three years in a row. Many home-schooling families are quite entrepreneurial, and it's fabulous to see families earning together!

Earning is an absolute essential step to any child becoming financially independent. Always let your kids know that you believe in their ability to earn and to have what they want, just resist the temptation to always be the one who gives it to them! Never underestimate your own child's resourcefulness when they want something bad enough and you don't simply pony up and give it to them. As they build confidence and skill in earning, they may surprise you. "Kid entrepreneurs" are on the rise and many of them have built million-dollar companies. As a FEE.org article on child entrepreneurs[73] suggests, it's easier to think outside of the box when you don't know the box exists!

9. **Teach Financial Consequences.**

Part of letting kids do their own growing means you don't shield them from the consequences of their mistakes or failure to follow through. Children must be allowed to learn from their experiences and mistakes.

In an episode of The Prosperity Podcast,[74] our friend Patrick Donohoe describes family loans with young borrowers that did not get paid off as planned. What happened? There were consequences!

"We do nice things with the kids, but if they want stuff, I never say no. I say 'Okay, of course!' and we set up a family intra-banking system. They have to borrow and figure out a way to make payments. And I've repossessed ipads, bikes... and there's tears, but if you just give stuff to your kids, you do a huge disservice."

Patrick admits that his methods and opinions aren't mainstream (and we do give our kids gifts), but it's important to hold kids to financial agreements that they make. Whether your kids are 5 years old or 50, teach them that if they don't follow through on an agreement, they won't be bailed out!

Of course, Family Financing is an ideal financial strategy to teach kids of all ages the cause and effect of money realities! Learning to borrow money and pay back loans is a valuable skill that teaches discipline and responsibility. And while you'll also want your kids to build their credit rating when they are old enough to do so, the advantage to Family Financing is that they don't have to "qualify" at a bank, which gives much more flexibility. (Last we checked, our bank wasn't loaning 15-year-olds money anyways!)

Remember that even "negative" consequences can make for *positive* lessons about how money works. It's not mean—it's part of life to learn that causes have effects! After all, what child learns to walk and then run without falling down a few times in the process? In the same way, you've got to allow your child the possibility of failing. Let them take a loan for something they want, even if you're not positive they can pay it back. Just be prepared to stick to the rules if they've bitten off more than they can chew.

Of course, the "consequences" of actions can be positive, too! Some parents link allowances to chores. Sites and apps like Allowance Manager and FamZoo can help parents assign and track chores and allowance. Other parents provide financial rewards for good grades or positive efforts with homework, sports, music practice or other goals.

10. Foster Independence.

In *The Cycle of the Gift: Family Wealth and Wisdom*,[75] the authors tell the importance of allowing children to "pay their dues" and make their own way in the world. For instance, you don't do a child a favor by hiring them for positions in family businesses for which they are not qualified. Sometimes it is better to let them earn their experience elsewhere first.

Children of any age that are repeatedly rescued, subsidized or promoted without earning it lose the ability and confidence to help themselves. Often, they live beyond their means without a clear sense of responsibility or the value they bring to the marketplace. And they will keep coming to the "Bank of Mom" (or Dad) for their next financial fix.

Thomas Stanley, author of *The Millionaire Next Door, The Millionaire Mind,* and other books, calls such financial gifts "economic outpatient care," and is adamant that such gifts usually backfire. The research gathered from many interviews with millionaires shows that the more a child is given, the less they tend to save, and the less financially responsible they end up being.

The fundamental lesson that Stanley repeats again and again in his books is this: *If we want our children to be self-supporting, we have to stop supporting them.*

11. Trust Is Earned.

We feel strongly that children should not be spoiled just because their parents (or grandparent or uncle) can afford to do so. This does not build trust—it only builds expectations and entitlement!

Yes, our kids have been given much. We have helped them in many ways—financially and otherwise. One day, they will inherit more. We are confident they will be ready. They have earned our support and, most importantly, our trust.

The Ultimate Gift is a movie about an entitled young man who ends up being the sole beneficiary of his grandfather's fortune—if only he can prove to his Trustees that he can be trusted with the money. The journey ends up being much longer, more difficult and more rewarding than he imagines—in more ways than one.

Trust is built a step at a time. A child doesn't graduate from learning to manage a $5 allowance to managing a multi-million dollar inheritance. Start small, go slow and keep building. As they learn to manage their own money, they will someday be trustworthy with yours.

12. Cultivate Gratitude and a Prosperous Mindset.

Gratitude is the *opposite* of entitlement. It is directly opposed to the bad habits you pray your children don't adopt at any age: whining, demanding, bragging, jealousy, shaming of self or others, or demanding "I want it now!" like Veruca Salt, the famously spoiled girl in the original *Willy Wonka and the Chocolate Factory*.

Gratitude is perhaps the most essential part of a broader mindset rooted in prosperity. And to THINK from a prosperous mindset is the *first* of our 7 Principles of Prosperity™! (We have written more about the principles elsewhere, such as our previous book, *Financial Planning Has Failed*.) The relationship of gratitude to lifetime success and happiness cannot be underestimated.

You'll want to establish family traditions and model a grateful attitude to help your children become habitually grateful. Some things we do in our family and also in our business:

- Begin meetings, family gatherings and conversations with a positive focus. Have each person share something happening in their lives for which they are grateful.
- Establish a morning and/or evening routine that includes gratitude journaling or sharing with a gratitude partner or group.
- Always look for the "silver lining" and the positive side of a challenging situation. Sometimes asking what you are *learning* through challenges can help show you the positive.
- Follow Shawn Achor's 5-step formula for happiness. Positive Psychologist Shawn Achor has a fabulous TED talk about this topic, and we've outlined his 5 steps in an article on ProsperityEconomics.org titled, "Happy Wealth."[76] The first two steps involve writing down three things each day for which you're grateful, and spending an additional two minutes journaling about a positive experience each day. This retrains your brain to scan for the positive first!

Thinking from a Prosperous Mindset determines how we handle our money. The Parable of the Talents (generally interpreted through a "spiritualized" lens), has much to say about investing. In this story, a wealthy man leaves for an extended trip, entrusting three different servants with his assets. The first two double what is given them through investing wisely, but the third is fearful and buries the money, claiming that he was afraid to make a mistake, thus, he chose to keep the money safe by *not* investing it.

Of course, that was the wrong strategy! The master was furious. "That's a terrible way to live! It's criminal to live cautiously like that! If you knew I was after the best, why did you do less than the least? The least you could have done would have been to invest the sum with the bankers, where at least I would have gotten a little interest."
—*The Message*[77] *(translation of the Bible by Eugene Peterson)*

A scarcity mindset leads us to handle our money fearfully, timidly and ineffectively. It leads us to cling tightly to every dollar, thinking that we are keeping it safe. But in reality, our tight hold eliminates growth, prevents profits and even takes opportunity out of our hands. Thinking abundantly increases the flow of our money by allowing us to use it in multiple ways, not simply "bury it" or lock it up to slowly accumulate interest.

This, of course, is the foundation of Family Financing: putting money to USE!

This chart demonstrates some of the differences between Prosperity Thinking and Poverty Thinking:

UNBELIEVABLE THINKING

Poverty Thinkers	Prosperity Thinkers
Focus on cutting costs	Brainstorm ways to increase income
Reduce involvement	Work on self improvement
Stop dreaming	Set attainable goals
Decrease motivation	Celebrate baby steps
Hoard cash	Keep money moving
Paralyze their decision making process	Trust that crises=opportunity
Hold back constantly	Move forward in some form
Complain	Give gratitude
Seek outside approval	Build internal confidence

22790 HWY 259 SOUTH • MT. ENTERPRISE, TX 75681 • T 877.889.3981 • F 602.532.7915
www.Partners4Prosperity.com

How do you THINK? Is your mindset aligned for prosperity and abundance? To download a book, video and recording that describes all 7 of Partners for Prosperity's Principles of Prosperity, go to Partners4Prosperity.com and sign up for our Prosperity Accelerator Pack.[78]

13. Practice Generosity.

Whether through tithing to a church or donating to charity organizations, having children donate a portion of their allowance or participate in family donation decisions is a powerful way to teach them discipline and values. "This can be as simple as having children divide their allowance into three jars marked 'Spend,' 'Save,' and 'Share,'" says Ellen Remmer, vice president at The Philanthropic Initiative, Inc., a nonprofit consultant.

According to author Thomas Stanley, the habit of giving can also make them *more* likely to acquire wealth! His research for books such as *The Millionaire Next Door* led him to conclude that the discipline required to tithe and give is the same discipline needed to budget and spend wisely. It's also well documented that givers do better in business, and in building networks. So perhaps it should be no surprise that the biggest givers do just fine, not in spite of their gifts, but perhaps because of them!

Generosity should be a way of living and also a habit. Your family may also wish to use policy dividends or a portion of proceeds from death benefits for philanthropy. Structured, planned giving provides a powerful use of family assets as well as a unique opportunity for family members to work on a project that will leave a lasting mark. It's a powerful strategy for making a difference as well as bringing the family closer together around a common goal and purpose.

THE BOTTOM LINE

Wealth education starts young—and it's not all about dollars and cents! Children who grow up to be responsible with money are typically exposed to money management early in age-appropriate ways. They are given responsibility, taught independence, and allowed to learn from their mistakes.

Teaching about money can happen formally and informally. Whether it's a Family Council meeting to discuss Family Financing, a conversation around the dinner table, or a response to a "teachable moment" in real time, take advantage of the myriad of opportunities to help your children become financially aware and responsible people—no matter their age.

Building character is essential and paying dues is important. Parents who try too hard to protect children from financial failure often disempower them by giving them money. Rather than subsidizing children, instead model a prosperous mindset, gratitude practices and generosity. And of course... saving! Help your kids become savers, too, and they'll be on their way to self-sufficiency.

CHAPTER 14:
The 7 Phases of Prosperity

The second family retreat was a bit different from the first. In addition to family-led activities and lots of sharing and bonding, a special guest was invited to speak. Jerry Lee, John and Carol's financial advisor, came on Saturday to make a presentation on the 7 Phases of Prosperity. John and Carol spoke highly of him and the girls had gone to him for assistance with the new policies. Yet at the same time, John and Carol noticed their families were still following a lot of typical financial advice that might not be the best for building long-term wealth. It was time to get everyone on the same page!

"I'm grateful that Jerry was willing to come and speak about the 7 Phases of Prosperity," John told the gathered group in his introduction. "I'm grateful because this stuff works, and our family is proof of it. Coming from the banking world, I thought I knew all I needed to know about money, but Jerry's guidance and advice has done so much to grow and secure our family's future!"

John had everyone's attention.

"I'm also glad Jerry's here because he truly is an expert, and I know you'll have great questions that Carol and I won't be able to answer," John said with *a smile, even though everyone knew they were no slouches when it came to finances.*

Carol added, "I'm grateful for Jerry because I consider him a true friend of the family. It can be HARD to talk about money, but he has made it easy. Remember what we've learned—generational wealth can only succeed with long-term thinking and strategies, effective communication, and cohesive family vision and values that gets us all rowing in the same direction."

"If these retreats were your idea… Thank you, Jerry!'" declared James, as some scattered applause and smiles broke out.

"We have a good start by putting whole life policies for each of us in place, but now Jerry can show us how it all fits with the Big Picture," said John.

"I would encourage each of you to take notes and also jot down any questions," added Carol. Oh—and I almost forgot, you boys—the grandkids, I mean—you're free to go play games or start the campfire after Jerry goes through the first phase, unless you'd like to stay and learn more. The big thing for you to focus on in your teens is simply developing the right mindset and habits. Jerry and the Council will help you with the rest when it's time."

The grandsons nodded and made plans to build a fire as it got dark. Sheldon was eager for the opportunity to put his scouting skills to the test.

"S'mores in 90 minutes!" Ellie called out, after confirming the schedule with Cyndi.

Jerry smiled. He truly enjoyed the Johnson clan, and was honored to be the warm up act for a family campfire. And what a gift it was to have a family so committed to building wealth together! He felt such gratitude as he positioned his white board and got out his notes on the Phases of Prosperity.

. . . . .

"Do This, Be Wealthy!"

While the following seven phases are no substitute for individual finan-cial advice, they offer ideas and "best practices" for wealth-building. Based in Prosperity Economics thinking, they are intended to serve as a general guideline for a lifetime of prosperity.

You'll notice that the recommendations run counter to much typical financial advice. This is no accident, as these seven stages are the "antidote" to typical advice that—as we outlined in chapter one—can *sabotage* long-term wealth.

Prosperity Economics offers an alternative to typical financial advice and "money as usual." Strategies often include alternative investments and real estate investing as well as whole life insurance to store cash, provide protection and create liquidity for investments or Family Financing.

A note about the 7 phases: You might not "fit" the age range of each phase as far as capability, and not every step or strategy will necessarily be a match for your family. Use it as a starting point, or as a challenge to see what might be missing from your family's financial picture. You may be 50 years old and just getting serious about saving or buying a home. So be it—it's much better to start now than never! What's most important is not the age or the details, but how the strategies are *sequenced* to build wealth *synergistically*.

Phase 1: Building Prosperous Habits

Typically age 20-29

This is the time to set yourself up for a lifetime of success. Establish positive habits, start saving and put protections in place to avoid losses. Most importantly, start building—building up your savings, building equity in a home, building your own traditions and values. Many young people spend a decade or two consuming and acquiring debt, then another decade digging out. These steps will get you started right. Don't worry if you can't do everything or can't do it perfectly, focus on what you *can* do, and build from there.

- Develop a separate "emergency/opportunity" fund with 3 months of living expenses.

The first thing you should do when you start working is create an emergency fund. This will become your Family Fund as it grows, eventually providing cash for investments as well as unexpected expenses.

For now, your emergency fund should be in an account where the money is easily accessible when needed, such as an account at a bank or credit union. Preferably it WON'T be connected to your checking account so it won't be tempting to spend it. Do not get an account with monthly fees; they can drain your savings. If your bank pays next-to-nothing on savings, check out online banks such as Ally, Synchrony, Discover, or Alliant Credit Union.

- Save 15-20% of your income into a Prosperity Flow-Through Account as soon as you have your emergency fund set aside.

A Prosperity Flow-Through Account is a checking account set up separately for control and tracking. It's used only for transactions that relate to your financial and economic growth—your savings, life insurance premiums, disability insurance premiums, outlay for investments and cash flow from investments. It is not for household expenses, emergency monies, vacations and other spending.

A Prosperity Flow-Through Account prevents the commingling of funds and gives you a clear picture of the cash flow in your personal economy. It provides a financial case history carried forward from year to year and a monthly financial statement documenting all transactions.

Can't find 15-20% of your income to save? Start where you can, even if it's just 5 or 10%. You may need a higher paying job, or you may benefit from tracking what you're spending to help you see where you cash is going. Tools such as YNAB.com (You Need a Budget) or Mint.com can be helpful. (Soon we will also have a Prosperity Economics finance tracking software that will be even better, as it will be able to integrate cash value savings and help you measure assets and liabilities more effectively.) Ultimately, if you are able to establish excellent savings habits, you won't need a budget!

The key here is to start SAVING before investing. Young adults get talked into saving in a 401(k) before they have savings, and then they have no liquidity for emergencies or opportunities. The other common challenge is over-spending, especially when a young person has friends with more income than they do. Defining needs vs. wants and developing discipline will lead to success!

- Buy term life insurance equal to 15-20 times your income with 30-year term.

This may seem like a lot of life insurance at the time, but they key here is that you want to lock in your insurability and aim for your "Human Life Value," rather than using needs analysis. (See Chapter 7, "12 Things to Know about Life Insurance for Family Financing.")

Half or more should be convertible term insurance—convertible to whole life. (We can help with this, contact Partners4Prosperity.com.[79]) This protects your insurability. If your parents or grandparents started a whole life policy for you, you might be expected to take over payments once you are self-supporting.

- Obtain property and casualty (car and home or rental) insurance, health insurance (or health insurance alternative, such as the medical bill sharing ministry that Kate uses and has written about on our blog, see "Medical Cost Sharing Plans"[80]) and possibly disability income insurance.

Raise policy deductibles as your savings grows. Deductibles should be as high as you can handle. With all car and home insurance, it's better to have a larger deductible than to scrimp on coverage, such as liability coverage and PIP (Personal Injury Protection). If you are renting a home or apartment, add renter's insurance to your car insurance.

- Purchase a home when you can afford to do so.

Ideally, you should be in a position where you don't anticipate moving for a few years, or would be prepared to rent out your home if you did move.

Obtain a 30-year mortgage and put no more than 20% down. Expect that your payment may be higher than renting for now, but realize that long-term, renting will cost more while producing no equity or asset. You can also rent out a room or "Airbnb it" if the home has extra space and a desirable location.

For more on buying a home including a buy vs. rent analysis, see the "Savvy Homebuyer's Guide" chapter in *Busting the Interest Rate Lies*.[81]

- Consider starting a 401(k) or other retirement fund.

Once your emergency fund is in place, you are saving regularly, and you have a home down payment (if buying a home is a possibility for your situation), then it's time to start your retirement account. (Most people begin this too early in the sequence.) If you have the capability, contribute to retirement plans *only* up to the "match" level—the contribution amount your employer makes matching contributions on. We prefer a Roth 401(k) or Roth IRA as those provide tax-free growth *and* tax-free distributions.

- Manage debt wisely, avoiding consumer debt.

Apply for one or two credit cards or store cards and use sparingly to establish credit. (For instance, finance a laptop or household appliances and pay off ASAP.) Pay cards off monthly; resist holding "revolving" debt on credit cards.

Pay the minimum on mortgages, focusing on saving elsewhere rather than prepaying "cheap" or efficient debt.

Pay the minimum on student loans unless the cost of money (interest rate) is 8% or higher, or unless student loans are preventing you from purchasing a home. We prefer you focus on building savings.

- Finance cars with the least expensive cost of money.

Car financing will vary according to the type and age of car, as well as your credit and qualifications. Depending on the circumstances, the lowest interest rates could be a credit union, bank loan, dealer financing or a life insurance loan. (Beware of dealer financing for new cars—you're usually better off finding your own financing so you can get a cash rebate!)

See Kim's book *Busting the Interest Lies*[82] for information on saving money when purchasing a car, also our article, "Drive Away with a Deal."[83] And if you live in a city where Uber and public transportation abound, consider carefully whether or not you need a car... you might not!

- Get a simple will.

We'll have different recommendations for you as you grow assets along with potentially, a family, but for now, simple and "done" is your goal. Kim got her first will from an office supply store for $35. You can do this online through websites such as RocketLawyer.com, LegalZoom.com or LawDepot.com. Another good way to get a simple will is through Legal Shield, which can prove to be helpful in other ways as well. (Note: these are *not* substitutes for a proper estate planning process—only easy ways to get something in place temporarily.)

Phase 2: Creating Capital

Typically age 30-39

Continue your good habits and build your financial foundation. Even if you are a family of one at the moment, this is the perfect time to build long-term savings, begin investments and establish permanent insurance. What you begin now will pay big dividends later.

- Start to convert the term life insurance to whole life insurance. Or purchase your second, third or fourth whole life policy if you don't have term insurance.

You can do this bit by bit, policy by policy as your income grows and you have the capability to save more. The goal is to have $10-20k in savings and the rest of your Family Fund in whole life cash value.

When you convert term life to whole life, you are also *transitioning* much of your savings to whole life cash value. This gives you tax-advantaged growth, increased privacy, and other benefits mentioned earlier in this book.

Aim for 3-12 months living expenses in your emergency/opportunity fund at this stage, depending on predictability of income and comfort level. Your cash value will eventually become a large emergency/opportunity fund that can be leveraged as needed, as well as an ideal wealth transfer vehicle.

Maximize your Paid-Up Additions (PUA) rider to maximize cash value. When you have the ability to save more, consider other Whole Life policy riders that offer additional protections such as Waiver of Premium, Critical Illness and Long-Term Care riders.

- Purchase whole life insurance on children, if applicable.

Cash value will typically grow more quickly on a child's policy, and it becomes part of your family's liquidity and emergency/opportunity fund. Some parents use it as a 529 replacement to save for college because of its greater flexibility, safety and ability to borrow against it, if desired.

- Build your Prosperity Flow-Through Account to $25,000 and beyond.

There are excellent investment opportunities (we think of these as "real investments") that require $50k minimums. Without saving lump to invest, people end up investing only in mutual funds and stocks, which is terrible asset allocation and leaves them subject to systemic market risk. Building ample savings and liquidity allows you a wider range of investments.

- Apply for a home equity line of credit (HELOC) to bolster your emergency/ opportunity fund.

This allows you to utilize the cash in your Prosperity Flow-Through Account for investments and still have the capacity to respond to financial emergencies or opportunities. (Never use home equity for speculative investments. It can make sense to "borrow to invest," but only in opportunities with predictable outcomes.)

If you purchased a home with a small down payment or if the market has depreciated, it may take time to build sufficient equity to obtain a HELOC.

- Consider purchasing rental property if it positively cash flows.

  As you build your whole life cash value, that can be a good source for the down payment. You will typically need at least 20-25% down payment for non-owner occupied properties at reasonable rates.

  If you "move up" to a different or larger home, consider keeping your old home as a rental if it would have positive cash flow. You can potentially "season" funds (putting in the bank for 60+ days) from your home equity line on your current home to use for the down payment on your next home.

- Make emergency preparation an annual priority.

  Use a tool such as TheTorch.com[84] to communicate the many things that someone would need to know to navigate your life should something happen to you. Also, make it your business to find out how to manage your parents' affairs, should something happen to one of them. Know where accounts and keys and passwords are, how to pay the mortgage, find medical records, etc.

- Continue all other strategies from Phase 1:

  - Purchase a home if you have not yet done so. (Don't get stuck in the rent trap! It's difficult to build wealth when 20-40% of your income goes towards rent and is lost forever.)
  - Consider more convertible term life insurance as your income and assets grow.
  - Adjust car and home insurance deductibles upwards if appropriate.
  - Continue to fund your 401(k) or similar to match level only.
  - Manage debt wisely, avoiding consumer debt.

Phase 3: Parenting and Projects

Typically age 40-49

Often times this is a phase in which you are using the capital you've built, as you continue to also build more. If you have kids with school sports and activities, you'll find that kids are expensive (but worth it)! Or perhaps you have "fur kids" (sometimes they are expensive, too!) and other projects that keep you busy. Some people start businesses or become real estate investors in this phase.

These are excellent years to begin new saving and investment vehicles that will pay dividends for decades to come. And if you have followed the strategies outlined thus far, you will have access to new types of alternative investments that can dramatically accelerate your wealth-building.

- Consider life settlement funds for your IRA and/or long-term money ($50,000 minimum.)

  Life settlements are one of our favorite investments, yet you may not have even heard of them! They cannot be purchased from typical brokerages but are available for accredited investors. (Net worth $1 million or income of $200k/year, $300k for couples.)

  By this time, you have probably built your 401(k) to the point where you can do a self-directed IRA. We recommend life settlements for long-term growth investments because they are backed by life insurance companies and not subject to stock market risks. (Contact Partners for Prosperity for more information at Partners4Prosperity. com/contact.[85])

- Use bridge loans or other private lending investments for cash flow ($50k minimum).

  Private lending is simply loaning out money in exchange for an agreed-upon return. Bridge loan investments are typically secured by real estate and used as temporary financing to purchase or develop real estate. Mineral rights leases also function in a similar way, secured by business interest and equipment. You'll find some generalized information about bridge loans and mineral rights leases on the Prosperity Blog at Partners4Prosperity.com/blog.[86] You can contact Partners for Prosperity at Partners4Prosperity.com/contact[87] for further education.

- Take the cash flow from investments and convert term life insurance to more whole life insurance.

- Continue to start whole life policies for children and/or purchase new policies for yourself.

- Continue to maximize paid-up additions/use dividends to purchase more PUAs.

- Work with your kids to devise a way to pay for college.

  If needed, consider using life insurance loans or home equity to help with college tuition. We don't recommend 529 plans for a number of reasons, including market risk and limitations due to rules and restrictions. It is more efficient to build up assets you can borrow against that will continue to earn or grow rather than save money in a 529 plan that has only one use.

- Purchase additional rental properties.

- Continue to fund your 401(k) to match level only.

- Continue to manage debt wisely, avoiding consumer debt. Do not prepay mortgages; focus instead on expanding assets and investments.

- Update wills and trusts as needed, as well as your family's TheTorch.com[88] or Everplans.com[89] account or other emergency preparation system.

Phase 4: The Expansion Years

Typically age 50-59

At this stage of life people are often "hitting their stride" in their profession or business. If you have children, they are typically more independent by now. You may be feeling the pressure to double down on saving and investing, especially as the typical retirement age approaches. We encourage people to "rethink retirement" and continue to contribute and earn for as long as possible. Nevertheless, this is a great phase to be productive. So focus on your finances—just never to the detriment of your health or relationships. Maintain balance and treasure all that life has to offer.

- Skim the profits off bridge loans/private lending and investment real estate to buy more whole life insurance on yourself and/or your children.

- Borrow against the whole life for private lending deals (with appropriate due diligence and caution).

  Borrowing at a low interest rate and lending at a higher rate is a primary way that banks make money. You can leverage your cash value by taking policy loans or by using cash value as collateral at a bank, which may give you a better rate. Never borrow against cash value for speculation, only a reliable investment based on a contractual agreement for repayment.

- Use the cash flow from bridge loans to pay off whole life loans or home equity lines of credit.

- Reinvest gains from life settlement funds.

- Use whole life dividends to pay off loans/lines of credit if necessary.

  It is best to pay off loans out of your income as that allows your dividends to buy PUAs, which is essentially reinvesting them. However, you never want to let life insurance loans sit and accumulate interest year after year.

- Consider more cash flowing real estate investments.

- Update wills, trusts, beneficiaries and your family's emergency preparation as needed.

Phase 5: The Transition Years

Typically age 60-69

At this phase, your focus may be transitioning from your current career to what you will do "next." It's a time for new choices about how you want to live and work—or contribute, if you will. This could include volunteerism, new hobbies, a new career or business, freelancing, consulting, cutting back to part time, or retirement. Some people use retirement income from one career to transition into something else. You might retire from traditional work to spend more time managing investments, if you enjoy it. Some people retire to become more actively involved with grandchildren and hobbies. This is also a popular time to buy second homes and expand travel horizons.

During this phase, the biggest financial challenge is preparing for potentially *decades* of future inflation. Just 3 percent inflation will turn $1,000 of expenses into *over $2400* in 30 years. (See calculation using TruthConcepts.com[90] Future Value calculator.) In other words—things will be MUCH more expensive at age 95 than age 65!

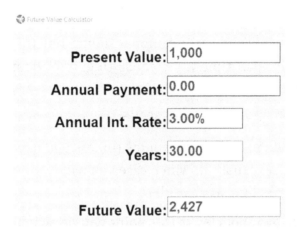

Retirees also may not be prepared to pay for extra help they might need around the house and yard, or the significant expense of future assisted living or long-term care. That's why we all need to stay productive and prepare to live to 100—or beyond!

- Keep working at least part time.
- Continue to build a life settlements portfolio and bridge loan/private lending portfolio.
- Pay off all whole life loans.
- Keep paying whole life premiums.
- Consider purchasing whole life insurance on grandchildren.
- Update estate plan and emergency plan as needed.

Phase 6: The Wisdom Years

Typically age 70-79

During this phase, many people retire from traditional work if they have not already done so. (We recommend you stay productive!) With or without work, this is an active time of life. People in this age group spend more time reading, cooking, socializing, and tending to house and garden than the rest of the population, according to USNews.com, "How Retirees Spend Their Time." Staying healthy is a priority for wise seniors, as is spending time with grandchildren. Those who are well-prepared financially are often engaged in philanthropy, perhaps serving on a non-profit board of directors, rallying others around causes or volunteering.

- Keep contributing and earning money doing something you enjoy—perhaps part time work, consulting, freelancing or as a "senior-preneur."

- Start taking dividends from whole life in cash.

- Stop paying life insurance premiums (unless you have investment income above expenses in which case you will want to keep paying premiums for as long as possible).

  Ideally, your own policies at this point will be switched to "paid up." This change can be made typically after about 10 years of payments with maximum PUAs or 18-20 years without PUAs. (Contact your company or advisor to set this up.) Of course, you'll likely want to pay into a policy for much longer as it is your savings!

  If you have policies with adult children or grandchildren as the insured, they can assume payments and you can transfer ownership to them so they can keep making the premium payments, or you can keep them for yourself if you'd like to continue to control and utilize the asset.

- Enjoy spending the cash flow from bridge portfolio, private lending and real estate investments.

- Continue to skim the profits from life settlements for enjoyment or reinvest into cash flow investment vehicles. (A life settlement fund is a 7-10 year commitment.)

- Spend down IRA and other qualified retirement money before other assets for tax-efficiency. (You can download a special report that demonstrates the importance of sequencing how you spend your assets, *Permission to Spend: How To Spend Your Principle, Save a Fortune on Taxes, Increase Your Cash Flow... and Never Run Out of Money!* at ProsperityEconomics.org/permission.[91])

- Update estate plan and emergency plan as needed.

- Even if you are healthy and active, get all of your ducks in a row legally and financially so that should something happen to you, the family will be prepared.

Phase 7: The Legacy Years

Typically age 80-100

Opportunities to spend quality time with children, grandchildren and the little ones (great grandchildren and beyond) become more precious than ever. Pew Research polled senior citizens and found their most treasured pastime was spending more time with family. Relationships are highly valued at this age, and 90% of respondents said they speak with a family member or friend on a daily basis.

No longer in a rush, there is time to learn as well as teach. There is also time to focus on what you are leaving behind, from treasures and stories to family recipes and (hopefully not) an attic full of clutter. Staying active at this age is the key to health and longevity.

- Spend down tax-deferred assets such as traditional retirement accounts (assuming you have other assets/income).

- Develop exit strategy on rental homes. An outright sale, inheritance or Charitable Remainder Trust are all options. (A Charitable Remainder Trust allows you to donate a rental property or other income-producing asset, avoid the taxes a sale would create, and still benefit from its cash flow while you are living. You can download a special report on this strategy at BustingTheRealEstateInvestingLies. com.[92])

- Continue taking life insurance dividends in cash and enjoying income from bridge loans or other private lending investments.

- If additional cash flow is desired, consider:

- An immediate annuity. You can annuitize all or part of a whole life policy, which will produce more cash flow than dividends alone at this stage of life. (Be aware your policy's cash value, death benefit and living benefits will go away.)
- A reverse mortgage or home equity conversion mortgage (HECM). This converts your home equity into a line of credit or an income.
- Selling a life insurance policy if you have been diagnosed with a terminal illness. If your policy is desirable to investors, they will pay you more than your cash value for it. A family member may also be interested in purchasing the policy if they know you intend to sell it.
- Part-time work or freelancing. We have known many people who remained productive—and earning—into their 80s and beyond. (See GrowingBolder.com,[93] an excellent resource.)

- Update estate plan and emergency plan as needed.

- Allow the family to help you downsize your possessions, clear your basement, attic or garage. Pass treasures to heirs while living, or donate them to charities.

- Record memories, wisdom, advice and family stories to be archives for future generations.

THE BOTTOM LINE

Your financial foundation starts with good habits that build savings and protection. Continue with building equity in a home and taking advantage of 401(k) plan matches.

As liquidity grows, purchase non-correlated growth investments and assets that produce cash flow. Your ultimate goal is *not* building the biggest net worth possible. It is having cash flow you can rely on for your expenses. By sequencing your savings and investments and following Prosperity Economics principles, you'll be able to reduce your taxes, increase control over your assets, and have greater financial certainty.

CHAPTER 15:
Wills, Trusts and Wealth Transfers

What will happen to your assets?

So you're not a billionaire. You may not even be a millionaire—or not yet. If you are financially secure, having provided adequately for your future, you'll probably be leaving something for someone. The question is: who? Here are the usual suspects that will end up with your money:

- **The federal government.** The less estate planning and financial strategizing you do, the bigger Uncle Sam's cut will be of the assets intended for your heirs. For instance, even with modest wealth transfers, heirs will pay income taxes on distributions from inherited traditional IRAs and 401(k)s.

- **The state.** Each year, billions of unclaimed assets are surrendered to the state after the rightful owners cannot be contacted. These include bank accounts and CDs, dividend or payroll checks, life insurance policies, retirement accounts, stocks, bonds, and safe deposit box contents. (We'll share some of our favorite resources for preventing this in the next chapter.)

- **Heirs.** Typically a spouse and then children and/or grandchildren will likely be beneficiaries of an estate. Nieces, nephews, siblings and friends are also often included in wills. (Believe it or not, pets can also named as heirs. Increasingly, trusts for "fur children" are included in estate plans.)

- **Non-profits.** Charities, foundations, churches and colleges and donor-advised funds[94] are also common recipients of bequests.

If you don't determine what will happen with your assets, *someone else will.* And if you are part of the 60% of Americans who don't have a will, we urge you to change that right away. Contacting the National Network of Estate Planning Attorneys[95] or obtaining a recommendation from your financial advisor is a good place to start.

Wills and Trusts: What's the Difference?

People sometimes ask, "Should I have a will or a trust?" Yet the two really go hand-in-hand, along with an estate planning process from which both the will and trust emerge.

A will directs who will receive your property at your death and appoints a legal representative to carry out your wishes. *Wills* are necessary in that if you don't have a will (or a trust) then the state and the courts will decide who get what because you die intestate—a term that indicates there is no will.

One main difference between a will and a trust is that a will determines what happens only after you die, while a trust can go into effect as soon as you create it. A trust can be used to begin distributing property before death, at death or afterwards.

You can create a trust at any time while you are still alive and competent. Most trusts *include* wills, and wills can also create trusts.

A trust that is formed while its maker is still alive is a living trust, and the person who forms it is referred to as a grantor, trustor, founder or trustmaker. A trust that came into existence upon the death of its maker is called a testamentary trust. A testamentary trust must go through probate in order to get assets into it, so you can see the advantage of a living trust.

In their classic book, *Loving Trust: The Right Way to Provide for Yourself and Guarantee the Future of Your Loved Ones*, co-authors Robert A. Esperti and Renno L. Peterson point out that will planning is really death planning. Living trusts, in contrast, can deal with lifetime issues. Unlike wills, living trusts deal with all of your property.

(Note that "living wills" are sometimes confused with living trusts. A living will determines a person's medical treatment in circumstances in which they are no longer able to make decisions for themselves. It does not deal with a person's assets or property.)

While we provide some general information here as well as a bit of education regarding how trusts pertain to Family Financing, it's important to add this caveat: we aren't estate planning lawyers and don't give legal advice! Our best recommendation is *to meet with an estate planning lawyer*. You will be much better served by personalized help than general advice or cookie-cutter forms. (If you aren't already working with someone, we suggest contacting the National Network of Estate Planning Attorneys through their website at NNEPA.com.[96] See further information about the Network and Rick Randall, Chairman of NNEPA, at the end of this chapter.)

That said, something is better than nothing and "done" is better than perfect. If your situation is fairly simple and/or you're likely to procrastinate due to budgetary or other concerns, you can create at least a temporary will with do-it-yourself forms through LegalZoom,[97] Nolo's Online Will,[98] Quicken's Willmaker[99] or the Tomorrow.me[100] app. (Yes, there's an app for that!) If you have children and/or significant assets or any sort of complex situation, we recommend using an estate planning attorney. Just don't delay getting a will if you don't currently have one. It can always be updated or replaced, which typically happens multiple times over a lifetime.

. . . . .

John walked in the house with two bags of groceries, fresh from "hunting and fishing" at the grocery store, as he liked to say.

"I talked with Sylvia today," said Carol. "We set up an appointment for next week."

"Excellent! I know we're probably overdue to update our estate planning strategies, especially in light of the Family Financing system we've employed."

"Yes—speaking of which, Sylvia confirmed what Jerry had told us—that we can change the ownership or beneficiary of a life insurance policy to a new or different trust at any point in time. And there may be some good reasons to do that..."

"Oh really?" said John, pausing as he placed the broccoli in the vegetable drawer. "Give me just a moment to put the day's catch in the fridge."

Sylvia was John and Carol's estate planning attorney. She had assisted them with updating their will and beginning a trust several years ago when they acquired their first rental home. Now with the Family Financing project well under way, it was high time John and Carol revisited their wealth transfer strategies in more detail.

As John settled into his chair at the kitchen table, Carol continued.

"Well, Sylvia confirmed that the revocable trust we have now might not be the best solution for asset protection. It doesn't provide us with much creditor protection should a lawsuit be levied against one of us."

"She thought we might benefit from a different type of trust... probably not instead of, but in addition to, as there are pros and cons to various strategies and structures. And apparently, there are ways to set up an irrevocable trust so that they actually do have some flexibility."

"Got it. Well, I'd definitely be interested in learning more."

"Also, we have a living trust, which is the most common type of trust. And in recent years, something called a 'Spousal Lifetime Access Trust,' or SLAT, for

short, has become popular. She can explain the reasons for that when we meet with her."

"I've heard of those, but couldn't tell you much about them. I do know that we're no longer in any danger of exceeding the federal estate tax exemption with the new limits! So you can check that off the list of things we have to be concerned about."

"What are the new limits?" asked Carol.

"Currently here in 2019 with the new tax plan, the exemption is $11.4 million for individuals and twice that for couples."

"Yup—don't need to worry about that... I'm pretty sure that's a tax bill for a different zip code!"

"No doubt," John chuckled. "But did you know that if we ever made good on our threat to live out the rest of our days on the Oregon coast... Oregon would take a slice of everything over one million?"

"Ouch! I'm not sure easy access to the Sandcastle Contest would be worth that." said Carol. "But I'm not leaving the kids anytime soon!"

"I know, Dear. Neither am I. But in ten years... who knows where we—or the kids—could be!?"

"Yes—and I guess that's the point, our estate plan has to allow for contingencies and future possibilities. Even the higher estate tax exemptions could possibly get rolled back, I suppose. But there's a 100% chance of our grandsons growing up! So that's a possibility we will have to prepare for."

"Right now, the girls are our beneficiaries after we both go since the boys are so young. Plus, we never really came to a conclusion about what instructions or stipulations we would put into place if the boys were our direct beneficiaries. But that is just a temporary solution."

"Agreed—it's probably time to name the grandsons in our will—with specific instructions for the trust to make sure they will be treated equally in an inheritance. I mean, just because our daughters will receive equal amounts doesn't mean the boys would benefit equally."

"And of course, we don't want them to receive too much too soon. And maybe we need a 'no Ferraris' clause for Sheldon!"

"Adding to the list!"

"Perfect; I'm glad you set this up, I think we have more to talk about than I realized."

"Sylvia's office has also just updated their beneficiary education process. That's something we should get the girls and their husbands involved with."

"Absolutely! And updated or not, I know we've got to be continuously having conversations with the big kids so they know what we've set up... and making sure they are prepared in an emergency."

"I have to say... I think our Family Financing project has gone a long way towards facilitating that. And you know... it's not too early for them to start their own trusts."

"You are absolutely right," said John. "Actually, I think Jackson got some simple revocable trusts for the new whole life policies he and Julie started. But we need to do a deeper dive on this topic. Do you think perhaps Sylvia would speak at our next Family Retreat?"

"I don't know... but I'll let her know there will be free S'mores in it for her!"

"That's a deal if I've ever heard of one! Plus... she'll get a chance to spend time with the most awesome family ever."

"Hard to put a price on that!" smiled Carol. "I'll add it to the list of 'Sylvia' topics."

. . . . .

Wealth Transfers 101

A trust is a legal arrangement through which one person (or an institution, such as a law firm), called a "trustee," holds legal title to property for another person, called a "beneficiary." Often, a trust will have two types of beneficiaries—one that receives income from the trust during their lives (such as a spouse) and another set that receives whatever is left over after the first set of beneficiaries dies (usually children or other heirs).

There are living trusts, revocable trusts, irrevocable trusts, dynasty trusts, incentive trusts, asset protection, charitable, special needs, spousal lifetime access trusts, and many of other types of trusts, plus many combinations thereof. A revocable living trust is sometimes referred to as a "family trust."

But before we drill down to further detail, let's get a bigger picture of trusts—the 30,000 foot view, if you will. There are several things you should understand—or not misunderstand—about trusts and estate planning.

One misconception about trusts is that they are often assumed to be only for "rich people."

It's true that they are an effective way to avoid probate or estate taxes, but not many people have estates taxes these days, and there are many ways to avoid probate. Still, trusts are something that almost everyone should consider. They are widely used by middle class couples and families as well as the affluent, and regardless of where you place yourself on that continuum, if you're reading this book, they're probably for you.

Secondly, a trust is optional in many cases.

While a trust is useful, it is *not* necessary to have a trust in order to obtain a whole life insurance policy and start your Family Fund. While we routinely suggest considering having a trust own and be the beneficiary of a life insurance policy, it is not always practical. If you are starting to save $100 or $200 per month in a life insurance policy and have little in the way of assets, an estate planning process may be premature. Get a simple will done (see suggested resources a few pages back), designate beneficiaries for your bank accounts, keep your life insurance beneficiaries updated and pat yourself on the back that you are off to a great start!

When a trust is not optional: If the beneficiary of your policy is a minor, we *strongly* recommend you have a trust in place. A life insurance company will not pay death benefit proceeds directly to a minor. If you have not created a trust or made legal arrangements for someone to manage the money, the court will appoint a guardian—at no small expense—to handle the proceeds until the child reaches 18 or 21, depending on the state. (Alternatively, YOU could designate a guardian in advance who would receive and manage the funds... but we strongly prefer a trust.)

There are two other problems with having a court make decisions. First, the judge will have to approve investments if paid to a minor. Second, your child could end up with a lump sum payout at too young of an age. Gradual or limited payouts over a longer period of time allow the beneficiary a better opportunity to become a good steward as they mature. Thus, it's critical to have a trust for family control and appropriate instructions!

Third, be aware that rules, laws and protections vary state to state.

Protections against creditors vary state to state. Some states have inheritance taxes and others have estate taxes—sometimes with a lower exemption than the federal estate tax. A wealth-transfer strategy that makes sense in Florida or Texas might not make sense in Oregon or Connecticut. And advice found on the internet—even from reliable sources—might not be accurate for your location or situation. Our friend Rick Randall reminds us that "Standard" rules of thumb must be considered in light of state law.

> "In some states the client LOSES protection by transferring property to a living trust as opposed to naming the individuals protected by state law. In those states, the importance of creditor protection must be balanced against the other advantages provided by the living trust during lifetime (disability access/instructions) and after death when proceeds are paid out and when the living trust becomes irrevocable (creditor, divorce, remarriage, illness and instructions)."

Still, Rick says most clients opt for making the trust beneficiary after weighing the pros and cons.

Fourth, don't confuse a trust or estate plan with a mere legal document.

A trust is, primarily, a *relationship* that is formed when someone "entrusts" their money to a third party who—sometimes rather uncomfortably—stands between the trust and the beneficiary of the trust. This third party, the trustee, is responsible for making sure the money is managed or distributed as the Grantor of the trust intended.

The trustee also owes a fiduciary responsibility to the beneficiaries, so they are tasked with acting fairly and honorably towards both parties. However, it can be much more complex than simply "following instructions." The relationship between trustee and the beneficiary has been compared with that of an arranged marriage—a complex and delicate personal and legal relationship in which both parties may be virtual strangers who did not choose each other.

Fifth, almost anyone can be a trustee. (But not everyone should.)

Other than being an adult of sound mind and body (a trustee should be around for awhile, ideally), there are no special qualifications to serve as a trustee. Of course, they should be "trustworthy," as it is their job to make sure the trustmaker's wishes are honored and the rules of the trust are followed. A trustee can be a family member, a friend, or an individual or an institution with no beneficial interest in the trust, such as a bank or trust company, a professional trustee, an investment advisor, accountant or lawyer. Sometimes co-trustees are chosen, such as two family members, or perhaps a family member and a lawyer or professional trustee.

Trustees are sometimes characterized as an antagonist to the beneficiary, especially when great wealth is represented. Unfortunately, that can be the reality. James E. Hughes, Jr., Esq, author of *Family Wealth*, argues that both beneficiaries and trustees are often to blame when the relationship goes awry. Hughes builds a compelling case for why and how the trustee should act as a *mentor* to the beneficiary in his enlightening essay, "Trustee as Mentor."[101] Hughes's publications are most useful for very high net worth families, but his points should be well-taken that beneficiaries as well as trustees have responsibilities, and relationships already based on communication, mutual respect and trust produce the best results.

There may be wisdom in giving the beneficiary some influence in the choice of a trustee, when that seems appropriate. In many situations—such as when the beneficiary is a grown, responsible adult—the trustmaker will provide for the beneficiary to be a co-trustee—or even his or her own trustee! While not the most usual arrangement, this can make a lot of sense.

Sixth, estate planning is a process—not a document.

In addition to being a relationship, a trust should be the result of a *process* in which a trusted professional engages in inquiry and education as well as legal advice and representation. Too many people are focused on just getting a trust *document* they perceive will protect the money—preferably as quickly and cheaply as possible. Yet it is actually the *process* with the estate planner, and the *relationship* between the trustee and beneficiary, that will determine if the trust succeeds according to its originator's intentions. Properly done, the process facilitates participation and communication from both trustees and beneficiaries.

Finally, beneficiary education and preparation is a critical piece of the estate planning process.

Too often, parents and their estate planners spend much time, effort and money constructing an estate plan. Unfortunately, this plan exists on paper—not in people's lives—and it remains under lock and key until a death or disaster happens.

Then, when heirs are in grief and shock, they are given instructions on what to do next. *This is the worst possible moment to try to educate beneficiaries.* People do not learn or absorb information well when a loved one passes.

This is why we do drills. Fire drills, evacuation drills, and other disaster drills. You've done drills since at least elementary school. We do drills so that when an emergency actually happens, people know how to respond to it. They have practiced their response and they can act even when under stress or pressure.

Perhaps this sounds morbid—but we need "death drills" to prepare beneficiaries, trustees and other helpers. Yes, you should give instructions. But don't stop there. Periodically remind people and ask, "Now, if something should happen to me, what will you do? Who do you contact? Where will you find the necessary documents?"

When your children are minors, if something happens to you, they will not be in charge of handling your finances or your affairs. Other adults will handle these matters—and those adults need to be prepared. Then, the older your children are, the more they need to know.

Of course, passing wealth successfully isn't merely a test of a beneficiary's ability to contact the right people in an emergency. Beneficiary education happens throughout a lifetime, in both formal and informal ways. This book gives you an excellent head start on various ways that families can communicate about money. A good estate planning attorney will continue that process.

Utilizing Trusts for Perpetual Wealth

Trusts often serve multiple purposes. A trust can be a vehicle for holding and growing wealth or a tool for disbursing money (lump sums or income streams). They can last for generations or be put into place for a very specific time and purpose. Often, properly constructed trusts preserve and protect wealth from creditors and predators—folks like divorcing spouses, medical bill collectors for end-of-life illnesses, not to mention, in many cases, the IRS.

Some trusts also aim to protect beneficiaries from themselves. One way a trust might do that is to ensure the beneficiary does not receive more wealth than they can manage at too young of an age. Another way is through what's commonly known as incentive trusts. This is a trust that "incentivizes" certain behavior, for instance, requiring a beneficiary to have a full time job in order to receive disbursements from the trust. (We'll review some pros and cons later in this chapter.) In extreme cases such as drug addiction, a trust may be combined with a guardianship or provide for an independent trustee to ensure an inheritance does not endanger the well-being of the beneficiary.

There are many different types of trusts, some of which we mention below. These are not necessarily exclusive. For instance, you could have a living trust that is also a revocable trust and that functions as an incentive trust and a special needs trust.

Revocable Versus Irrevocable

There are two kinds of living trusts: irrevocable and revocable. With an irrevocable trust, the maker cannot change the trust instructions after he or she has signed the trust. With a revocable trust, on the other hand, the maker can change the trust or even cancel it at any time—for any reason. After the maker has died, however, a trust cannot typically be either revoked or changed.

There are pros and cons to each. In general, we are believers in revocable living trusts. People change, and it is best to leave your options open—and change the trust accordingly, if you so desire. However, a creditor with a judgment can demand money from a revocable trust, and there is little recourse. You can protect trust assets from creditors or predators much more effectively with an irrevocable trust, as long as the trust was not established in order to defraud a creditor.

The most common type of irrevocable trust would be a marital or family trust created by one spouse for the other. Upon death, the proceeds go straight to the beneficiary and creditors of the policy-owner cannot stop this. (If the beneficiary has a creditor, however, proceeds transferred in individual name are fair game for creditors.)

Is there a way to get "best of both worlds?" Perhaps. As NNEPA's Rick Randall explained in a Prosperity Podcast episode,[102] "Estate Planning with Rick Randall," there is a creative and perfectly legal approach by which even irrevocable trusts can be changed by a trusted third party, even after their death, in accordance with their intent. This is accomplished through the appointing of a *trust protector*, who ensures that the intent of a trustee is indeed carried out, whether they are still living or not. The protector can act according to the trustee's wishes in many ways, such as replacing a trustee who is found not to be trustworthy, changing investment strategies to address economic upheaval, or altering other provisions of the trust, according to written instructions provided by the trustee during the creation of the trust.

Such a trust, properly drafted and maintained, can provide personal protections. Lawsuit creditors can be held off, marital division in many states can be "controlled" so that bloodline distribution and not division in a later divorce is achieved. Provisions protecting the proceeds in the event of remarriage of the beneficiary can be included. Through the trust protector, in many states the proceeds can be protected from Medicaid spend-down in the event the beneficiary has a long-term illness.

Also keep in mind that you may have more than one trust. Therefore, a portion of your assets can receive the potential protection granted to irrevocable trusts, while another portion of assets could be placed in a revocable trust.

When it comes to asset protection, the basic rule of thumb is this: You cannot use a trust to avoid your own creditors. So if you establish a revocable living trust, where you are both trustee and beneficiary, creditors can get at your assets. If you die, however, leaving the assets of that trust to your children as the beneficiaries, creditors no longer have access to the trust's assets. The critical difference here is who set up the trust on whose behalf. If the trustmaker and beneficiary are different people, the assets can be protected.

This principle can also be used for big medical bills at the end of life. Children, for example, can set up a trust for their parents so medical creditors cannot take all the assets in the trust—assets the children placed there. Parents, likewise, can establish living trusts for their progeny thereby protecting whatever assets are in the trust from creditors and predators. (But remember: Your other assets are fair game.)

Life Insurance and Trusts

Life insurance—often combined with trusts—is a common strategy to protect and preserve wealth. In general, we recommend policies be owned in trust and be payable to trust. (Again, this is an option but not a requirement.) If a trust is the beneficiary of a policy, the death benefit or other inheritance is paid into the trust, which can then disburse funds to—or hold funds for, depending on the circumstance—beneficiaries.

Properly drafted, access to the cash value is the same for living trust owned policies, and for irrevocable trusts, it can be accessed easily for health, education and (the big one) maintenance. These are very liberal standards if a family-controlled trusteeship is used, which is generally recommended.

Spousal Lifetime Access Trust (SLAT)

A great tool for couples using Family Financing strategies is the SLAT. Each spouse creates an irrevocable trust for use and benefit by their spouse. The husband can reach and use the cash value of the wife's policy and vice versa through the health, education and maintenance standards. Some families allow only the beneficiary spouse to access funds during his or her lifetime while children and grandchildren benefit after the beneficiary spouse's death. Other families structure SLATs to permit distributions to the beneficiary spouse and children simultaneously.

A SLAT allows all the advantages of the irrevocable trust protections, without compromising access much at all. Protection against disability and divorce can be added in case a problem arises with one or both spouses during their lifetimes. The SLAT allows for personal protections while the grantors are alive, including creditor protection. This is important in states such as North Dakota which has a very low creditor protection limit. (It is the trust itself that provides the lifetime protection, not the state law.)

Wealth Replacement Trusts

Sometimes combined with a charitable remainder trust strategy, a wealth replacement trust replaces all or a portion of assets given to charity by purchasing life insurance. For example, perhaps the grantor would love to make a sizeable gift to their favorite charity or university, but they don't want the gift to negatively affect the heirs within their family. A wealth replacement trust can be used to purchase life insurance to *replace* the money (or property, securities, retirement account or other assets) gifted to charity.

There can be significant tax benefits from this strategy, especially when donating appreciating assets to charity. Then when the grantor passes, their heirs receive an inheritance in a similar amount as what was gifted to the charity. The insurance carrier pays the tax-free death benefit to the trust, which replaces the assets donated. The trust can now use that money on behalf of the grantor's heirs, the beneficiaries of the trust.

You can use a similar idea with Family Financing strategies to ensure *Perpetual Wealth*. When a family member passes and the death benefit is paid into a trust, the trust can be instructed (or the beneficiary can be encouraged or required) to use some of the proceeds to purchase new policies on the beneficiaries (or their heirs).

The ability to add instructions to the receipt of the proceeds is one of most obvious advantages of trusts, yet it is often overlooked. The beneficiary can be encouraged or required to get certain training, help from trusted advisors, or save and invest proceeds in a certain manner.

We suggest such encouragements and instructions are best received when they have been previously discussed. Heirs are frequently eager to honor the wishes of their dearly departed, though it helps if they are not blindsided by expectations that may be perceived as limitations on "their" assets.

Incentive Trusts

Some parents fear that their own child or grandchild is likely to blow through their inheritance "Prodigal Son style," spending until it's gone rather than using the money wisely and investing for the future. Therefore they attach "incentives" to the money, rewarding heirs for behaviors such as staying in school, maintaining employment, carrying on the family business or staying drug-free.

There are pros and cons to incentive trusts. It's true that money can be a motivator, and there's also no doubt that many young people aren't capable of wisely handling sudden wealth. Yet, beneficiaries of incentive trusts tend to be resentful that the grantor is using money to "control them from the grave." The role of the trustee in this case becomes more of a babysitter than trusted advisor, which can add to the strain.

Should incentives or conditions be put in place, care must be taken that the terms are adequately defined and flexible. One trust recipient obtained seven degrees to satisfy conditions of an incentive trust that required him to "stay in school." He was sixty years old, yet never held a job! Similarly, if the beneficiary must remain employed according to the terms of the trust, could this prevent a beneficiary from successfully starting their own business, taking maternity leave or retiring to volunteer work following a career?

If an adult child has shown signs of concerning behavior, we can understand why a parent may put conditions on the money. It may be better to focus on beneficiary education and finding a trustee who can function as a mentor to the beneficiary. Ultimately, you know your own children. And context matters, such as age, experience, and the amount of the gift.

This might be something you discuss directly with them, sharing your thoughts or proposed solutions with them. If children feel like they have input, they are more likely to feel like their parents have partnered with them to serve their best interests. And you never know what a conversation will unearth! Sometimes, the beneficiary may suggest a solution the parent hasn't thought of—a solution they will be able to take ownership of.

If you have read this far, you probably understand how Family Financing nurtures the human capital of the family and could make an incentive trust moot. By building trust between family members, and confidence in beneficiaries, they can grow into family members who can be trusted with wealth.

The Beneficiary Checklist

One final but important detail… There are a handful of critical mistakes we see people make when it comes to naming beneficiaries. Follow these seven rules to avoid unintended consequences!

1. **Always keep policy and beneficiaries up-to-date.**

    Often estate plans are updated only once a year at most. But when there is a death, divorce or other major change in the family, don't wait!

    Also note that while some companies allow you to change a beneficiary online, other companies might require paperwork to be signed and sent back.

2. **Always have secondary and tertiary beneficiaries.**

    Let's say your spouse is your only beneficiary. What happens if you and your spouse are in an accident and neither of you survive? You would want to make sure there are other beneficiaries. An ideal beneficiary would be a trust that would receive and disburse the death benefit to other heirs and/or charities.

3. **Never name minor children as beneficiaries without a trust in place as the beneficiary.**

    (Don't even think about it!) The insurance company would be unable to distribute the funds to a minor and it would end up in the courts.

    A trust (or at the very least, a guardian you appoint) will need to be in place to distribute monies after the child is old enough to receive the funds. Depending on the amount, you may want several disbursements over a period of years to phase in control over assets as they mature.

    If hiring an estate planning attorney[103] to put a trust into place isn't a possibility for your current budget, one temporary solution is to put a simple trust into place yourself with Tomorrow.me[104] (an app created by lawyers).

4. **Never name your estate as your life insurance beneficiary.**

This subjects the life insurance proceeds to probate, creditors, and potentially taxes. Again, a trust can be a good solution.

5. **Always specify the details.**

When you name beneficiaries, don't just say "my children." List names, Social Security numbers and addresses/contact information. Don't make the insurance company launch a search.

Want to distribute proceeds equally to multiple heirs? When naming multiple beneficiaries, specify whether you want the money divided per capita (per head) or "per stirpes" (by branch of the family). Example: You have three children. Your first child has no children. Your second has two children. The third has four children. All of the children are minors and cannot currently receive proceeds. Do you want your three children to receive equal amounts, or do you wish for each grandchild to also receive equal inheritances to be distributed later? There's a big difference.

6. **Never name a beneficiary dependent on government assistance as a direct beneficiary.**

A financial inheritance can disqualify a disabled or otherwise dependent person from receiving benefits. Instead, you can create a "special needs trust" to support a special needs child or dependent without disqualifying them from receiving assistance.

7. **Don't assume your will trumps the life insurance policy.**

The life insurance company will pay proceeds to the beneficiaries you name on your policy. If you intend to make changes, you must make the changes with the life insurance company. A will or trust won't override the beneficiary designation on the life insurance policy.

Trust-worthy Help

Whether you decide to utilize a living trust or a testamentary trust, and employ a revocable trust and/or an irrevocable one, we recommend going through an estate planning process, such as the one implemented by attorneys who are part of the National Network of Estate Planning Attorneys (NNEPA). You can contact the Network through their website at NNEPA.com,[105] or you can call 1-800-638-8681. Rick Randall, the Chairman of NNEPA, has been very helpful with our clients and with this book, as well as helpful to us personally with some of our own questions as well. Rick knows attorneys throughout the country and also runs his own private firm with two other attorneys: Randall Law Offices. If you need an attorney in a certain state or focused on a certain practice area (such as eldercare law), he can help you find a good match.

Another worthwhile resource that may prove to be helpful, particularly for trustees and beneficiaries, is the book, *Trustworthy: New Angles on Trusts from Beneficiaries and Trustees*, which contains 25 short stories of relationships that went right—often after some initial challenge. The book could also be instructive for founders or anyone with a role on a Family Council.

If you need help with a life insurance policy, contact Partners for Prosperity through our website at Partners4Prosperity.com/contact,[106] by emailing us at hello@Partners4Prosperity.com[107] or give us a call at (877) 889-3981 ext. 120. We are happy to provide a quote in the form of an illustration, answer your questions, and (if you like), get your policy started!

THE BOTTOM LINE

Wills and trusts go hand in hand and are both important estate planning tools. It is best to go through a process with a professional, although "done" can be better than "perfect" if you do not have a will. There are apps and affordable options for those with few assets and simple estates.

Trusts are a useful tool that can enhance *Perpetual Wealth* life insurance strategies. A living trust can be the owner and beneficiary of a life insurance policy (unless a SLAT—spousal access lifetime trust—is preferred). After a death benefit is paid, the trust distributes (or holds) the life insurance proceeds according to the wishes of the grantor.

Trusts are either revocable or irrevocable. Revocable trusts are the most flexible, but do not offer the same asset protection as irrevocable trusts. Trust protectors and SLATS can provide greater flexibility for irrevocable trusts.

You'll want to make decisions that address your concerns and priorities with the advantage of expert advice. State laws vary, as do families. Avoid common mistakes when naming beneficiaries and update your estate plans when there are major changes.

CHAPTER 16:
Leaving the Legacy You Intend

Wills, trusts, paperwork, policies and processes... sometimes Family Financing was technical, even complex, at times. The Family Retreats always put things in perspective. After all, the reason John and Carol went through the paperwork and process in the first place was for the people they loved most.

Momentary frustration with an estate planning decision or a life insurance application passes. For John and Carol, what remained were the memories and the satisfaction of watching their family—and their family's legacy—grow and flourish. All the temporary inconveniences and learning curves were all worth it to see the family grow in love and devotion and support each other in fulfilling dreams.

After each retreat, Carol would include her favorite memories of the retreat in her gratitude journal. Labeled, "What I want to remember about this year's family retreat," she would list the things—big and small—she never wanted to forget about the days they spent together.

For now, she kept these memories to herself, although she knew she would one day share them at a future Family Retreat. Beginning with the 10th annual retreat, she would read her highlights from a decade earlier.

Today, Carol entered these entries in her journal about the third annual Johnson Family Retreat that had just come to a close:

What I want to remember about this year's Family Retreat:

The way the grandson's faces lit up when they saw Uncle Paul.

The "oohs and ahs" and obvious delight expressed by all at this year's scrumptious annual "Thanksgiving in June" dinner.

The gratitude shared around the table, and the thought that went into the acknowledgement of each family member.

The announcement by the Family Council (and the excitement afterward) that the Family Fund had grown this year by a record $100,000... and then some!

The first report of the Family Giving committee. The research presented by John and the grandsons about the non-profits, and the pride I saw in our daughter's faces as they listened.

The earnest discussion and vote that followed to select our first three non-profits to receive Family Giving funds. The realization that I will likely live to see our family make a "six-figure difference" in the world through our giving!

The badminton game in the yard... the laughter and delight, the friendly competition, the miracle "winning shot" by Cameron.

Our video conference with Phyllis and the wonder of watching her interact with her great-grandsons across the miles. (And I'm so grateful we thought to record that on Zoom... what a precious video to have for all time!)

Watching the way that the grandsons have come to trust and rely on the aunts and uncles, and watching Cyndi, Julie, Sam and Jackson become true mentors to them.

The day we spent at the lake picnicking, swimming, hiking and enjoying the beauty of Colorado. The photos Ellie took that perfectly captured the day.

Spontaneously singing and playing the Hokey Pokey before breakfast.

The presentation by Syvlia and the way she made it relevant to the entire group. The "Q and A" that followed and the conversations that went long into the night around the campfire later.

The way the concept of "legacy" is expanding in this family.

. . . . .

The Elephant in the Room

According to the consulting firm Accenture, boomer parents will be distributing about $30 trillion to their millennial descendants over the next 30 or so years. While it would seem that the subject would spark some lively and important inter-generational discussions, quite the opposite is true.

A 2014 study from Wells Fargo revealed that the most challenging topic to discuss with others is personal finances (44%). The second-most challenging topic was death (38%). Politics (35%), religion (32%), taxes (21%), and personal health (20%) ranked as less difficult.

Martin Halbfinger, a private wealth manager at UBS Wealth Management, outlines four main reasons why families are hesitant to discuss the $30 trillion elephant in the room:

- Parents are resistant to disclosing their financial affairs to their children and other heirs.
- People tend to avoid discussing the uncomfortable subject of death at almost all costs.
- Parents don't want their children to know what they might receive in case it causes friction between siblings.
- They are concerned about how their children handle money and hesitant to create expectations.

Families sometimes find it very challenging to discuss financial topics. However, when money can be discussed openly and lovingly without blame, shame or manipulation, it is a relief to all.

Of course, before you can discuss your estate plans with the family, you have to decide them for yourself. A few rules of thumb:

First, make sure that your own needs are met.

The greatest gift you can give your children is your own independence. Parents may be tempted to neglect their own needs in favor of their children's. For instance, parents have paid for children's college expenses, only to become dependent on their children in later years when challenges arise and they have not taken care of their own needs first.

When most commercial airliners take off, the flight attendant goes over the emergency procedures. If the cabin loses pressure and the oxygen masks pop out of the ceiling, we are instructed to secure our own mask and start to breathe normally BEFORE we help someone else with their mask. The point is that you can't properly help someone else until you've seen to your own needs first.

This bit of advice applies to estates as well. Your own health care and long-term living expenses must be provided for first, and you can't predict your own longevity or future health care or caregiving needs.

Remember that your assets will remain *your* assets to use as long as you need them—and don't be afraid to communicate this fact clearly with heirs. Your legacy gifts will be just that—gifts. They are not "legacy obligations." Your first responsibility is to secure your own financial oxygen mask.

Second, communicate clearly—not necessarily specifically—with your heirs.

Despite the reluctance of parents and children to discuss the inevitable, such communication is essential. Mark Accettura, a Detroit area elder law attorney, notes that while "estate planning is not a democratic process," parents should let their heirs have a sense of their financial situation.

Atlanta Financial Psychologist Mary Gresham is a proponent of having a family meeting around the issue. These meetings are a great forum for going over instructions on where important documents are kept and who to contact should you pass away. This is also the perfect time to discuss your intentions and any questions your beneficiaries have about how assets might be distributed.

No matter how well-intentioned, avoid setting up unrealistic expectations. While you should definitely discuss money matters with children, it is best to not lead them to assume all assets will be "theirs" someday. Take care not to make promises that cannot be guaranteed. Refrain from committing certain assets or dollar figures to heirs.

Focus on the big picture of your intentions, not the specific numbers. Always qualify that your heirs will receive assets when you no longer have need for them, and that unforeseen expenses can arise. You always want your children to be saving and investing for themselves—not waiting for an inheritance to remedy poor financial habits.

There is a certain amount of awkwardness built in to these discussions, but that is nothing compared to the potential explosiveness of unpleasant surprises after you've gone. Take the trouble to explain the logic of your decisions with your children and allow for feedback. You may find estate planning attorneys or other professionals can be helpful in communicating about money. A good estate planner has processes and tools that help facilitate such conversations effectively.

The importance of communication in money matters is one of the big takeaways of *The Cycle of the Gift: Family Wealth and Wisdom* (Hughes, Massenzio, and Whitaker). Money given without communication as to the giver's intention can be misinterpreted and misconstrued.

> *Does a gift of money mean your parents love you and want to support your dreams? Is it an indication that they don't think you and your spouse can make it on your own without subsidies? Or were they just playing the game of beating Uncle Sam out of taxes—and you happened to benefit?*

Family members who think they know each other well can be poor mind-readers. And even more important than the *money* you give to your heirs is ensuring that the *spirit* of the gift is not lost. This is a good mindset to have when talking with heirs. What's the spirit of the gift and your intention for giving it? What positive impact do you hope it will make in the life of the receiver?

Third, strive for fairness in distributing your estate.

Mark Accettura advises, "If you want to minimize fighting, leave it as equal as you possibly can." Not only does this apply to assets, but also to assigning responsibility for settling your estate. He suggests that anyone with a level of capability should be assigned a small role at the very least. One common scenario involves an adult child who struggles financially and gets occasional (or regular) help from Mom and Dad. Whether assistance is doled out in your lifetime or via your estate, this kind of help can be counter-productive. In *Millionaire Women Next Door*, Thomas Stanley refers to such coddling as "economic outpatient care" or (EOC).

Stanley's research led him to conclude that, over time, such gifts actually make the recipient *less* able to provide for themselves. Such favoritism also can lead to resentment and does little to foster healthy relationships between siblings. Relationships can be sorely tested by the inequitable distribution of your estate.

Those who receive the most assistance while their parents are alive generally receive a disproportionately large share of the estate as well. The successful children are essentially given negative reinforcement for achieving their own measure of success.

Regardless of what your concerns are, it is always prudent to consider the dynamics of your family. You may wish to discuss such issues in a family meeting or privately with each adult child.

One advantage of Family Financing is that it helps families talk about money. This in itself is a huge gift! If you practice communicating with your children about money matters, you will instill a positive, open and practical attitude toward finances that they will benefit from in many ways. They're likely to experience lower stress, better health, more harmonious marriages and greater wealth.

A Legacy of More than Money

> *"Every one of us receives and passes on an inheritance. The inheritance may not be an accumulation of earthly possessions or acquired riches, but whether we realize it or not, our choices, words, actions, and values will impact someone and form the heritage we hand down."*
> —Ben Hardesty

An estate plan helps you prepare for the transfer of your wealth and assets after your death. Your estate involves everything you *own*—investments, properties, life insurance and belongings—plus, often, what you *owe*—your debts. An estate plan involves documents, tasks, processes and people such as lawyers and trustees. It may be simple or complex.

Your legacy *includes* your estate, yet legacy goes far beyond assets. Your legacy includes everything you want to leave for future generations—all that you consider important—your core values, relationships, family history, and so on.

What is the unique legacy you wish to leave? We encourage you to think beyond the dollars. What do you know that you want future generations to know, too? What else do you want to pass down to your heirs? What do you value? The list might include things like:

- **Family stories and history.** This can include oral histories, family sayings, inside jokes, source maps, and stories of lessons learned and hero's journeys. Some families hire documentary filmmakers who specialize in memoir and legacy videos, such as Family Line Videos,[108] Your Heritage Films[109] or Scratch Made Media.[110] These services are wonderful, but archiving family stories does not need to be complicated or costly. It can be as simple as asking questions and recording conversations on a smart phone.

- **Photos, letters, scrap books, documents.** At a recent memorial of a family matriarch, grand-and-great-grandchildren gathered to read the sweet love letters that had been exchanged between the matriarch and her husband-to-be when she was still a teenager and he left for military service during World War II. These are treasures that should be kept and shared for generations.

Handcrafted gifts from children can also be precious treasures. Don't feel compelled to keep everything—select your favorite memorabilia and let go of the rest (unless the child that created it wants to keep it!)

- **Jewelry, antiques and other heirlooms.** It is most helpful to keep or write down any pertinent information about heirlooms, such as when and how they were purchased or passed down, any appraisals or certificates of authenticity.

  However, be warned; many children don't want their parents' "stuff." There is a saying: "One person's treasure is another person's trash." This is becoming increasingly true of antiques and heirlooms. Young people are traveling lighter these days. Plus—we hate to be the ones to tell you—but a lot of your favorite things have gone out of style.

- **Family traditions and recipes.** These may be lived and taught more than passed on in physical form, but it can help to document even living traditions to ensure they do not become lost. Not only does wealth often falter by the third generation—so do oral histories. This is another area where digital recordings can come in very handy!

- **Family wisdom and values.** These may be rooted in the past, yet also connected to, even foundational for the future the family is creating. Family mission statements and constitutions are ideal structures to capture family wisdom and values. They can also be valuable documents that support the vision and mission of Family Financing.

- **Cultural traditions and history.** Does your family identify with one or more ethnic heritages? Do you have a strong religious background? Were you part of a sorority, fraternity, or other organization you valued? These are important stories and traditions to pass along. Continue to share traditions if they are meaningful. Even if you no longer participate in cultural practices or religious ceremonies, record memories of their meaning and significance to you or your ancestors.

Think long-term. Look to both the past and the future. Ask yourself questions such as:

- What values did generations before me pass down to me?
- How can I help my heirs understand how family wealth was built?
- What challenges did I or other family members overcome?
- What do I want future generations to know and remember about this family? Consider what family stories you would like to keep alive.
- What NEW traditions would the family like to start? Family retreats, talent shows, open mics, "show and tells" and sharing... note what activities your family is enjoying and make it a tradition.
- How can I help ensure my children will keep loving each other after I'm gone? Model and convey the importance to you of family connection, support and affinity.

It's *your* family's heritage. You get to both remember it and create it however you want!

Preserving—and creating—heritage with technology.

There is also a practical aspect in how to best preserve and pass along parts of your family legacy. As precious as the "originals" are, strongly consider digital reproductions. This not only protects your treasures against fire or loss, but it allows valuable items to be shared and remembered by multiple family members.

Just as your beneficiaries need to be updated when things change, so changing technology requires periodic updates. Perhaps there is a new way to store and preserve treasured family memories. Perhaps it's time to get those VHS tapes converted into digital files, or update CD-Roms to DropBox files.

Some families create family films, logos, websites, biographies and more. You are only limited by your imagination! Some families may hire graphic designers, videographers, ghostwriters, branding and other professionals. But you need not spend a lot of money—especially if it's not in your family's budget. Family branding, family storytelling and preserving heritage in new formats can also be a fun family project to use or develop your "in house" talent!

5 Things You Should NEVER Leave to Your Children

> *"You will only be remembered for two things: the problems you solve or the one you create."*
> —Mike Murdock, American preacher

While inheritances are largely thought of in terms of financial legacies, there are many things that we "leave" for our children, including things they may not want! Our financial, emotional, physical, intellectual and spiritual legacy is hopefully a positive one, not one that burdens them.

Whether or not you have life insurance, assets, or a sizable estate that may one day be a financial legacy, here are five things that your children—however young or old they may be—are hoping you DON'T leave them.

1. **A house full of clutter.**

    A friend of ours just took 8 months off of work to sort through the packed basement, attic, closets and rooms of her father's home after his passing.

    We know a woman who left her four-bedroom house full of things to her surviving sister to deal with. It took a high emotional and physical toll to have to clear the home of decades of "stuff," not to mention deal with overdue repairs.

    Another woman we know took trips from Seattle to the East Coast for well over a year to clear the mountain of belongings and paperwork out of her father's home... and she was not without assistance.

    Yes, there are those who can be hired to help in such circumstances, such as professional organizers who specialize in clearing estates.

However, it can be difficult for family members to delegate the task of sorting through family treasures—and family junk—to strangers. The financial cost of such help can also be significant, although the personal cost of *not* getting help can also be high.

Start giving things away now. Don't leave all the "stuff" stored in your attic, basement, garage or junk room for your loved ones to sift through someday. Give the treasures to family members who appreciate them, and don't stop until the clutter is gone and nothing but a few boxes of holiday decorations remain.

"Is an object 'actively used or deeply cherished'?" asks "Lighten Up" workshop creator Laura Lavigne. "If not, let it go."

If you need help or find yourself overwhelmed to the point of inaction, hire out or call on family members. It is far more satisfying to have a family garage sale and recycle/donation weekend during the good times than to have to sift through piles of belongings during a time of grief.

Lightening your load lessens your burden and helps you leave the legacy you intend.

2. A paperwork mess.

An acquaintance of ours shared a heartbreaking story on his blog about the aftermath of his father-in-law's passing and the legacy he didn't intend to leave. Unfortunately, his family's experience is not uncommon.

His father-in-law was a good man with good intentions. However, he left one heck of a mess for his loved ones. Not only did the family have to confront a storage locker full of useless, outdated junk, they had other, more difficult challenges left by his unfinished business.

The father-in-law had always *planned* on "getting his accounting records together and filing several years of delinquent, back taxes." But he passed away unexpectedly before he even turned 65, leaving his children with the impossible task of preparing tax returns with incomplete records.

And the hassle was only the beginning. "They had to personally sign and take on liability for those back taxes," explained the son-in-law. "He planned on living longer and eventually getting around to these things, but he never did. Life had a different plan...."

Don't leave the paperwork you didn't want to deal with to others. If you don't want to tackle this burdensome task, your children certainly don't either! Hire a bookkeeper, an accountant or whoever you need to sort it out. Ask for help from the family if you are unable to deal with it yourself. Chances are, they would much rather help you now than be left with your mess later.

3.   A mountain of debt.

The woman who left behind her 4-bedroom house full of things also left behind tens of thousands in credit card debt from years of living beyond her means.

Our acquaintance's father-in-law had dropped his health insurance because it was "too expensive." He thought he could do without it until he was old enough for Medicare to replace it, but he never made it. His children were left to negotiate and settle a pile of medical bills that consumed their father's life savings and bankrupted his estate.

Every day, people die without proper estate planning or trusts that leave their heirs responsible for settling debts.

One reason we advocate for whole life insurance is that the death benefit can replace assets that must be spent when "life happens," or when the paid-off house must be sold or mortgaged to fund long-term care. Now the long-term care benefit riders available on whole life insurance policies can be very helpful. But do read the details of the contract—it takes time before the benefits can be fully realized.

One way or another—find a way to resolve your debts. If you have whole life cash value, this can help you pay off high-interest debts faster. Pay off the debt with a lower interest policy loan and work to pay off the policy loan.

If you are unable to repay your debts, try to settle them for a negotiated amount. If that does not work, bankruptcy could be a viable alternative. A major reason people enter into bankruptcy is because it offers them protection from their creditors. Bankruptcy also offers the same protection to a person's estate, thus protecting heirs who would otherwise have to pay debts from the proceeds of the liquidated estate.

4. **A Family Fued.**

One way to start a family feud is to leave siblings with differing amounts of an estate. And regardless of their financial habits or history, anything other than an equal split is likely to leave someone crying "unfair!"

Another way to start a family feud is to not have an up-to-date estate plan in place. Too many people "intend" to organize their financial affairs and assemble an estate plan. Instead, they left a mess of contradictory documents and incomplete plans that pit family members against each other.

Failure to keep beneficiaries up to date can also create chaos and ill will. Sometimes, divorced spouses or divorced spouses of children are still listed as beneficiaries of an estate, while younger grandchildren, nieces or nephews (born since the last updated will) have never been added! Clearly, that was not what was intended.

Kate's mother discovered after 34 years of marriage—shortly before her husband passed—that his first wife was still listed as the beneficiary on his life insurance accounts. "If you died," she told him, "I would have to kill you again!"

Be clear, consistent, and complete with your estate plans. Establish a will, and a trust, if applicable to your situation. Update it every few years, or at the very least, when there is a change in the family structure of a family, such as a death or divorce.

Need help to get started? Contact the National Network of Estate Planning Attorneys,[111] they have an excellent process to help families communicate effectively.

5. **Confusion and a lack of communication.**

When our friend Lenore's father became suddenly very ill, he was temporarily unable to run the household or pay the bills. Lenore and her mother had to figure everything out—and it was no easy task!

Following that experience, Lenore had a pregnant friend who lost her boyfriend and father of their unborn child in an accident. The family searched for weeks, not knowing if there was a life insurance policy or not.

Realizing how many families are left to "figure things out" in the wake of illnesses and tragedies, Lenore created an online platform that gives people a way to organize, document and communicate essential information. We've mentioned it previously—it's called TheTorch. com,[112] and it offers a way to provide important details to your loved ones in the event of an emergency. If someone else has to suddenly to navigate your life, pay your bills, contact your doctors, find legal documents, and care for your home, children or pets, they will need instructions!

Family members may talk frequently, yet are they having conversations about the things that would really matter in an emergency? Usually not. The lack of communication creates pain and confusion as those remaining are left to wonder:

- What lawyer, financial advisor, CPA or insurance agent should be contacted?
- Where are the important documents stored, and which documents should loved ones expect to find?
- Who is the family doctor, and is there a durable POA?
- How does the mortgage get paid, anyway? Knowing what bills are on "autopilot," which aren't, and how the family financials are tracked is crucial.

- Then there are the more personal logistics… Where are the extra car keys? Are there instructions for taking proper care of the dog? And the list goes on.

Communicate thoroughly and pro-actively. Kim's grandmother had a green notebook that listed all of the essential information and detailed where to find what, and everyone knew where the green notebook was.

TheTorch.com,[113] Everplans.com[114] and Tomorrow.me[115] do what my grandmother's green notebook did, but these electronic platforms make sharing and updating information much easier—especially across the miles. Best yet, these platforms prompt you to think of many important things you might otherwise overlook!

Find and use a strategy or platform that works for you. Maybe it's a Google doc of instructions and DropBox.com. Maybe it's a well-labeled file cabinet in the family home that everyone has a key to. But you *must* have a system for storing, updating, and communicating essential information!

Get Started on Your To-Do List Now

It's easy to feel overwhelmed when you read something like this. But if *you're* overwhelmed by your unfinished business, do you really want to leave it to your loved ones to complete?

Anything that drains your energy will become an energy drain for your loved ones if—or rather, *when*—something happens to you. So start finishing your unfinished business today. It doesn't matter that you may well live 30 or 40 more years, because who wants to live that long with unfinished business hanging over their head!?

Envision what you would like to leave for your loved ones—beyond the financial legacy. And if you assess that you are in danger of leaving a legacy of clutter, confusion, and unfinished business, then start taking action now. Make a list and set aside time to work on your list. With regular action-taking, you'll be able to celebrate having your "ducks in a row" before you know it.

Communicate with your heirs about your intentions, read *Perpetual Wealth*, and start preparing them to be successful beneficiaries and wealth stewards. Use money to continue your legacy of love and care, to support the people and causes you care about.

The Legacy Beyond Your Lifetime

As we've said, *long-term thinking is the mindset required for Perpetual Wealth*. Legacies generally start with thoughts of what you will leave your family—or perhaps, a determination not to let Uncle Sam take what could instead go to your heirs or the non-profits you care about. But legacies often extend much further than we anticipate.

What is Steve Job's legacy? How can one estimate the legacy of the man who envisioned the personal tech revolution?

What will Oprah Winfrey's legacy be—the first black female billionaire who shattered ideas of limitations and inspired a generation of people to realize their potential for success?

What will Bill Gates and Warren Buffet's legacy be—not only their personal legacies as titans of business, investing and philanthropy, but the impact of The Giving Pledge,[116] which has inspired over 200 other business leaders and billionaires to give the majority of their wealth to charitable causes?

Chances are, your legacy will be comparatively modest, yet never underestimate the impact you can have.

One of Kim's missions has been to form a movement that will change how our nation does personal finances. The Prosperity Economics Movement teaches people how to move away from strategies that place our money in volatile securities out of our control and move onto firmer financial ground.

One of Kate's missions is to become a "6 Figure Giver"—giving more than $100,000 to charity over a lifetime—and inspiring others to do the same (Even better... what about six figures per year!?)

Your legacy isn't limited to what you can do yourself—but by the change you can inspire.

Family Giving

Your family may or may not have a philanthropic focus. It is something to consider as charitable giving can do so much good—not only in the world, but in your family as well. Giving:

- nurtures generosity
- requires discipline
- supports worthy causes
- brings ideas to life
- and (often) provides a tax incentive, too.

As our fictional family does, you could use a portion of death benefits or dividends to fund Family Giving. And again, while this is a noble thing to do for the "worthy cause," there are other important benefits, such as opportunities for bonding, mentorship, teamwork and leadership development.

An article from Fidelity, "How to Make Giving Back a Family Affair" has wonderful suggestions, including:

- Pair grandparents and grandchildren together (from 8 or 10 on up) to explore giving opportunities. (The middle generation may have their own favorite charities, but this is a unique opportunity for bonding and mentorship.)
- Offer Family Grants to non-profits and allowing grandchildren to research and visit (if possible) different charities to select possible recipients.
- Have the children make presentations to the rest of the family about various charities, explaining what they do and why they are worthy of support.
- Hold a contest between cousins to have "their" chosen charity receive the most votes or funds. This develops presentation and negotiating skills, and encourages children to stand up for their own beliefs.

- Have an annual meeting to review Family Giving outcomes, lessons learned, future goals and grants for the coming year.

The amounts are not as important as the participation... even small grants of say $250 or $500 could create meaningful engagement. (Of course, more is wonderful and even more motivating.) But never let a modest budget stop your family from being active givers. Family Giving isn't so much about giving to charity as it is growing a generation of givers. You aren't just raising funds—you are *raising up* wise and generous stewards of wealth!

Also consider giving of your family's time and talents. Volunteering together is another way to give and create positive memories. There are opportunities to combine travel and sightseeing with service work all over the world.

Legacies are Multi-Generational

Usually when we hear a phrase like "multi-generational legacy," we think of money and making sure that family wealth is preserved. This is not what we mean here—or not *only* what we mean—when we say legacies are multi-generational.

What we mean is that your children, grand-children and great grandchildren *will leave legacies of their own*. And *their* legacies will become part of *your* multi-generational legacy. The good you inspire them to do, the support your family provides to see them through to success, the financial resources you invest in your children and their dreams, and the lives they change through fulfilling their own life's vision and mission all become part of your family's multi-generational legacy.

Kim: My son Robby is fundraising for Principia, the college that both Robby and I attended, as well as my father, Dan Hays and my sister Tammi Brannan. When Robby helps to raise money that can pay for a scholarship that allows a student to attend college, that is part of our family's multi-generational legacy.

My daughter Kaylea went to South Africa to volunteer at an afterschool program for orphans and vulnerable children—and later published a book about her experience (*Every Day Is a Miracle: Lessons from Susan Rammekwa*). That book and experience is part of our multi-generational legacy.

Kate: When my daughter writes a song or helps someone relieve pain and heal through massage therapy, that is part of our family's multi-generational legacy.

Each person has their own legacy to leave. In a family, these legacies have compounding effect throughout multiple generations.

Invest in Your Children's Legacies

Your children's legacy is not—or not just—to carry on *"your"* legacy. Yes, you may well pass down dreams and visions and a mission that they will carry forward. This is a wonderful thing. And they will have their *own* dreams and passions.

Sometimes, it is most challenging for children from strong, driven, wealthy and/or influential families to find their own way in the world. They can grow up in the "shadow" of their parents and their parents' accomplishments.

The Cycle of the Gift, mentioned previously, was written for parents seeking to transfer legacy gifts to children in a way that truly enriches their lives rather than subsidizing their lifestyles. In a sequel of sorts, the authors wrote another book aimed at the beneficiaries of such gifts. *The Voice of the Rising Generation* explores how such children can find their own voice and way in the world.

On a blog devoted to supporting family businesses, we found this moving personal reflection inspired by a main lesson of the book:

> The authors talk about a session with a group of young people, members of the same extended family, entirely devoted to identifying each of the participants' own personal dreams. Toward the end of the session, after the participants had defined their dreams and shared them with the group, the parents joined the meeting. Each parent

interviewed his or her son or daughter, heard about their dreams, and then asked, "How can I invest in your dream, my child?"

I believe this is a wonderful question, perhaps the best out of all the questions a parent can ask his or her young son or daughter.

Why?

First, simply asking the question proves that the parent is truly interested in getting to know his/her child's world, dreams and ambitions. Second, the parent comes to understand that to succeed a person must seek to realize his or her own dreams, and not the dreams of others. The question frees the young person from the obligation of realizing his/her parents' dream and places the parents' resources at the young person's disposal. And third, the word "invest" is not, of course, limited to money—it can include advice, mentoring, connections, a blessing, emotional support, etc.

…We don't have a family business, and each of my three children has chosen a different career path. But my partner and I certainly live by what I teach my clients: we invest in our children's dreams.

When our son returned from abroad with his artist bride, it was clear to all that in the absence of a facility and equipment enabling her to engage in her plastic art, she would have to give up her dream. She might be able to teach art classes at the community center in the afternoon, but she definitely wouldn't be able to create works of her own or to realize the abilities she acquired while studying abroad.

However, she had a crystal-clear, well thought-out dream—a center where young graduates of the Bezalel Academy of Arts and Design [Israel's oldest institution of higher education] who lacked the facilities that would enable them to persevere in their art could work. We decided to pitch in and help out, and first of all provided the wherewithal to rent a location and build the equipment. I was involved in the negotiating the lease, screening the candidates who would work with her and planning the moves. I served as a mentor, a sympathetic ear and sounding board, and sometimes, a shoulder to cry on, while my significant other spent hours in shared thinking about marketing and financial planning.

Today, four years later, the dream has still not completely become a reality. But there is no one happier than I when I visit the studio, see the work that's being done, and meet the young artists who work there and the people who come to learn their craft. Sometimes, seeing my daughter-in-law's hard work and the difficulties she faces, the physical exhaustion, pressures and disappointments, I feel a tug at my heartstrings, but I also see how our investment in her dream is helping her to make it a reality.

I must point out that we don't give our children extra cash: we don't cover their overdraft at the bank or solve the budget problems of a young couple with kids. But we do invest in their dreams!

This mother-in-law is not an artist—but now, part of her legacy is a center for artists.

The author of the post goes on to say that many business owners are preoccupied with how their son or daughter can help the *parent's* dream come true. There may be nothing wrong with this—other than the fact that "it lacks the dimension of passion." What would happen if parents were committed to helping their children find and realize their own missions, whether they were similar or quite different from their own?

"One way or another, talk to your children, young and older alike, and ask them that wondrous question, 'How can I invest in your dream, my child?'"

How can you help your children realize the legacies they were born to fulfill?

THE BOTTOM LINE

Legacies go far beyond dollars, and far beyond our lifetimes. Family history, stories, wisdom, traditions, memories, heirlooms, photos and videos are often an important part of your legacy and should be treated as such. Use digital technology to update, preserve, and create memories.

The ability to communicate about money is key to successful wealth transfers and legacies as well as financial education.

Family Giving can be a meaningful part of a legacy and a rewarding part of Family Financing.

Legacies are multi-generational. To maximize yours, learn to invest in your children's dreams using your human capital as well as your financial capital.

CHAPTER 17:

Winning the Long Game of Wealth

As the apple pie was served for dessert at tonight's family dinner, Carol started the evening's Family Financing discussion with an unexpected question.

"What do you know about Leonardo da Vinci?" Carol inquired, looking especially at her grandsons.

"Wait—Is this a pop quiz or something? Because I didn't study for it!" said James, Julie's oldest boy, who was rarely shy in expressing himself.

"No, no, nothing like that," assured Grandpa John with a chuckle. "We're all going to watch a couple of short videos after dinner. They relate to a very important lesson we're learning from the example of Leonardo's life and work."

"He was a scientist... and a famous painter, right?" asked Jeffrey.

"Exactly," replied a pleased grandmother. "But what you might not know about Leonardo da Vinci is how he worked in obscurity for most of his life. To put it bluntly, he thought he was a failure for much of his own lifetime!"

"Really!?" asked James. "And yet he is still famous, hundreds of years later!"

"Yes—it seems ironic, right?" replied John. "Da Vinci was playing what I'll call 'the long game.' He worked for decades to pay his dues and hone his craft. He was always learning, always improving. Eventually, he became one of the greatest artists the world has ever known. But it took a very long time.

"A lot of things worth doing will take longer than you think... and perhaps more effort than you expect. That doesn't mean you shouldn't do those things. As a matter of fact, the things that require a long-term commitment—those are often the things most worth doing."

Sam cleared the pie dishes as they all moved into the family room to watch the videos. Everyone was engaged and the videos—aptly titled "The Long Game"— prompted a wonderful discussion afterwards. Sam shared about his experience of running marathons—his favorite "long game." John and Carol shared more of their signature family stories and wisdom.

As they discussed how Leonardo da Vinci has been remembered, a question from Cyndi prompted each family member to consider how they wanted to be remembered long after they were gone. What would their legacy be? It wasn't your typical after-dinner conversation, but then again, the Johnsons were becoming quite atypical. They were now on the road less traveled. They were becoming a family with an uncommon commitment to each other and a long-term vision for a future of Perpetual Wealth.

. . . . .

The Myth of Overnight Success

> *"The path from dreams to success does exist.*
> *May you have the vision to find it, the courage*
> *to get on to it, and the perseverance to follow it."*
> —Kalapna Chawley, American astronaut

When it comes to "making it," the media loves to report on overnight successes, lottery winners and tech start-ups that seem to come from nowhere to capture the imagination of the market. It is exciting to contemplate being handed a fortune and fantasize about spending it.

Exciting, but also quite misleading.

Those who seem to have suddenly appeared out of nowhere to achieve "overnight success" include:

- Actress Betty White, who worked for 10 years in radio after told she was too "un-photogenic" for movies. After finally landing work in TV, she worked for 20 more years until her role on *The Mary Tyler Moore Show* led to her first Emmy.
- George R. R. Martin, who published novels for 37 years (taking a temporary break after his 4th novel was a flop) before selling the rights to his epic fantasy series to HBO, upon which the wildly popular "Game of Thrones" series is based.
- Rowland H. Macy's first five department stores failed, according to Success.com. It wasn't until R. H. Macy moved to New York and applied all of his lessons learned that Macy's department store became a household name.

History's biggest achievers haven't counted solely on talent or serendipity to attain their goals. Stories of patience, practice and determination aren't quite as exciting as guessing the winning answer on *So You Want to be a Millionaire*, yet all of these factors are essential in finding wealth and success. Perhaps Ray Kroc said it best, "I was an overnight success alright, but 30 years is a long, long night."

The other key factor that never makes headlines is perseverance. A majority of millionaires took the "slow climb" approach to building wealth through earning, saving and investing. It shouldn't be a surprise, but those who try to "get rich quick" rarely do. And as a survey of bankrupt celebrities and lottery winners would reveal, those that do succeed quickly often fail to retain the money gained. In other words, there are no shortcuts to lasting success.

What it Takes to Develop True Expertise

"How do you get to Carnegie Hall? Practice, practice, practice!" goes the old show business saying.

In 2008, Malcolm Gladwell published his controversial best-seller, *Outliers: The Story of Success*. Basing his theories on a study by Anders Ericsson, Gladwell posits that "researchers have settled on what they believe is the magic number for true expertise: ten thousand hours." He uses The Beatles as one example. From 1960 through 1963, the unknown band played 1200 shows in Hamburg, Germany, amassing more than 10,000 hours in concert (and, as per the quote above, their second US concert took place in 1964 at Carnegie Hall).

Gladwell also cites Bill Gates, who had access to a high school computer starting at 13 years old. Again, he put in the time—about 10,000 hours of programming—before he graduated. Gates then went on to partner with Paul Allen to start a company you may have never heard of... Traf-O-Data. Yes, before there was Microsoft, there was Traf-O-Data, which attempted to track traffic data. According to a *Newsweek* article from April of 2011, between 1974 and 1980, Traf-O-Data totaled net losses of $3,494 before they closed up shop.

Both examples also indicate a willingness to do whatever it takes for as long as it takes. As Gladwell says in the book, "Success is not a random act. It arises out of a predictable and powerful set of circumstances and opportunities."

Was Leonardo da Vinci a Failure?

The inspiration for this chapter came from "The Long Game," a two-part video essay by Adam Westbrook. The video still for part one shows an image of Leonardo da Vinci's famous painting, *The Last Supper*, labeled with this provocative statement: "The Guy Who Painted This Was a Loser (and what that means for the rest of us)."

In the video, Westbrook blasts commonly held ideas of success. With a fresh perspective on "the other side" of da Vinci's life that we may be less familiar with, he makes the case that our quintessential renaissance man dealt with failure for a great deal of his life. Most of the projects he worked on were too ambitious, and many went unfinished. His reputation suffered so much as a result of his inability to complete projects that by the age of 30, the only job he could get was drawing portraits of dead criminals for authorities.

Despite a history of setbacks, Leonardo never gave up or stopped working on his craft. His big break did not come until 1498 when he won the commission to paint his signature piece, "The Last Supper." He was 46 years old (which was quite old in 1498!)

Westbrook describes a common thread that connects all of the lives of eventually-successful people he examined: "The Difficult Years." Much like da Vinci, other heroes go through long periods of struggle during which they hone their chosen disciplines. The Difficult Years are defined by a quote from *Mastery* author Robert Greene: "A largely self-directed apprenticeship that lasts 5-10 years and receives little attention because it does not contain stories of great achievement or discovery."

The Difficult Years could be seen as the period during which someone puts in their 10,000 hours:

- Marie Curie spent seven years in abject poverty while she studied radioactivity.
- The great saxophonist John Coltrane practiced every day for 17 years until he had his first hit in 1960.
- Stephen King wrote every day for nine years before he sold his first novel.

All the greats played The Long Game.

Are you pursuing your own "long game"? Are you willing to power through your own difficult years in order to achieve your legacy? If we want lasting prosperity, we must practice the habits that produce it with persistence.

To contemplate your own long game (or your need for greater perseverance) in your own lifewatch Adam Westbrook's excellent and thought-provoking video essays. You can follow the links below to watch them on YouTube, or find them both (along with a version of this chapter) at ProsperityEconomics.org: "Winning the Long Game of Wealth."[117]

The Long Game, Part 1[118]

The Long Game, Part 2[119]

Playing the Long Game of Wealth

"Do any of us have the patience?" asks Westbrook. The philosophy of The Long Game runs counter to our general culture of fast food, faster computers and instant gratification. Yet when it comes to wealth, as in other areas of life, there is something to be said for patience and perseverance.

When we seek quick results in our finances, our actions can lead to disappointment instead of mastery and success. Speculation of all types turns an investor into the proverbial "hare" that rarely beats the predictable, steady tortoise in the end.

Sadly, we've seen people start whole life policies and not follow through. It turns into wasted effort and dollars. It takes long-term thinking and consistent action over years to build a financial legacy with whole life—but it *works*. Every time.

In seeking out quick results, we do a disservice to our peace of mind as well as our dollars. We find ourselves glued to market results, crossing our fingers that lady luck will be kind. But *Perpetual Wealth* isn't about luck… it's about taking strategic, consistent actions over a long period of time.

While the masses chase after the latest "hot stocks," those practicing the long-game of wealth practice prosperity by investing consistently for the future. Building long-term equity in a home, a solid business or a whole life insurance policy are proven reliable long-game strategies.

When starting to learn a craft, it is impossible to know for sure if you will be able to invest 10,000 hours.

Likewise, no one can guarantee that they will have 30 years or even 3 months to save the money they intend to guarantee that their loved ones will be taken care of properly. Whole life insurance ensures that every policyholder can play the long game of wealth whether they are beginning at age 25 or 75.

Whole life insurance was built for the long game of wealth. It was built to last for generations. It was built for *Perpetual Wealth*.

You *can* leave a legacy.

You *can* invest in the future of your children, grandchildren, great grandchildren, and the children that will come after them... perhaps long after you are gone. With the Family Financing practices in this book, your legacy will outlive you.

You can build virtually unshakeable prosperity. You can invest in what—and who—matters most to you. And you can leave a legacy that lasts.

Acknowledgements

From Kim:

To Todd Langford, my husband and best friend. When a person is conceptual as I am (Kolbe 4492) having a partner who proves things numerically is the best addition to a business one could ask for. For 25 years now (that's when I first took his training), his ability to help overcome my original incorrect training is amazing. He is patient, thorough, analytical, and specific, yet able to communicate any analysis with his Truth Concepts software in a way I and others can understand. I am amazed literally every time I help him conduct a training for advisors. In addition, our shared values of give first, humble confidence (due to proof), and love of what whole life insurance does for our family and others make working together an absolute joy.

To my other best friend and sister Tammi Brannan, who first created our characters John and Carol and who made significant contributions to the book and the letter to heirs.

My mom, Nancy Lea Hays, was the person who helped me realize typical financial planning was a silly process. When we started going over the questions like what age do you want to retire? She said "How am I supposed to know that?" How much income do you want? "Enough plus some extra?" (And my mom was not a "generalize it" person!) She had faith in me to support my entrepreneurial quest when I left my job at a bank to start a business helping people with their finances without any salary at all. I will always be grateful for her.

My dad, Dan Hays, continues to support that entrepreneurial spirit by referring me to people I can help and attending our Summit4Advisors. He is also "busting the retirement lies" by continuing to work in his early 80s while also maintaining our family's farm in Oregon. Together they taught Tammi and me the value of money and hard work when they bought us milk cows and helped us sell the milk from 4th through 12th grade. I knew about savings accounts, balance sheets and income statements by middle school as I had to keep records for all my 4-H projects. We have been involved with "Family Financing" for decades!

My son Robby Butler and daughter Kaylea also have learned about and implemented the ideas in this book as they have inched into adulthood. Two of my proudest moments as a mother were Robby buying his first policy literally the day he turned 18 and Kaylea asking if she had to save 10 percent of her second job she had in college since she was already saving 10 percent from her first job.

Todd's children, Jake and Jessica, have also taken many of the steps we've suggested here, and all know they can ask us questions regarding money and there will not be any judgmental answers.

We have started to use a few of the family retreat ideas and I love knowing our kids will continue to build their financial knowledge. Money IS a talked about subject in the Butler-Langford "house of both."

To Kate: I'm grateful to have such a skilled and balanced left brain/right brain writer as a team-mate for this effort. Thanks for your persistence and all that you brought to the table.

Special thanks to the P4P team that serve our clients at Partners for Prosperity: Theresa Sheridan, Rae Ann Vitense, Mercedes Berg, the entire SCIcreations crew and Kate.

Much gratitude to the PEM team who fuels the Prosperity Economics Movement: Mimi Klosterman, Patrick Donohoe, Tammi Brannan, Spencer Shaw, and many others.

And thank you to the Truth Concepts software team: Katie Jackson, David Jehlen, Elizabeth Hagenlocher and Todd Langford.

From Kate:

I want to acknowledge the generational legacies that precede and follow my own. To my mother, who is my undying supporter, cheerleader, and occasional proofreader. (I think I might *still* be working on the book without the long hours sitting in the recliner with my laptop while you cooked and took care of me and my broken ankle!)

To my daughter Maddie, the best daughter and travel companion who inspires me to be the best Mom I can be! Thanks for sharing your love and light, and for your openness to talk about life and all kinds of important topics: including budgets and life insurance!

To my step-father, my role model of devotion and lifelong learning. To my father, who never let the small stuff stop you from being "happy as a clam." You are both missed.

To Jim, my partner who has never known me when I wasn't writing this book! Thank-you for your unconditional love, support and patience.

To my friends who support me in so many ways. Special thanks to Bryan Rust (who also contributed to "The Long Game" chapter), Bill Roman, Merilee Lovejoy, Connie Gulick, my local yoga/fitness/gratitude sisters Shay, Natalia, Johanna, and Beverly, and especially to Diazina Mobley and Afrin Khan for coaching and support, to my Red Elephant tribe and the whole P4P team.

Most of all, I'd like to acknowledge my co-author Kim Butler for entrusting me and partnering with me on this project. Your endless knowledge and commitment to constantly expand and "help more people in more ways" is inspiring. *Perpetual Wealth* and the good it will do in the world would not exist without you!

About the Authors

Kim D. H. Butler is a leader in the Prosperity Economics Movement and an often-interviewed expert on whole life insurance and alternative investments.

Kim got her start in banking and then worked as a financial planner, obtaining her Series 7 and Series 65 licenses, and her CFP® designation. But she grew disillusioned over time, realizing that the practices of typical financial planning were irrelevant, misleading, and even harmful!

Driven to find a better way, Kim studied the commonalities between wealth builders. She observed what worked and what didn't, which led her to identify the Principles of Prosperity that really worked—and co-found the Prosperity Economics Movement.

In 1999, Kim created Partners for Prosperity, LLC, dedicated to the principles of Prosperity Economics. Rather than seeking "assets under management," the firm shows people how to build sustainable wealth by controlling and benefiting from their own assets. Partners for Prosperity serves clients in all 50 states.

Kim's work as an advisor has been recommended by financial thought leaders and authors such as Robert Kiyosaki (*Rich Dad, Poor Dad*), Tom Dyson, publisher of the Palm Beach Letter investment newsletter, Tom Wheelwright (*Tax Free Wealth*), and Garret Gunderson (*Killing Sacred Cows*). Kim has been named to the Investopedia 100 of influential advisors three years in a row and has appeared on many popular financial and leadership podcasts. Kim now co-hosts The Prosperity Podcast with Spencer Shaw.

Kim lives in Texas with her family, a large dog, two cats, and 16 alpacas. Find out more about Kim D. H. Butler and on our website at Partners4Prosperity.com.

To work with Kim and her team to diversify away from the stock market and build generational wealth, send an email to hello@Partners4Prosperity.com or give us a call at (877) 889-3981 ext. 120. If you are ready to play the long game of wealth, we're here to help!

Kate Phillips has worked with Kim Butler and Partners for Prosperity since 2011 as a writer, editor, and marketing coach, helping to further articulate the principles and strategies of Prosperity Economics through the "P4P blog," the Prosperity on Purpose ezine, and various books.

Kate is also the founder of Total Wealth and creator of programs such as "The Financial Stress Solution," "ReWrite My Money Story" and "Total Wealth School." Kate helps people get to the root causes of why they struggle with money so they can free themselves from financial stress.

Kate sees money as a tool for personal transformation and spiritual growth as well as financial wealth. She has a knack for helping people get unstuck with the personal stuff (beliefs, emotions, self-sabotage) that keep them from moving forward. She loves to help people start saving and investing by making money fun and accessible.

Additionally, as a coach and a wealth educator, Kate delights in helping clients brainstorm solutions and action steps that are often "outside the box" of what is typically recommended.

Kate is the author of a mini-ebook, *Break Through to Abundance: Why You're Stressing About Money (and how to break the cycle forever!)*, available as a free download at TotalWealthCoaching.com). She is also co-author with Kim Butler of *Financial Planning Has Failed*, available at Partners4Prosperity. com.

Kate lives east of Seattle and loves to hike in the Cascade foothills when she's not writing on her laptop or helping clients. She is also a singer-song-writer who believes in the transformative power of music and creativity!

Find out more about Kate and Total Wealth at TotalWealthCoaching.com or at Facebook.com/TotalWealth.

Notes

Introduction

1. https://partners4prosperity.com/blog
2. https://partners4prosperity.com/subscribe/
3. https://prosperityeconomics.org/permission

Chapter 1

4. https://www.ibisworld.com/industry-statistics/market-size/
   financial-planning-advice-united-states/
5. https://www.cfp.net/knowledge/reports-and-statistics/professional-demographics
6. https://partners4prosperity.com/subscribe
7. https://amzn.to/2EihWhv
8. http://www.demos.org/publication/
   retirement-savings-drain-hidden-excessive-costs-401ks
9. https://partners4prosperity.com/
   life-insurance-commission-shock-whole-life-commissions-vs-mutual-fund-expenses/

Chapter 2

10. https://partners4prosperity.com/healthcare-sharing-plans/
11. https://data.oecd.org/hha/household-savings.htm
12. https://prosperityeconomics.org/401k-risk-assessment/

Chapter 3

13. https://partners4prosperity.com/contact
14. https://partners4prosperity.com/contact

15. https://prosperityeconomicsadvisors.com/
16. https://amzn.to/2su8BQD

Chapter 4
17. https://partners4prosperity.com/contact
18. hello@Partners4Prosperity.com
19. https://partners4prosperity.com/
20. https://www.amazon.com/Tax-Free-Wealth-Permanently-Lowering-Advisors/dp/1947588052/
21. https://wealthability.com/show/
22. https://prosperityeconomics.org/20-ways-to-save/

Chapter 5
23. https://en.wikipedia.org/wiki/Patronage

Chapter 6
24. https://lifehappens.org/videos/facing-the-unexpected/
25. https://partners4prosperity.com/contact/
26. https://partners4prosperity.com/contact/
27. https://partners4prosperity.com/contact

Chapter 7
28. Hello@pem.email
29. https://nnepa.com/
30. https://prosperityeconomics.org/stop-paying-life-insurance-premiums
31. https://prosperityeconomics.org/seniors-getting-life-insurance/
32. https://partners4prosperity.com/contact/
33. https://partners4prosperity.com/best-whole-life-insurance-company/
34. https://prosperityeconomics.org/convertible-term-insurance/
35. https://partners4prosperity.com/contact
36. https://partners4prosperity.com/disadvantages-of-universal-life/
37. https://prosperityeconomics.org/questions-about-life-insurance/
38. https://prosperityeconomics.org/life-insurance-questions/
39. https://partners4prosperity.com/
40. hello@Partners4Prosperity.com

Chapter 8
41. http://money.cnn.com/2013/12/13/retirement/american-inheritance/index.html
42. https://www.cnbc.com/2017/06/06/68-percent-of-millennials-expect-an-inheritance-only-40-percent-of-them-will-get.html
43. https://www.marketwatch.com/story/one-in-three-americans-who-get-an-inheritance-blow-it-2015-09-03
44. http://money.cnn.com/magazines/fortune/fortune_archive/1986/09/29/68098/index.htm

45. https://www.ted.com/talks/bill_and_melinda_gates_why_giving_away_our_wealth_has_been_the_most_satisfying_thing_we_ve_done?language=en

46. https://www.cnbc.com/2017/09/21/warren-buffet-is-the-most-charitable-billionaire.html

47. https://givingpledge.org/About.aspx

48. http://library.columbia.edu/locations/rbml/units/carnegie/andrew.html

49. https://books.google.com/books/about/The_Gospel_of_Wealth_and_Other_Timely_Es.html?id=q5ALvRp61wgC&printsec=frontcover&source=kp_read_button#v=onepage&q&f=false

50. https://www.forbes.com/sites/chloesorvino/2014/07/08/whats-become-of-them-the-carnegie-family/#12c479a67b55

51. https://investorplace.com/2013/08/woolworths-heiress-outspent-a-near-billion-dollar-fortune-died-penniless/

52. https://prosperityeconomics.org/sudden-money-inheritance/

53. https://partners4prosperity.com/contact/

Chapter 9
54. hello@Partners4Prosperity.com

Chapter 10
55. https://www.artofmanliness.com/articles/creating-a-family-culture-how-and-why-to-create-a-family-mission-statement/

56. https://home-school-coach.com/

57. https://www.amazon.com/Habits-Highly-Effective-Families/dp/0307440850

58. https://www.amazon.com/Secrets-Happy-Families-Improve-Mornings/dp/0061778745/

59. https://www.amazon.com/What-Would-Rockefellers-Do-Wealthy/dp/069263536X/

60. https://www.artofmanliness.com/articles/creating-a-family-culture-how-and-why-to-create-a-family-mission-statement/

Chapter 11
61. https://partners4prosperity.com/borrow-against-assets/

62. https://partners4prosperity.com/collateral-assignment-banking-on-your-life-insurance-policy/

63. https://partners4prosperity.com/business-financing-secret/

64. https://truthconcepts.com/how-do-i-tell-if-my-real-estate-deal-is-a-good-one/

65. https://www.youtube.com/watch?v=cgK_dOIesZo

66. https://theinsuranceproblog.com/direct-recognition-vs-non-direct-recognition/

67. https://partners4prosperity.com/best-whole-life-insurance-company/

68. https://prosperityeconomics.org/stop-paying-life-insurance-premiums/

Chapter 13
69. https://nnepa.com/

70. http://partners4prosperity.com/talking-with-your-kids-about-money

71. https://www.foxnews.com/us/college-student-blames-parents-after-she-blows-90g-college-fund

72. https://fee.org/

73. https://fee.org/articles/forget-lemonade-stands-these-kidtrepreneurs-are-running-million-dollar-companies/

74. https://partners4prosperity.com/category/podcast/

75. https://www.amazon.com/Cycle-Gift-Family-Wealth-Wisdom/dp/1118487591

76. https://prosperityeconomics.org/happy-wealth-secrets-of-success/

77. http://www.biblegateway.com/passage/?search=Matthew%2025:14-30&version=MSG

78. https://partners4prosperity.com/subscribe/

Chapter 14

79. https://partners4prosperity.com/

80. https://partners4prosperity.com/medical-cost-sharing-plans/

81. https://www.amazon.com/Busting-Interest-Rate-Lies-Discover/dp/0991305418/

82. https://www.amazon.com/Busting-Interest-Rate-Lies-Discover/dp/0991305418/

83. https://partners4prosperity.com/car-financing-tips/

84. https://thetorch.com/

85. https://partners4prosperity.com/contact

86. https://partners4prosperity.com/blog

87. https://partners4prosperity.com/contact

88. https://thetorch.com/

89. https://www.everplans.com/

90. https://truthconcepts.com/

91. https://www.prosperityeconomics.org/permission/

92. https://bustingtherealestateinvestinglies.com/

93. https://www.growingbolder.com/

Chapter 15

94. https://partners4prosperity.com/donor-advised-funds-pros-cons/

95. https://nnepa.com/

96. https://nnepa.com/

97. https://www.legalzoom.com/personal/estate-planning/last-will-and-testament-overview.html

98. https://store.nolo.com/products/online-will-nnwill.html

99. https://www.amazon.com/Nolo-Quicken-WillMaker-Trust-2020/dp/B07WG484LW/Q==

100. https://tomorrow.me/

101. http://www.jamesehughes.com/articles/TrusteeMentor.pdf

102. http://partners4prosperity.com/estate-planning-rick-randall-episode-183

103. https://nnepa.com/

104. https://tomorrow.me/goals/living-trust-fund/

105. https://nnepa.com/

106. https://partners4prosperity.com/contact

107. hello@Partners4Prosperity.com

Chapter 16

108. https://familylinevideo.com/

109. https://yourheritagefilm.com/family-legacy-films/
110. https://scratchmademedia.com/
111. http://nnepa.com/
112. https://thetorch.com/
113. https://thetorch.com/
114. https://www.everplans.com/
115. https://tomorrow.me/
116. https://givingpledge.org/

Chapter 17
117. https://prosperityeconomics.org/the-long-game/
118. https://youtu.be/IV6tZEj4yY0
119. https://youtu.be/r7hraQwMKIw

CPSIA information can be obtained
at www.ICGtesting.com
Printed in the USA
LVHW020455110621
689903LV00011B/1129